# Critical Pedagogies for Modern Languages Education

## BLOOMSBURY GUIDEBOOKS FOR LANGUAGE TEACHERS

This series brings together books that enhance language educators' teaching practice. The books provide practical advice and applications, suitable for use in a range of contexts and for different learning styles, which are evidence-based and research-informed. The series appeals to practitioners looking to develop their skills and practice and is also suitable for use on a variety of language teacher education courses. The books feature a range of topics and themes, from critical pedagogy, to using drama, poetry or literature in the language classroom, to supporting language learners who have anxiety.

### FORTHCOMING IN THE SERIES:

*Using Theories for Second Language Teaching and Learning*, Dale T. Griffee and Greta Gorsuch

*Teaching Beginner Level English Language Learners*, Lesley Painter-Farrell and Gabriel Díaz-Maggioli

*Psychology-Based Activities for Supporting Anxious Language Learners*, Neil Curry and Kate Maher

### ALSO AVAILABLE FROM BLOOMSBURY:

*Researching Education for Social Justice in Multilingual Settings*, edited by Jean Conteh

*Education for Critical Consciousness*, Paulo Freire

*On Critical Pedagogy*, Henry A. Giroux

# Critical Pedagogies for Modern Languages Education

## Criticality, Decolonization and Social Justice

EDITED BY
DEREK HIRD

BLOOMSBURY ACADEMIC
LONDON • NEW YORK • OXFORD • NEW DELHI • SYDNEY

BLOOMSBURY ACADEMIC
Bloomsbury Publishing Plc
50 Bedford Square, London, WC1B 3DP, UK
1385 Broadway, New York, NY 10018, USA
29 Earlsfort Terrace, Dublin 2, Ireland

BLOOMSBURY, BLOOMSBURY ACADEMIC and the Diana logo are trademarks of Bloomsbury Publishing Plc

First published in Great Britain 2023

Copyright © Derek Hird and Contributors, 2023

Derek Hird and Contributors have asserted their right under the Copyright, Designs and Patents Act, 1988, to be identified as Authors of this work.

For legal purposes the Acknowledgements on p. xiii constitute an extension of this copyright page.

Series design by Grace Ridge
Cover image © franckreporter / Getty Images
Series logo © warmworld / Adobe Stock

All rights reserved. No part of this publication may be reproduced or transmitted in any form or by any means, electronic or mechanical, including photocopying, recording, or any information storage or retrieval system, without prior permission in writing from the publishers.

Bloomsbury Publishing Plc does not have any control over, or responsibility for, any third-party websites referred to or in this book. All internet addresses given in this book were correct at the time of going to press. The author and publisher regret any inconvenience caused if addresses have changed or sites have ceased to exist, but can accept no responsibility for any such changes.

A catalogue record for this book is available from the British Library.

A catalog record for this book is available from the Library of Congress.

ISBN: HB: 978-1-3502-9877-4
PB: 978-1-3502-9876-7
ePDF: 978-1-3502-9878-1
eBook: 978-1-3502-9879-8

Series: Bloomsbury Guidebooks for Language Teachers

Typeset by Deanta Global Publishing Services, Chennai, India
Printed and bound in Great Britain

To find out more about our authors and books visit www.bloomsbury.com and sign up for our newsletters.

# CONTENTS

*List of Figures* vii
*List of Tables* viii
*List of Contributors* ix
*Acknowledgements* xiii

Introduction: What Is Critical Modern Languages Education? *Derek Hird* 1

**PART I** Interculturality, Decolonization and Decanonization 21

1  Existential Literacy: Promoting the Culture of Dignity for All Languages in Modern Language Classrooms *David Balosa* 23

2  English Teaching in the Global South: Interculturality, Postcoloniality and Critical Pedagogy *Hamza R'boul* 45

3  Pedagogical Stylistics and World Literature in Upper Secondary Schools *Isabella Marinaro* 62

**PART II** Multilingualism, Translingualism and Linguistic Diversity 83

4  From Babble to *Babel:* Engaging Linguistic Diversity in the College Classroom at Home and Abroad *Lucile Duperron* 85

5  Bridging Languages, Bridging Cultures: AFL Learners' Translingual Journeys *Sahar Alshobaki* 104

## PART III  Beyond Stereotypes and Discrimination  121

6   Modern Language Pedagogy beyond *Sombreros* and *Toreros*  Candace Skibba  123

7   Third-Person Pronouns, Gender and the Han Gaze in the Chinese Modern Languages Classroom  Derek Hird  134

8   On Facing Racism in ELT: Black Teachers and Racially Relevant Pedagogies in Discussion  Gabriel Nascimento  149

## PART IV  Textbook Discourses  163

9   The First Encounter: Representations of Gender and LGBTQ+ in Textbooks for Learners of Dutch and Swedish as a Foreign Language  Josef Wikström and Juul Wolters  165

10  'For Us Foreigners, Licking Our Fingers Clean Is a Good Habit': On Learning Chinese and Learning about Discourse from Chinese-Language Textbooks  Séagh Kehoe, Paul Kendall, Gerda Wielander  183

## PART V  Teacher Education  199

11  Translanguaging in Austrian Primary Teacher Education  Theresa Guczogi  201

12  Learning Language in All Subjects – The Key for More Equal Opportunities: A Mixed Methods Study on the Concept of *Sprachliche Bildung* (Integrative Language Learning) in Primary Schools in Vienna and Lower Austria  Golriz Gilak  218

13  English for Creative Resistance: Critical Pedagogy in a Teacher Education Programme in Palestine  Maria Grazia Imperiale  235

*Index*  253

# FIGURES

3.1 Frequency of the third-person and of the first-person pronouns 72
3.2 'The beauty around me' 75
3.3 'Underneath the cordiality' 77
4.1 Poster exhibition opening event 96
8.1 School parade in Banco Central 158

# TABLES

3.1  First-person Subject Pronoun 'I' and Transitive Use of Verbs  73
3.2  Intransitive Verbs Referred to 'He'/Friday  73
8.1  Conception of Self and Others by Culturally Relevant Teachers and Assimilationist Teachers  156
9.1  Representation in the Dutch Textbooks  173
9.2  Representation in the Swedish Textbooks  176

# CONTRIBUTORS

**Sahar Alshobaki** a Research Associate at the University of Glasgow (School of Education), UK. She has taught languages (English and Arabic) online and face to face in the UK, Austria, Turkey, and Palestine in the primary and secondary school sector, as well as in higher education. She is interested in language learning and teaching, in particular the use of vision and strategies in teaching and learning a foreign language. Sahar is also interested in researching second-language motivation, translanguaging, self and online teaching and learning.

**David Balosa** teaches world languages at the School District of Philadelphia, Pennsylvania, USA. His research interests focus on sociolinguistics, intercultural communication studies and minority languages' rights. He has published on the use of L1 in second-language teaching and learning, the relationship between language and human dignity and on integrationism, diversity and artistic creativity. His most recent publication, a book chapter entitled 'Existential Sociolinguistics: The Fundamentals of the Political Legitimacy of Linguistic Minority Rights' (2022) appeared in Makoni et al. (eds.), *The Languaging of Higher Education in the Global South: De-Colonizing the Language of Scholarship and Pedagogy*.

**Lucile Duperron** is Associate Professor of French and Francophone Studies at Dickinson College, PA, USA. As a teacher-scholar trained in applied linguistics, she examines Instructed Second Language Acquisition (ISLA) from both a cognitive and sociocultural perspective. Her most recent publication, 'The Transition from the Foreign Language to the Study Abroad Classroom: Mediating Writer Culture Shock' (2019) examines learners' evolving perceptions of writing in a second language. A language educator with thirty years of experience, she is committed to developing transdisciplinary curricular initiatives that harness academic collaboration, pedagogical innovation and linguistic diversity locally and internationally.

**Golriz Gilak**, born in Tehran, started her career in higher education at the Private University College of Teacher Education Vienna/Krems in 2015. Currently, she is a Lecturer in the Department of General Secondary Education (Center for Evidence-based Competence Development) at the University College of Teacher Education Vienna. Her teaching and research focus on multilingualism, migration and language promotion. In her teaching she shares her intercultural experiences with (prospective) teachers. She has worked in secondary education with a high number of immigrant students for several years. Since 2015, she has been volunteering for the Austrian Integration Fund, primarily to motivate immigrant students through personal (success) stories.

**Theresa Guczogi** is Lecturer in Primary Teacher Education in the Department of English at the Private University College of Teacher Education in Vienna/Krems, Austria.

**Derek Hird** is Senior Lecturer in Chinese Studies at Lancaster University, UK. His research interests focus on Chinese middle-class masculinities, Chinese male beauty cultures, happiness and health in Chinese populations and critical pedagogies for modern languages. He is co-editor of the *Transnational Asian Masculinities* book series. He has published widely on Chinese masculinities. His book-length publications include the co-authored *Men and Masculinities in Contemporary China* (2013), and the co-edited volumes *Chinese Discourses on Happiness* and *The Cosmopolitan Dream: Transnational Chinese Masculinities in a Global Age* (both 2018).

**Maria Grazia Imperiale** is Lecturer in Adult Education at the University of Glasgow, Scotland. Her research interests focus on language education for adult refugees and migrants, multilingualism and intercultural education. She has conducted research in several contexts, including Palestine, Lebanon, Ethiopia, Ghana, Italy and Scotland. She has worked as a language teacher and a teacher trainer. She has been part of the QAA (Quality Assurance Agency for Higher Education) Advisory Board leading the Linguistics subject benchmark statement review for 2021–22.

**Séagh Kehoe** is Lecturer in Chinese Studies at the University of Westminster. Their research interests focus on Chinese media representations of ethnicity and race, gender and sexuality, nationalism and military. They have published in *China Quarterly, positions, Media, Culture & Society*, and *Asian Ethnicity*, and are co-editor of *Cultural China: The Contemporary China Review 2020*.

**Paul Kendall** is Senior Lecturer in Chinese cultural studies at the University of Westminster. His research interests include urban space, everyday life, animation, translation and reception. His first book, *The Sounds of Social Space: Branding, Built Environment, and Leisure in Urban China*, was published in 2019.

**Isabella Marinaro**, independent researcher, is a Teacher of English Language and Literature at Liceo Scientifico Statale 'G. B. Morgagni', Rome, Italy.

She has a PhD in Textual Studies/English Studies from Sapienza, University of Rome. Her main research focus is on Pedagogical Stylistics applied to Upper Secondary Schools, especially in comparing 'traditional' English literature with world literatures in English. She has also published in the field of stylistics applied to ecocriticism. She authored the article 'Using Pedagogical Stylistics to Teach World Literature in English in Italian Upper Secondary Schools: Going Beyond Traditional English Literature Syllabi' (2020), and her latest article is 'Pedagogical Stylistics in Upper Secondary School. Connecting Dickens and Instapoetry: Linguistic Strategies to Catch the Readers' Attention. A Case Study' (2022).

**Gabriel Nascimento** is Assistant Professor of Language Studies at Universidade Federal do Sul da Bahia, Brazil. He received a PhD in Language Studies from the University of São Paulo and holds a master's degree in Applied Linguistics from the University of São Paulo. He served as Visiting Scholar at the University of Pennsylvania and has published and worked collaboratively with international groups in the United States and in South Africa, as well as contributing to refereed journals like *Applied Linguistics*, *Critical Studies in Education*, *Journal of Sociolinguistics* and so on.

**Hamza R'boul** is a research assistant professor in the Department of International Education at the Education University of Hong Kong. His works examine interculturality, power relations and the skewed geopolitics of knowledge as they shape education and society at large. They also address inequalities and discuss the demands for more epistemic justice in intercultural communication education and research, sociology of education, internationalization of higher education and English language teaching. His research interests include intercultural education, (higher) education in the Global South, decolonial endeavours in education, cultural politics of language teaching and postcoloniality.

**Candace Skibba** is Associate Teaching Professor in the Department of Modern Languages at Carnegie Mellon University in Pittsburgh, PA, USA. She specializes in contemporary Spanish literature and film and has concentrated her research on investigating the intersection between literary and film studies and studies of the body, including gender analysis, dis/ability studies, and health humanities. The convergence of her literary and cultural studies interests and pedagogical foci has led her to investigate agency and empathy in both artistic expression and classroom practices. Her most recent book is a co-edited volume titled *Trauma-Informed Pedagogy: Addressing Gender-Based Violence in the Classroom* (July 2022).

**Gerda Wielander** is Professor in Chinese Studies and Associate Head of the College of Liberal Arts and Sciences at the University of Westminster, UK. Her research interest lies in the link of the personal and spiritual to wider social and political developments in modern and contemporary China. She is the author of *Christian Values in Communist China* (2013), as well as several book chapters and articles in leading peer-reviewed journals. Her most recent work includes a volume on *Chinese Discourses on Happiness* (2018) and *Cultural China 2020* (2021). Gerda Wielander is the director of the Contemporary China Centre at the University of Westminster and editor of the *British Journal of Chinese Studies*.

**Josef Wikström** is Lecturer of Swedish at Osaka University in Japan. His research interests focus on bilingualism and political language.

**Juul Wolters** is Lecturer in Dutch Language and Culture as a Foreign Language at the International Business department of The Hague University of Applied Sciences, the Netherlands. Previously she taught Dutch as a foreign language at the Comenius University in Bratislava, Slovakia. Her research interests focus on Dutch as a foreign language, business communication, interpersonal and intercultural skills and presentation training.

# ACKNOWLEDGEMENTS

The interest and motivation to embark on this book project grew from conversations with colleagues in languages over many years. When I worked in the Department of Modern Languages and Cultures at the University of Westminster, a major curriculum review helped me think more deeply and critically about the integration of language and culture. I benefitted from many discussions with colleagues in Chinese, including Gerda Wielander, Cangbai Wang and Paul Kendall. During my time at Westminster I also had the good fortune to speak at and attend events organised by Language Acts and Worldmaking, an AHRC-funded Open World Research Initiative, led at Westminster by Debra Kelly. Discussions with colleagues at Westminster including Debra Kelly, Alexa Alfer, Rob Williams, Saskia Huc-Hepher, Elizabeth Waters and many others helped me better understand the pedagogical and institutional challenges facing the languages sector.

At Lancaster University, where I am now based, the enthusiasm of colleagues for critically integrating culture and social issues in language teaching has inspired me immensely. Sascha Stollhans' incredibly successful workshops on gender-inclusive language were a particularly strong source of inspiration. The level of attention to pedagogical excellence in the Department of Languages and Cultures at Lancaster has always impressed and stretched me in positive ways. I value the many discussions about language pedagogy I have had with Lancaster colleagues, including, but not limited to, Olga Gomez-Cash, Charlotte Baker, Amit Thakkar, Romain Bardot, Alana Jackson and Jocelin Lingxia Zhou.

I could not do my job at Lancaster, particularly since 2019 as Head of Department, without the amazing support of Sarah Elliott, Brigitte Theunissen-Hughes, Colette Webb and other Professional Services colleagues. Long may the integration of academic and PS colleagues in departmental culture continue at Lancaster!

My thanks also go to Godela Weiss-Sussex of the Institute of Modern Languages Research in the School of Advanced Study, University of London, for inviting me to speak at the AMLUK Symposium on Pedagogies in Modern Languages, Area Studies and Linguistics in March 2021. I took that opportunity to scope out the vision of critical language pedagogy – and the challenges facing it – that underlies this project.

More broadly, I learned much during my time as East Asian Studies representative on the University Council of Modern Languages about the inspiring work taking place across the country on languages pedagogy at all stages of the education pipeline.

This book project would never have happened if Maria Giovanna Brauzzi Martínez, my wonderful commissioning editor from Bloomsbury Publishing, had not contacted me after the AMLUK Symposium to ask if I wanted to write a book on critical pedagogy in languages education. Throughout the gestation of the project, Maria has been a supportive voice *par excellence*. The same is true for Laura Gallon at Bloomsbury, whose attention to detail and patience with me has brought this project to this happy result. The three anonymous reviewers contributed invaluable and encouraging comments on the book proposal and the manuscript that have significantly enriched and sharpened the arguments in this volume.

My intellectual development in general, in particular its critical dimensions, has been indelibly shaped by my discussions with Harriet Evans over many years, first as her doctoral student and then as colleague. Harriet's enduring commitment to teaching, research and engagement with the world remains an inspiration to me.

My family, as always, have been a loving and dependable source of support. Jamie, my partner, continues to be my rock and soulmate.

This book is dedicated to Sinéad Wall, my friend and colleague at the University of Westminster, whose fearless critical voice inspired students and academics alike. Taken from us much too soon; always remembered for the warmth and light she brought to this world.

# Introduction

# What Is Critical Modern Languages Education?

*Derek Hird*

In the context of Black Lives Matter, decolonizing initiatives, #MeToo, climate emergency protests and other movements for social and environmental justice, this volume posits a simple question: How can modern languages be taught so that they challenge rather than reinforce social inequalities? Covering eleven languages across five continents, its contents engage with this question from a wide range of perspectives and settings, reflecting the diversity of backgrounds and approaches of the volume's contributors. The themes examined in the book include interculturality, decolonization, decanonization, multilingualism, linguistic diversity, stereotypes, discrimination, textbook discourses and teacher education. The book covers a wide range of concepts, theories and viewpoints, such as critical discourse analysis, activist pedagogy, culturally sustaining pedagogy, linguistic justice, translanguaging and LGBTQ perspectives. The chapters offer insights and methods for language educators across different educational levels to adapt and use in their own teaching.

Despite the multiple languages, geographical settings and array of theoretical and methodological approaches in the volume, the chapters share a common enthusiasm for languages education as a means of social transformation. This is a book by language teachers for language teachers, drawing on the contributors' collective vast experience in the field of modern languages. It brings a critical and decolonizing lens to the ways that languages are taught, and it responds to the deep desire of many language educators across the globe to do all they can through their work in the languages classroom to make this world a better place.

## What Is the Purpose of This Volume?

Language learning is still mostly taught as a technical process of decoding and encoding (Kramsch 2020). Yet, languages are never neutral (Phipps and Guilherme 2004): they are often used to legitimize social inequalities and marginalize minorities in ways that serve the interests of elites (Bauman and Brigg 2003). The languages and cultures of dominant groups are set as standards to be aspired to; conversely, the languages and cultures of minority groups are viewed as intrinsically deficient. A dominant 'standard' language is enforced through state language and educational policies, which enact linguistic symbolic violence by stigmatizing 'non-standard' speech (Alim and Paris 2017; Kramsch 2020). Language teaching that uncritically seeks to reproduce 'standard' forms of language unwittingly or otherwise enforces the normative aims of state authorities. Unfortunately, an assumption of 'ideological neutrality' pervades dominant models of language teaching and learning (Morgan and Mattos 2018). Reinforcing an iniquitous status quo is not 'ideologically neutral', hence this book's call for a critical pedagogy for modern languages that recognizes the political nature of languages. If languages can produce discrimination and inequality, they can also challenge and subvert oppressive practices (Pessoa and Urzêda-Freitas 2012: 757).

Bringing the politics of language into the language classroom is desirable for several reasons: it enhances the intellectual respectability of language teaching in an academy that values critical thinking; it addresses the status gap between language specialists and culture specialists by turning language teachers into combined language *and* culture specialists; and, by making language learning relevant to important sociopolitical issues, rather than viewing it as a neutral technical process, it attracts more students into the language classroom. An activist pedagogical stance that 'exposes, acknowledges and unpacks social injustices [and] is founded in a commitment to personal and social change both inside and outside the classroom and the academy' (Preston and Aslett 2014: 514) reshapes language teaching into a critical discipline committed to making a difference in the world. Bringing critical pedagogy into the languages classroom transforms students, teachers and society in positive ways.

A critical, activist pedagogy of language identifies and critiques oppressive linguistic systems and recasts the language classroom as a site of linguistic and cultural resistance and diversity. It advocates a shift away from the view of language learning as technical skills development and towards critical language learning that (i) calls out language that reproduces unjust relations of power and (ii) fosters progressive linguistic solutions to social inequalities. Unmasking the ideologies and hegemonies that lie behind keywords (Heller and Duchêne 2007; Heller and McElhinney 2017) affirms the value of minority linguistic and cultural practices.

With student–teacher collaboration at its heart, it 'build[s] a community of activist learners and educators in the classroom with tangible and meaningful opportunities to initiate and advocate for change' (Preston and Aslett 2014: 514).

This volume reimagines modern languages by transforming linguistic practices in the classroom. This endeavour requires a heightened critical awareness of the reproduction of linguistic and social hierarchies in the languages classroom. Decolonizing the language classroom requires a critical deconstruction of language standards. Decanonization of the language classroom entails pluralizing language materials so that they include differing voices, accents, vocabularies and grammars, as well as multiple viewpoints on language issues in the target culture (Phipps 2019).[1] This reimagined language pedagogy draws inspiration from translanguaging approaches, by emphasizing actual practices of speakers of the target language, rather than relying on the 'standard' language of state language policies and uncritical textbooks. It puts everyday language interactions at the heart of languages education and problematizes norms imposed through language policies, textbooks and normative discourses of correct and incorrect linguistic practices (García et al. 2021: 205).

This volume's ethos responds to the principles informing Paulo Freire's (2005) critical pedagogy and H. Samy Alim and Django Paris' (2017) culturally sustaining pedagogy. It exposes the ways in which conventional language teaching abets the interests of elite state actors and advocates inclusive linguistic and cultural pluralism as a means to resist and transform oppressive linguistic practices. The volume provides transformative approaches to languages teaching and learning that respond to the key social concerns in the contemporary world. By critically transforming the ways languages are taught, the modern languages sector can not only strike a blow for social justice, but it can also improve the status of its own language teachers, win more influence in the academy and society and attract learners from more diverse backgrounds into studying languages.

This volume does not take sides in a left-right struggle over educational methods, nor in an imagined culture war in which one side fights for social justice and the other side fights to prevent it. In this volume, social justice is conceived of as a common good that societies can reach some degree of consensus on through constructive debate. This volume is not a project of the radical left, nor a 'woke' attempt to 'cancel' certain views in the languages classroom. Quite the opposite: this volume is an attempt to increase the diversity of viewpoints in the languages classroom, to enhance the breadth and depth of pedagogic quality in the languages classroom; and to encourage the language learning and teaching community – educators, students, publishers, administrators and all – to reflect on how open-minded critical thinking can be more deeply practised in the languages classroom.

## What Is This Volume's Significance?

This volume breaks new ground in modern languages research, drawing on the rich and diverse experiences of modern languages practitioners, researchers and teacher trainers, as well as insights from cognate research in applied linguistics and education studies and more broadly from critical pedagogy research. This is a book that speaks directly to modern languages educators about social justice issues across many linguistic and cultural contexts.[2]

The volume addresses a gap in the literature on critically informed languages teaching, which is currently dominated by publications written by education and applied linguistics specialists (e.g. Macedo 2019b; Norton and Toohey 2004; Phipps 2019). Existing works often focus on retheorizing languages and cultures education (e.g. Osborn 2021); sometimes even explicitly excluding discussion of teaching approaches and the integration of culture into language teaching (e.g. Reagan and Osborn 2020). They may contain only one or a small number of case studies (e.g. Guilherme 2002; Phipps and Guilherme 2004), limit their scope to one national context (e.g. Reagan 2022; Wassell and Glynn 2022) and do not necessarily cover multiple languages or foreground a social justice agenda (e.g. Díaz 2013). Some focus exclusively on English language classrooms and teacher education (e.g. Crookes and Abednia 2021; Godley and Reaser 2018); others approach language education through the lens of intercultural communication pedagogy (e.g. Dasli and Díaz 2017);[3] Such works demonstrate that sociolinguistics and education specialists have analysed language education's participation in the production of unjust relations of power and have developed progressive linguistic pedagogies to challenge and reduce social inequalities. However, despite their relevance and insights, linguistics-heavy books have had limited impact in changing modern languages teaching practice, primarily because they do not speak to modern language educators in an idiom with which modern language educators are familiar. *Critical Pedagogy for Modern Languages Education* fills that gap.[4]

Three key features of this book are: (i) it contains practical and accessible examples of case studies grounded in deep concern with mobilizing social justice goals in language education; (ii) it is written by languages educators from diverse backgrounds specifically for languages educators; and (iii) it covers a variety of teaching contexts across primary, secondary and higher education, in many different locations across multiple continents. While key themes such as criticality, decolonization and social justice are threaded through the volume, the individual chapters illuminate the specificities of their particular contexts, so as to not homogenize the kinds of interventions and concerns potentially applicable.

The volume's key contribution to the field is the critical stance to the teaching of languages that it brings into the modern languages classroom.

For too long, the modern languages classroom has neglected the kind of critical approach to linguistic reproduction of power asymmetries that is taken in sociolinguistics, education and cultural studies. Each chapter in its own way advocates for language teaching itself to adopt a criticality hitherto largely absent from the language sector.

It is true that in modern language classrooms across the sector social justice issues are increasingly discussed (see e.g. Wassell, Wesely and Glynn 2019); and that textbook authors and publishers are under pressure to decolonize images and content (see e.g. Macedo 2019a: 16–22). Target languages themselves, however, are seldom put under forensic scrutiny. When sexism, racism, classism, ableism and other forms of oppression manifest in morphology, lexis, syntax and grammar, language educators should call them out. When textbooks, reading materials, curricula and language teacher training fail to critically examine power asymmetries in language, they should be revised and improved. Language teachers must work with students and stakeholders to raise awareness of the ways in which language reproduces oppressive social norms and to promote progressive change in languages. Critical language teaching and learning is not a simple matter of 'technical' skills development and uncritical 'immersion' that aims to produce 'near-native' standard speakers of the target language. The languages teacher can and should be repositioned away from the role of bureaucratic agent, measuring 'objective' progress in standardized tests, and towards being an advocate for criticality, decolonization and social justice (Pennycook and Makoni 2020: 98).

To change how languages are taught demands an overhaul of modern languages teacher training, with a need for much more emphasis on critical sociolinguistics, linguistic anthropology and other questioning approaches to languages. Conversely, much less emphasis should be placed on the mythical ideal of the 'native speaker'. Language pedagogy in the Western academy from the 1970s developed a focus on communicative competence through immersive exposure to mother-tongue speakers; yet the elevated status of the 'native speaker' has been under critique for decades for its assumption that mother-tongue speakers are invariably better speakers and teachers of the target language than non-mother-tongue speakers (Andreou and Galantomos 2009; Davies 2003; Kramsch and Zhang 2017; Rampton 1990; Savignon 1991). The most pressing issue in languages teaching is not the mother-tongue status of languages teachers, but training in critical language studies.

In some higher education contexts, the languages sector is divided between an elite of cultural studies lecturers equipped with PhDs and a substratum of 'workhorse' language tutors, by and large without PhDs; the latter are treated in second-class ways in terms of contract type, workload allocation and status in the academy (for a related sense of researcher-teacher hierarchies in applied linguistics and language teaching, see Allison and Carey 2007). From the author's own knowledge of the UK HE languages sector, research-active PhD-holding academics are allocated intellectually respectable cultural modules, substantial research time, and have well-delineated career progression pathways to professorships; whereas their non-PhD-holding colleagues – who are more likely to be foreign 'native speakers' – are employed on teaching-only contracts and deliver large amounts of less academically prestigious language teaching. If languages teachers are equipped with critical pedagogic skills, then we can begin to address the asymmetries that the modern languages sector currently perpetuates, both in the classroom and in the profession itself (Macedo 2019a: 9–10). The impact of translanguaging pedagogies, which disrupt 'seemingly common-sense notions as native speaker, standard language, first/second language, and academic language' (García et al. 2021: 218), can and should be replicated in the modern languages classroom.

The need for change in the modern languages classroom and profession could not be clearer; yet the struggle for change is not just a matter of transforming individual educators and the languages profession. Politicians are equally responsible for perpetuating the practice of language teaching as skills development, cloaked in the myth of neutrality, through language policies that reproduce colonial and asymmetrical linguistic regimes (Canagarajah 2005). Departments of education worldwide should audit their modern languages policies to evaluate where critical thinking manifests in the languages pedagogies that their language policies espouse.

## Target Audience, Scope and Limitations

The primary audience for this volume includes modern languages educators, trainee language educators and language curriculum developers in the primary, secondary and tertiary education sectors, as well as applied linguistics and language education researchers interested in social justice in language teaching. Critical pedagogy practitioners and researchers comprise the volume's secondary audience. The volume is intended to serve as a set text or recommended text for undergraduate and postgraduate students in modern languages, languages teaching pedagogy, including TESOL and TEFL, and educational linguistics. It is an important resource for PhD students who are interested in modern languages teaching, teacher education and social justice issues. The book's global appeal lies in its case studies covering eleven languages (Modern Standard Arabic, Dutch, English, French, German, Levantine, Mandarin, Portuguese, Spanish, Swedish, Tamazight) across thirteen countries and regions (Austria, Brazil, China, France, Italy, the Levant, Morocco, the Netherlands, Palestine, Spain, Sweden, the UK, the United States) and five continents (Africa, Asia, Europe, North America, South America).

Despite its extensive and diverse coverage of modern languages education across the globe, the volume is not equipped to address all issues of importance relating to critical language pedagogy. The field is fraught with inequalities and language hierarchies that fall outside the scope of the volume (e.g. indigenous languages, heritage languages, minority languages, less-widely taught languages, anthropocentric and Global North-centric notions of languages ontologies and epistemologies); it is important to acknowledge that language education theorists and practitioners may (un) knowingly be complicit in (re)producing them. For example, the choice of English as the volume's linguistic medium is driven by the role of English as an academic lingua franca around the world, which is a taken-for-granted aspect in the expected market and readership of this book (Pennycook and Makoni 2020: 96). And, as Boaventura de Sousa Santos points out, truly emancipatory changes in the global social order may require 'grammars and scripts other than those developed by Western-centric critical theory' (2014: viii), a notion with which this volume fully concurs but which requires a separate volume to develop in the context of languages education. Finally, the important topic of global digital technology falls outside the scope of the examples of praxis in the various contributions.

## Criticality and Decolonization in Critical Pedagogies for Modern Language Education

Criticality and decolonization are the two key principles of this book underpinning its aim to invest modern languages teaching and learning with a social justice mission. These two principles underscore that what is at the stake in the modern languages classroom is not just the development of linguistic skills, but also the opportunity to move society in a more positive direction.

This volume takes its understanding of criticality from the renowned Brazilian educationalist Paulo Freire (1921–97). Freire famously set out a critique of the 'banking model' of education, in which students passively 'receive, memorise, and repeat' (Freire 2005: 72) the information the teacher 'deposits' in them. In its place, Freire advocated a critical, dialogic, problem-posing pedagogy in which students and teachers work together to identify, challenge and reduce social inequalities (Freire 2005: 79–81). Freire's critical pedagogy was deeply influenced by Marxist anti-capitalist class struggle and its expression through the Frankfurt School, by Erich Fromm's notion of the fear of freedom in the mass unconscious, and by a sense of the virtue of individual dissent: it is from this conceptual synthesis that Freire's method of 'revolutionary empowerment' emerged (Aronowitz 2013: 5–7; Lake and Dagostino 2013). A believer in the potent mix of theory and praxis, he emphasized both and devalued neither (Aronowitz 2013: 5).

The understanding of decolonization in this volume is linked to Freire's critique of the banking model of education under capitalism, in that this volume takes capitalist modernity and colonialism as two sides of the same coin (Mignolo 2007: 450–51). Decolonizing languages education requires rejecting the banking model and its assumption of the neutrality of education. Instead, it involves teachers and students gauging their positionality in colonial hierarchies through open and critically reflective discussion (Kubota 2021); it calls for critical reflection on the role of languages teaching in furthering colonial and hegemonic oppression of minority languages (Macedo 2019a: 10); and it inspires the co-creation of 'new, multilingual ecologies of the postdecolony' (Phipps 2019: 93). This kind of radical dialogic collaboration between students and teachers builds a social justice model of education founded on criticality and decolonization. Moreover, decolonizing initiatives such as translanguaging can help disrupt the concept of a language as a neatly packaged standard aligned with (or marginalized by) national state cultures; at the same time, however, the potential of named languages to aid emancipatory sociopolitical projects should not be overlooked (Pennycook and Makoni 2020: 98).

## Volume Contents

The volume is composed of five sections that move from 'theoretical' pedagogical concerns, including decolonization, interculturality, decanonization, multilingualism, translanguaging and anti-racism, to more 'concrete' elements in the larger pedagogical ecosystem, such as textbooks and teaching materials, and finally to teacher education, which closes the cycle of the various stages involved in the volume's larger project for modern languages education.

The three chapters in Part I, on 'Interculturality, Decolonization and Decanonization', cover the main conceptual underpinnings of the volume. In this section, readers will find a productive mix of theoretical discussion and case study analyses, from the exposition of an integrated pedagogy of existential literacy (David Balosa) to Moroccan high school teachers' awareness of the politics of English (Hamza R'boul) and the decanonization of the Italian upper secondary English literature syllabus (Isabella Marinaro). While raising important questions about the ways in which modern languages are taught, they also set out theoretically informed modes of practice that aim to move the languages classroom in progressive directions.

Part I begins with David Balosa's systematic exposition of his concept of existential literacy, a pedagogy of the heart that places dignity and justice as the central values to be attained inside and outside the languages classroom. Defining existential literacy as a set of capabilities enabling the flourishing of human dignity and relationships, Balosa finds inspiration in Paul the Apostle's plurilingual model of intercultural relations. Paul built deep connections with different peoples by showing his loving appreciation of their languages, cultures and predicaments. Interculturality is key to Balosa's pedagogy, which he understands as the 'processes of recognition of human, linguistic, cultural, technological, moral and environmental diversity that constitute our integrated humanity or global life landscape'. With an emphasis on the importance of relationships and community building, Balosa makes a powerful argument for linguistic inclusivity, arguing that marginalization or inequitable treatment of students' languages in the classroom is damaging to the intercultural ecology of globally interconnected humanity. Encouraging an approach of critical philosophical reflection towards texts and discourses, Balosa sets out a simple yet powerful example of decolonization and existential literacy in his French class in South Philadelphia High School, in which young students discover dignity and confidence through a pedagogy of inclusive multilingualism that brings all his students' seven home languages into the classroom learning experience. Importantly, as Balosa points out, this approach helps deconstruct the cultural and linguistic prestige of dominant cultures and build the kinds of equitable intercultural relationships that are necessary for sustainable and just language learning environments.

Chapter 2, by Hamza R'Boul, continues with these themes of interculturality and decolonization through its investigation of the influences of English in Morocco and Moroccan teachers' understandings of the intersections of English, coloniality and imbalanced interculturality. Understanding interculturality as the 'dynamics and processes involved in the co-construction of meanings, identity and culture during intercultural interactions', R'Boul shows that it is not sufficient simply to include more diverse voices in debates when Anglophone spaces are already privileged and regional languages struggle to escape their subaltern status. R'Boul argues for a context-specific application of critical pedagogic principles to illuminate local specificities in the global spread of English. In a qualitative study of fifteen EFL pre-service and in-service high school teachers of English in Morocco, R'boul found that they took a practical, rather than critical, stance towards the increasing influence of English in Moroccan society. His informants viewed the spread of English as a positive development, especially in relation to its undermining the use of French, the language of the colonial elite. R'boul's findings underscore the need for language teacher training programmes to include input from critical sociolinguistics and linguistic anthropology, to highlight the implications of the increasing reach of English in the Global South for local languages and cultures.

Part I concludes with Isabella Marinaro's Chapter 3 on decanonizing world literature in Italian upper secondary classrooms, which develops the themes of criticality and decolonization through a decanonizing approach to English literature. Marinaro argues for a broadening of the Italian educational syllabus from its traditional focus on British literature to a much more inclusive world literature in English, encompassing authors of diverse backgrounds. A stylistics approach brings analytical attention to the function and effects of textual features, particularly when they deviate from the 'norm'. Through comparative close readings of the stylistics deployed in Daniel Defoe's *Robinson Crusoe* and Bidisha's *Venetian Masters. Under the Skin of the City of Love*, Marinaro explores the racism inherent in the former and the exposure of racism that the latter aims to effect. Through this practice of 'comparative intertextuality', Marinaro seeks to encourage teenage learners to embrace pluralism, polycentrism and inclusiveness by adopting this critically aware approach to literary criticism.

Part II, on 'Multilingualism, Translingualism and Linguistic Diversity', consists of two chapters that cover critical pedagogical techniques across the life cycle of a French degree at a US-based undergraduate liberal-arts college (Lucile Duperron) and multilingual approaches to teaching Arabic as a foreign language to beginners (Sahar Alshobaki). Criticality and decolonization impulses are still very much present in these two chapters; and they both illuminate highly inspiring yet distinctive ways in which capacious understandings of multilingualism can enrich critical languages pedagogy.

Chapter 4, Lucile Duperron's analysis of linguistic diversity in her French classroom in the US, adopts Claire Kramsch's (2017) standpoint of the educator as 'multilingual instructor', which foregrounds the importance of addressing the symbolic power of language. Duperron points out the usefulness of Piller's (2016) notion of linguistic diversity for capturing the stratification of languages and ensuring social justice as a core pedagogical aim. Continuing her conceptually rich discussion, Duperron discusses the benefits of including cultural sustaining pedagogy and academic service-learning as critical but also constructive modes of learning that de-stigmatize marginalized language varieties and emphasize mutually beneficial learning experiences. Duperron's account of the first-year seminar shows how her students and immigrant language learners gained critical awareness of linguistic discrimination from their interactions. The final-year seminar that Duperron discusses, a capstone course, involves the students' in-depth explorations and reflections on linguistic diversity – and associated inequalities – in southwest France, the location of a partner institution. Duperron provides a detailed breakdown of the syllabus and assessment practices for both seminars. She concludes that world language courses that nurture critical intercultural awareness and multilingual writing skills are well positioned to contribute to social justice ethics development in the languages classroom.

In Chapter 5, on the translingual journeys of Arabic learners, Sahar Alshobaki discusses the experiences of eight Arabic beginners whom she encouraged to utilize their full linguistic repertoire when reflecting on their progress. In this way, Alshobaki forefronts the value of translanguaging as a learning technique in the modern languages classroom. In the Arabic-speaking world, translanguaging is a common phenomenon, as speakers move between dialects and Classical Arabic, depending on the formality of different contexts. Translanguaging approaches in the classroom disrupt and question the hierarchy of Arabics that is often presupposed in curricular models; yet as Alshobaki points out, there is resistance from teachers and learners to adopt translanguaging, despite Arabic's inescapable multiglossic characteristics. Through a study of learners' reflective comments on their language learning experiences, Alshobaki determines that translanguaging helped her learners avoid misunderstanding, provided a sense of empowerment and bonding with others, enabled them to convey their message, and added playfulness to their conversations. Crucially, through translanguaging, her students overcame the all-too-common feeling of shame at failing to be a monolingual in Arabic. Translanguaging techniques enabled them to expand their linguistic and cultural competencies through a framework of respect and space for home languages, minority languages and all forms of Arabic.

The chapters in Part III, 'Beyond Discrimination and Stereotypes', principally draw on and think through the role of critical and anti-racist pedagogies, strongly informed by decolonizing perspectives. Candace Skibba discusses anti-racist pedagogical initiatives in the languages programmes of a major private research university in the US; Derek Hird outlines a critical gender and anti-racist approach to teaching third-person pronouns in Chinese; and Gabriel Nascimento critiques the linguistic racism inherent in Brazilian society and education while highlighting the transformative potential of Black teachers on disadvantaged children.

At the outset of Chapter 6, Candace Skibba asks the reader to reflect on how they intentionally prioritize inclusivity and anti-racism in their own learning, teaching and research. Yet she cautions that rather than focus on changing the teacher or the student per se, a radical pedagogy of decolonization is most powerfully enacted through engagements between students and teachers, and teachers and institutions. Incorporating her own experiences, Skibba makes a case for the co-creation of knowledge that is possible when educators put their 'expertise' to one side and openly and honestly approach classroom dialogues as a means to mutual learning. Drawing on the work of Uju Anya (2021), Skibba shows how collective, respectful and inclusive efforts to integrate critical race theory with world language teaching can lead to liberatory practices of anti-racism and social justice in languages departments, curricula and classrooms. A simple yet powerful example is the way in which L1 contextualization of prepositions in Spanish can serve to disadvantage non-normative speakers of L1. Skibba's chapter compels all educators to reflect deeply on how apparently 'neutral' ways of teaching may in actuality perpetuate exclusionary effects.

In Chapter 7, Derek Hird tells the story behind the creation of the feminine third-person pronoun in Chinese in the early twentieth century, in a context of metadiscourses of colonialism/modernity that posited the gender binary as a norm and positioned Western European languages as the tongues of modern cosmopolitan subjects. Hird argues that the embedding of the feminine third-person pronoun was aided by the dominance of a patriarchal and Beijing-centric 'Han gaze', which continues to enforce a set of racialized and gendered norms that limit the expression of non-Han, non-Mandarin and non-binary sociocultural linguistic identities. Using a conceptual lens informed by feminist critical discourse analysis (Lazar 2014), linguistic performativity (Conrod 2020) and epistemological racism (Kubota 2021), Hird brings attention to the intersections of these normative gendered and racial linguistic regimes and their productive power in marginalizing and misgendering those who identify as non-binary. Hird argues that Chinese-language teachers should work with learners to create gender-inclusive practices for use in the classroom and society. Adapting Ryuko Kubota's (2021) anti-racist pedagogical framework, he sets out some practical suggestions for a critical gender pedagogy in the languages classroom as a means of connecting language learning with pressing gender and social justice challenges.

Gabriel Nascimento discusses language and racism in Brazil in Chapter 8, with a focus on the historical lack of recognition of the contribution of Black communities to the development of Brazilian Portuguese, due to what he terms 'linguistic racism'. To address this issue, Nascimento underscores the importance of ethnographic investigations of the lived realities of Black Brazilians, who comprise over half the population yet are hugely underrepresented in higher education, including Nascimento's areas of interest, linguistics and ELT. Drawing conceptually on postcolonial scholars, including Frantz Fanon, Walter Mignolo and Boaventura de Sousa Santos, Nascimento critiques epistemologies of the south that read the south as unique and homogeneous and write Black lives through the eyes of white scholars. In his rethinking of anti-racist teaching education in the Brazilian context, Nascimento adapts Ladson-Billings' (1994) notion of culturally relevant pedagogy into racially relevant pedagogy, because the notion of 'culture' has been used in Brazilian academic literature to underplay racism and explain it away as inevitable. Nascimento's chapter concludes with a powerful autoethnographic account of the transformative impact of Black teachers on his early education and life chances.

Part IV, on 'Textbook Discourses', applies a critical lens to teaching materials, in particular to textbook contents. Josef Wikström and Juul Wolters analyse representations of gender and LGBTQ+ in Dutch and Swedish language textbooks. The focus then switches to interrogating problematic discourses in Chinese-language textbooks, as explored by Séagh Kehoe, Paul Kendall and Gerda Wielander.

Chapter 9, by Josef Wikström and Juul Wolters, investigates the representations of gender and LGBTQ+ in seven textbooks of Dutch and Swedish as a foreign language. Wikström and Wolters' conceptual approach draws upon critical discourse analysis and the works of Paulo Freire; their key structuring framework is Kevin Kumashiro's (2002) theory of anti-oppressive education, which posits four different ways of understanding and challenging oppression in education. While recognizing that both the Netherlands and Sweden have strong global reputations for gender and sexual equality, Wikström and Wolters nonetheless paint a more nuanced picture of Dutch and Swedish progress towards linguistic equity. Before analysing the textbooks, they discuss gender-neutral pronouns and non-binary gender identities in the two countries, highlighting that while gender-neutral pronouns have become more established in Sweden than in Holland, it is not yet possible in Sweden to legally change one's identity to a third non-binary sex. In their findings from their analysis of the textbooks, Wikström and Wolters demonstrate that the Dutch textbook representations are generally male-dominant and show almost a complete absence of non-binary representations; as for LGBTQ+ representations fall between Kumashiro's 'Education for the Other' and 'Education about the Other' in that they fail to fully acknowledge the social structures upholding heteronormativity. The Swedish textbooks are varied in their coverage, with one exploring non-binary identities to a small extent, yet they are all also male-biased and heteronormative, although to a lesser degree than the Dutch ones.

In Chapter 10, Séagh Kehoe, Paul Kendall and Gerda Wielander discuss a critical language pedagogy that they have deployed in the Chinese programme of a large metropolitan university in the UK, which addresses issues in Chinese-language textbooks, including monolingualism, monoculturalism, heteronormativity, PRC dominance and Han centrism. A thorough reworking of the curriculum at their institution provided an opportunity to align weekly topics in culture and language teaching. The authors point out that thematic integration of culture and language has enabled even beginners to express views on complex social issues, has decanonized and decolonized the curriculum by allowing space for unorthodox materials and 'lesser' themes, has raised the perceived value of language pedagogy, and has provided a forum for critique of textbook discourses. The authors then discuss how their cultural studies lectures challenge three key discourses in the most popular Chinese textbooks in use, by complicating and identifying gaps in the textbooks' narratives. They use post-socialist dystopian animation to explore the legacy of the Mao era, dating site and cosmetics videos to discuss 'leftover women' and propaganda posters to explore representations of whiteness, blackness and Chineseness: all of which are topics unmentioned in the textbooks. They conclude that students have developed more powerful critical linguistic-cultural awareness and expression through the integrated curriculum model.

Part V, on 'Teacher Education', brings attention to critical modes of teacher training in languages, in recognition that the transformation of language pedagogies in the classroom equally requires transformation of teacher education. Theresa Guczogi explores the impact of translanguaging strategies in the education of primary teacher candidates in Vienna; Golriz Gilak discusses a mixed methods study on *Sprachliche Bildung* (Integrative Language Learning) with primary school teachers in Vienna and Lower

Austria; and Maria Grazia Imperiale analyses vignettes from her teacher training work with participants from the Gaza Strip in Palestine.

In Chapter 11, Theresa Guczogi argues that translanguaging strategies in primary education are important not just for their pedagogical power within the multilingual classroom, but also for their ability to challenge social linguistic hierarchies. Guczogi acknowledges the disjunctures between the high-level plurilingual aspirations the EU has for its citizens and the differing implementations of policies supporting plurilingualism in EU member states. Following Ingrid Gogolin's (2008) criticism of the 'monolingual habitus' dominating schools in Europe, Guczogi points out that plurilingual pupils are systematically disadvantaged if they are prevented from utilizing their full linguistic repertoire; translanguaging, she argues, has the potential to turn classrooms into more equitable spaces. Making all languages visible in a supportive pedagogical environment legitimizes the status of minority languages as appropriate modes of learning and communication for individuals as well as in broader social and national contexts. Guczogi draws conceptual inspiration from Leketi Makalela's (2018) Ubuntu translanguaging pedagogy, which emphasizes the premise of interconnectedness from which individual recognition and flourishing grow. Guczogi advocates for flexibility in teacher-trainee attitudes to allow for mother-tongue group discussion within a larger context of English language instruction and to facilitate multilingual modes of presentation. Guczogi lays out strategies and practical suggestions for effective ways of bringing translanguaging into teacher education, including highlighting students' language profiles, using contrasting experiences of the translanguaging versus the monolingual classroom, and exploring language prestige and power relations.

Chapter 12 emphasizes the benefits of integrative language learning, demonstrated through a mixed methods study that Golriz Gilak conducted with primary school teachers. In integrative language learning, language functions as a tool to deliver and understand the lesson content and takes into account all languages of students in the classroom. To facilitate integrative language learning requires a resource-oriented rather than a deficit-oriented perspective. Gilak points out that integrative language learning and content and language-integrated learning (CLIL) both help students to acquire educational language skills. CLIL's main goal is to extend the vocabulary in a foreign language through the use of an additional language in the CLIL classroom; integrative language learning, however, strengthens language skills in the language of instruction to improve content understanding. Integrative language learning is inclusive in that it aims to raise the cognitive academic language proficiency (CALP) of all students without discriminating against minority students, which requires special attention and systematic support, hence the starting principle that 'every lesson is a language lesson'. Gilak's findings show that among teachers currently there is only a partial awareness of the responsibility to train language skills outside of language subjects, especially to CALP standards. Moreover, only a quarter of respondents were aware that language barriers may act to exclude students from comprehending and participating in class discussions. Minority languages were not mentioned by respondents. Gilak argues that the implementation of an integrative language learning approach in teacher education would be an effective way to address these issues and to help connect classroom pedagogies with the larger goal of challenging social inequalities.

In Maria Grazia Imperiale's teaching training programme for pre-service English teachers from the Gaza Strip, discussed in Chapter 13, she was challenged by the trainees, who sought to re-appropriate English pedagogy in a critical and creative way for their own context. Inspired by critical engaged pedagogy (hooks 1994), the critical turn in applied linguistics (Pennycook 1994; Canagarajah 2003), James Scott's (1990) *Domination and the Arts of Resistance*, and decolonizing and participatory approaches, Imperiale developed and co-constructed localized critical and creative approaches through a teacher training course titled 'Using the Palestinian Arts of Resistance in English Language Teaching'. The course uses the arts as a multimodal, multi-genre way of protesting injustice. Imperiale shares two vignettes that show how participants developed critical responses to the course. The first vignette discusses the critique of a recipe-sharing activity by two students, which, while finding the activity meaningful, charged that it did not challenge relationships or power dynamics: that is, it did not render their critical voices audible. The second vignette concerns a simple drama performed by the students, which replaced symbols conventionally associated with Palestine, such as olives, oranges, barbed wires and olive trees, with roses, birds, rivers, sea, lakes and technologies. In doing so, Imperiale writes, her students 'affirmed their subjectivities as writers and agents and as young people engaging with contemporary challenges and opportunities'. Complicating existing conceptions of language as a tool for resilience, Imperiale concludes by celebrating her students' creative and critical performance as a transgressive form of 'resilient resistance', or *somoud* in Palestinian, which was meaningful and valuable for her students in their own struggle for social justice.

## Conclusion

Throughout all its component parts, this volume has a simple agenda: to transform the modern languages classroom into a site of critical pedagogy. Through decolonization, decanonization, interculturality, multilingualism, translingualism, anti-racist pedagogy and integrative language teaching, to name some of its key conceptual lenses, it aims to transform classroom teaching, textbooks and teacher education. The measure of its success will be whether it persuades languages teachers around the world not to continue teaching languages as if they were neutral tools of communication. Not only is that approach intellectually dishonest, it also reproduces the repressive sociolinguistic hierarchies that many languages educators profess to oppose. Moreover, there is no reason to believe that languages students are less committed to effecting positive social change in the world than students of other disciplines. It is time for languages teachers and students to work together to harness the transformative potential that their combined energies can bring to the study of languages; it is time to place a vision of social and linguistic justice at the heart of the modern languages curriculum.

## Notes

1  There is increasing recognition that 'decolonizing' processes cannot be reduced to the deconstruction of language standards; they must also refer to struggles of repatriation of Indigenous land and life (ontologies and epistemologies) or they may fall into the trap of becoming tokenistic/metaphorical ways of referring to the ongoing struggles of Indigenous peoples around the world. See Tuck and Yang (2012).

2  The term 'modern languages' is used extensively in the UK and Europe; in the United States the term 'world languages' is more prevalent, while in Australia, the preference is 'languages' without any qualifiers. While the 'modern' in modern languages ostensibly distinguishes the field from the teaching of classical languages no longer in daily use, it is also embedded in the matrix of coloniality/modernity. The term 'modern languages' is retained here because it is a widely spread terminology across contexts covered in the volume. Nevertheless, it cannot be exempted from decolonizing critiques, as categorizations of languages and named languages have been used in language education programmes to legitimize colonial languages and exclude the languages of the colonized. See e.g. García (2019).

3  See Crookes (2022) for a useful timeline of key publications on critical language pedagogy.

4  It is important to recognize advancement in language-specific contexts, e.g. Criser and Malakaj (2020) and Bouamer and Bourdeau (2022). These edited volumes have emerged from teaching and research collectives for transnational and transdisciplinary decolonization of German and French studies.

## References

Alim, H. S., and D. Paris. (2017), 'What is Culturally Sustaining Pedagogy and Why Does it Matter?', in D. Paris and H. S. Alim (eds.), *Culturally Sustaining Pedagogies: Teaching and Learning for Justice in a Changing World*, 1–24, New York: Teachers College Press.

Allison, D., and J. Carey. (2007), 'What do University Language Teachers Say about Language Teaching Research?', *TESL Canada Journal*, 24 (2): 61–81.
Andreou, G., and I. Galantomos. (2009), 'The Native Speaker Ideal in Foreign Language Teaching', *Electronic Journal of Foreign Language Teaching*, 6 (2): 200–8.
Anya, U. (2021), 'Critical Race Pedagogy for More Effective and Inclusive World Language Teaching', *Applied Linguistics*, 42 (6): 1055–69.
Aronowitz, S. (2013), 'Introduction: Paulo Freire's Pedagogy: Not Mainly a Teaching Method', in R. Lake and T. Kress (eds.), *Paulo Freire's Intellectual Roots: Toward Historicity in Praxis*, 1–10, New York and London: Bloomsbury.
Bauman, R., and C. L. Briggs. (2003), *Voices of Modernity: Language Ideologies and the Politics of Inequality* (Studies in the Social and Cultural Foundations of Language; no. 21), Cambridge and New York: Cambridge University Press.
Bouamer, S., and L. Bourdeau, eds. (2022), *Diversity and Decolonization in French Studies: New Approaches to Teaching*, Cham: Palgrave Macmillan.
Canagarajah A. S. (2003), *Resisting Linguistic Imperialism in English Teaching*, Oxford: Oxford University Press.
Canagarajah, A. S., ed. (2005), *Reclaiming the Local in Language Policy and Practice*, London and New York: Routledge.
Conrod, K. (2020), 'Pronouns and Gender in Language', in K. Hall and R. Barrett (eds.), *The Oxford Handbook of Language and Sexuality*, 1–45, Oxford: Oxford University Press.
Crookes, G. V. (2022), 'Critical Language Pedagogy', *Language Teaching*, 55 (1): 46–63.
Crookes, G. V., and A. Abednia. (2021), *Starting Points in Critical Language Pedagogy*, Charlotte, NC: Information Age Publishing.
Criser, R., and E. Malakaj, eds. (2020), *Diversity and Decolonization in German Studies*, Cham: Palgrave Macmillan.
Dasli, M., and A. R. Díaz, eds. (2017), *The Critical Turn in Language and Intercultural Communication Pedagogy: Theory, Research and Practice*, New York and Abingdon, Oxon: Routledge.
Davies, A. (2003), *The Native Speaker: Myth and Reality*, Clevedon and Buffalo: Multilingual Matters.
de Sousa Santos, B. (2014), *Epistemologies of the South: Justice against Epistemicide*, Abingdon, Oxon: Routledge.
Díaz, A. R. (2013), *Developing Critical Languaculture Pedagogies in Higher Education: Theory and Practice*, Bristol: Multilingual Matters.
Freire, P. (2005), *Pedagogy of the Oppressed: 30th Anniversary Edition*, New York: Continuum.
García, O. (2019), 'Decolonizing Foreign, Second, Heritage and First languages: Implications for Education', in D. P. Macedo (ed.), *Decolonizing Foreign Language Education: The Misteaching of English and Other Colonial Languages*, 152–68, New York: Routledge.
García, O., N. Flores, K. Seltzer, W. Li, R. Otheguy, and J. Rosa. (2021), 'Rejecting Abyssal Thinking in the Language and Education of Racialized Bilinguals: A Manifesto', *Critical Inquiry in Language Studies*, 18 (3): 203–28.
Godley, A. J., and J. Reaser. (2018), *Critical Language Pedagogy*, New York: Peter Lang Verlag.

Gogolin, I. (2008), *Der monolinguale Habitus der multilingualen Schule*, Münster: Waxmann.

Guilherme, M. (2002), *Critical Citizens for an Intercultural World: Foreign Language Education as Cultural Politics*, Clevedon: Multilingual Matters.

Heller, M., and A. Duchêne, eds. (2007), *Discourses of Endangerment: Ideology and Interest in the Defence of Languages* (Advances in sociolinguistics), London, New York: Continuum.

Heller, M., and B. McElhinny. (2017), *Language, Capitalism, Colonialism: Toward a Critical History*. Toronto: University of Toronto Press.

hooks, b. (1994), *Teaching to Transgress: Education as the Practice of Freedom*, New York: Routledge.

Kramsch, C. (2020), *Language as Symbolic Power*, Cambridge: Cambridge University Press.

Kramsch, C., and L. Zhang. (2017), *The Multilingual Instructor*, Oxford: Oxford University Press.

Kubota, R. (2021), 'Critical Antiracist Pedagogy in ELT', *ELT Journal*, 75 (3): 237–46.

Kumashiro, K. (2002), *Troubling Education: Queer Activism and Anti-Oppressive Education*, New York and London: Routledge.

Ladson-Billings, G. (1994), *The Dreamkeepers: Successful Teachers of African American Children* (2nd ed.), San Francisco, CA: Jossey Bass.

Lake, R., and V. Dagostino. (2013), 'Converging Self/Other Awareness: Erich Fromm and Paulo Freire on Transcending the Fear of Freedom', in R. Lake and T. Kress (eds.), *Paulo Freire's Intellectual Roots: Toward Historicity in Praxis*, 101–26, New York and London: Bloomsbury.

Lazar, M. M. (2014), 'Feminist Critical Discourse Analysis: Relevance for Current Gender and Language Research', in S. Ehrlich, M. Meyerhoff, and J. Holmes (eds.), *The Handbook of Language, Gender and Sexuality*, 180–99, Chichester: Wiley-Blackwell.

Macedo, D. P. (2019a), 'Rupturing the Yoke of Colonialism in Foreign Language Education: An Introduction', in D. P. Macedo (ed.), *Decolonizing Foreign Language Education: The Misteaching of English and Other Colonial Languages*, 1–49, New York: Routledge.

Macedo, D. P., ed. (2019b), *Decolonizing Foreign Language Education: The Misteaching of English and Other Colonial Languages*, New York: Routledge.

Makalela, L. (2018), 'Teaching African Languages the Ubuntu Way: The Effects of Translanguaging Among Pre-Service Teachers in South Africa', in P. Van Avermaet, S. Slembrouck, K. Van Gorp, S. Sierens, and K. Maryns (eds.), *The Multilingual Edge of Education*, 261–82, London: Palgrave Macmillan.

Mignolo, W. D. (2007), 'Delinking: The Rhetoric of Modernity, the Logic of Coloniality and the Grammar of De-Coloniality', *Cultural Studies*, 21 (2–3): 449–514.

Morgan, B., and A. Mattos. (2018), 'Theories and Practices in Critical Language Teaching: A Dialogic Introduction', *Revista Brasileira de Linguística Aplicada*, 18 (2). Available online: http://www.scielo.br/scielo.php?script=sci_arttext&pid=S1984-63982018000200213&lng=en&tlng=en (accessed June 7, 2022).

Norton, B., and K. Toohey. (2004), *Critical Pedagogies and Language Learning*, Cambridge: Cambridge University Press.

Osborn, T. A. (2021), *Critical Reflection and the Foreign Language Classroom (20th Anniversary Edition)*, Charlotte, NC: Information Age Publishing.
Pennycook, A. (1994), *The Cultural Politics of English as an International Language*, New York: Longman Group Limited.
Pennycook, A., and S. Makoni. (2020), *Innovations and Challenges in Applied Linguistics from the Global South*, Abingdon, Oxon: Routledge.
Pessoa, R. R., and M. Túlio De Urzêda Freitas. (2012), 'Challenges in Critical Language Teaching', *TESOL Quarterly*, 46 (4): 753–76.
Phipps, A. (2019), *Decolonising Multilingualism: Struggles to Decreate*, Bristol and Blue Ridge Summit: Multilingual Matters.
Phipps, A. M., and M. Guilherme, eds. (2004), *Critical Pedagogy: Political Approaches to Language and Intercultural Communication*, Clevedon: Multilingual Matters.
Piller, I. (2016), *Linguistic Diversity and Social Justice: An Introduction to Applied Sociolinguistics*, New York: Oxford University Press.
Preston, S., and J. Aslett. (2014), 'Resisting Neoliberalism from within the Academy: Subversion through an Activist Pedagogy', *Social Work Education*, 33 (4): 502–18.
Rampton, M. B. H. (1990), 'Displacing the 'Native Speaker': Expertise, Affiliation, and Inheritance', *ELT Journal*, 44 (2): 97–101.
Reagan, T. (2022), *Democracy and World Language Education: Toward a Transformation*. Charlotte, NC: Information Age Publishing.
Reagan, T. G., and T. A. Osborn. (2020), *World Language Education as Critical Pedagogy: The Promise of Social Justice*, New York: Routledge.
Savignon, S. J. (1991), 'Communicative Language Teaching: State of the Art', *TESOL Quarterly*, 25 (2): 261–78.
Scott, J. (1990), *Domination and the Arts of Resistance*, New Haven, CT: Yale University Press.
Tuck, E., and K. W. Yang. (2012), 'Decolonization is not a Metaphor', *Decolonization: Indigeneity, Education & Society*, 1 (1): 1–40.
Wassell, B. A., and C. Glynn, eds. (2022), *Transforming World Language Teaching and Teacher Education for Equity and Justice: Pushing Boundaries in US Contexts*. Bristol: Multilingual Matters.
Wassell, B. A., P. Wesely, and C. Glynn. (2019), 'Agents of Change: Reimagining Curriculum and Instruction in World Language Classrooms through Social Justice Education', *Journal of Curriculum and Pedagogy*, 16 (3): 263–84.

# Part I
# Interculturality, Decolonization and Decanonization

# CHAPTER 1

# Existential Literacy

# Promoting the Culture of Dignity for All Languages in Modern Language Classrooms

*David Balosa*

## Introduction

This chapter discusses the theory of *existential literacy* and the ways in which it may foster skills, reflections and mindsets needed in building and promoting a culture of happiness, courage, equity, diversity, inclusion and dignity for all. It also articulates strategies for better relationship-building as the main purpose of constructive and unifying communication (Celler, 1974; Gouhier 1974). I may use communication and literacy interchangeably to mean written, oral, technological, social media and arts as means of communication (Danesi 2004). (For example, Gouhier (1974) argues: 'communication is a relation from a subject to a subject' (p. 8). Neuliep (2021) states: 'Communication is everywhere. Every day, everywhere, people are communicating. Even when alone, people are bombarded with communication' (p. 8).) From this perspective we can deduce that communication or literacy is existential. This chapter intends to inspire and encourage people independently of their communication style, which I describe as an existential literacy, since life would be difficult to fully enjoy without communication. One would make sense to claim that an individual or a society that cannot communicate in any form of the different communication styles is a dead individual or a dead society. What kind of communication or literacy do we expect? The answer to this question is that we expect communication that builds better relationships among human diversity to bring happiness and build better societies for all. Failure to achieve this goal may create anxiety, misunderstanding and other multiple crises that may undermine the overarching culture of dignity for all (Canclini 2001; Danesi 2004).

Today's world still communicatively behaves under the heritage of colonization in which a politics of communication chose not to build better relations among different races, ethnicities, nations, languages, cultures, identities, personalities and continents, preventing individuals and communities across the globe from cultivating a *sustainable existential intercultural mindset* (SEIM) and better 'understanding' of human diversity (Fishman 1989: 20). To decolonize communicative behaviour and policies in and out of the classrooms, we need to promote intercultural or humane practices and discourses that counteract segregation, domination and humiliation of other subjects and cultures. In this regard, the anthropologist Néstor García Canclini reminds us that we live 'in a world so fluidly interconnected, the diverse ways in which the members of each group appropriate the heterogeneous repertoire of goods and messages available in the transnational circuits generate new forms of knowledge from various countries and cultures' (Canclini 1995: xxviii–ix). This is where the relevance of the theory of existential literacy prevails because to adjust to the imperative of the new forms of communication, literacies, and ways of life within the transnational circuits of the age of globalization, one must cultivate what I call a SEIM. Hence, we need to engage and encourage moral obligation embedded in communication as a relationship-building process for a dignifying intercultural world, where mutual human, cultural and linguistic respect and appreciation of equity, diversity and unity can bring happiness, peace, justice and prosperity for all. Within this context, the theory of existential literacy should play a crucial role – the role of (re)education, (re)construction and (re)adjustment in the building of relationships through a mechanism of SEIM to promote 'the courage to be' (Tillich 2014: 3) and a better existence for all (Gordon 1988; Marcel 1967; Miller 2013).

In his book *Society as Text: Essays on Rhetoric, Reason, and Reality* (1987), American sociologist Richard Harvey Brown writes: 'intelligible communication between groups and classes in a society is a precondition for the existence of a public in the classical, political sense of that term' (5). Existential literacy agrees that languages and cultures are parts of society as text. Thus, excluding certain languages in the management of a society is a destructive attitude that must be eradicated to adjust to the demand of intercultural ecology (Bateson 2000; 1980; Hornberger 2003; Hult 2014).

This chapter emphasizes the need for understanding cultural dependence and interdependence as a moral responsibility for mutual empowerment, and the respect and dignity of all languages as a sign of justice towards the representation of each society's life experience, which can be translated, interpreted and understood in any other life experience in any other society for the good of entire humanity. In my opinion, this interdependence or interculturality fosters literacy in all languages and the possibility to perform teaching that may be identified as a strategy for existential literacy. For example, the sociologist Milton M. Gordon argues: 'To attempt to understand human behavior is to me the most exciting intellectual challenge in the world. To use the results of whatever understanding is achieved to improve in substantial fashion the welfare of humankind constitutes the most impelling ethical imperative that our species collectively faces' (1988: 3). If we agree with Gordon, we must also agree with virtues such as love, courage, wisdom, patience, peace and joy that the theory of existential literacy may generate within individuals and communities. That is, an individual or a society needs to be equipped with a model of literacy – a model of epistemology – that guides him/her or it to appreciate, recognize and apply the understanding of various human behaviours across the cultures of the world for the welfare of humankind. This challenge should be addressed also in our modern foreign and local language classrooms. After the classrooms, we all, teachers and students, face an intercultural existence. We may reduce misunderstanding and anti-intercultural conflicts by acquiring and developing a SEIM.

In this chapter, I define interculturality as processes of recognition and integration of human, linguistic, cultural, technological, moral and environmental diversity that constitute our integrated humanity or global life landscape in fostering the culture of human dignity and common good (Maxwell 2014; Plummer 2021). That is, processes that highlight the need for a *sustainable existential intercultural mindset* to appreciate diversity and act in exemplary ways in re/constructing and strengthening political, educational and moral obligation for a better management of individuals' and communities' multiple and diverse identities in and out of the classroom (Balosa 2022a, 2022b; Rushkoff 2019; Stolle-McAllister 2019; Taylor 1995). Hence, interculturality nurtures empathy and equity in critical pedagogy and other processes related to public and social policies to cultivate mindsets of creativity, mutual mentorship, mutual understanding and mutual empowerment for better intercultural relationships. It is the backbone of existential literacy and the power to advocate for self-decolonization and decolonization of traditional educational practices and established oppressive and discriminatory discourses. In the age of globalization and interconnectedness, interculturality furnishes the insight to equitably treat life diversity with what I call *existential justice* (Balosa 2022b: 7289), rather than treating it 'on judgmental grounds' and oppressive and exclusive attitudes and practices that offend the liberty and the dignity of minorities and others (Dworkin 2006: 78; Mallon 2012: 43).

Existential literacy draws upon Nancy H. Hornberger's *Continua of Biliteracy: An Ecological Framework* (2003) – work that discusses bi/

multiliteracy 'as any and all instances in which communication occurs in two or more languages in or around writing' (xiii). Beyond *Continua of Biliteracy*, it encompasses all literacies including capacities for self-consciousness in fostering a culture of human dignity, building better and durable relationships with others and cultivating interest in global textualities of our modern life system – a system inescapably interdependent (Gee 2017; Schwartz 2019; Sorrells 2016; Tubino 2015). For example, in his article 'How Does Policy Influence Language in Education?' (2014), educational linguistics scholar Francis M. Hult articulates both 'the role of institutions and individuals' in the scales of policy and planning for languages in education (166–7). He argues that 'teachers are on the front line of language policy since the classroom is a key site where policies become action – teachers make decisions every day that amount to developing language policies for their classrooms' (159). Hult explains that 'teachers decide which language(s) to use during instruction, which language(s) to encourage when students speak to each other, what words are taboo, etc.' (Ibid). Bateson (1980) argues that the simplest but the most profound in the case of difference is 'the fact that it takes at least two somethings to create a difference – to produce news of difference or information, there must be two entities, real or imagined, such as the difference between them can be immanent in their mutual relationship' (76). Language teachers have the moral responsibility to articulate this difference in their classrooms and to play the role of transformational or decolonizing-mindset agents to promote a culture of dignity for all languages (Macedo 2019; Pirbhai-Illich et al. 2017; Wa Thiong'o 1986, 1993).

## *Definition of Existential Literacy*

I define *Existential Literacy* as 'the strategic capability acquired through various mindful life experience (family, schooling, community, friendship, media, sport, and so on) that facilitates the circumstantial adjustment to the acquisition of new mindful experiences and to the creation of new capacities leading one to living a more humane life and enjoying a dignified human existence within the responsibility for self and others' (Balosa 2022b: 7289) – that is, a comprehensive critical education that may help in managing life issues across intercultural encounters and building better and durable relationships in fostering 'existential justice and sustainable transformational interculturality' (Balosa 2022b: 7289–90) for individual and collective sustainable development (Sachs 2015; Tubino 2015). This set of capabilities provides necessary skills to help an individual or group of individuals adjust to life struggles for a happy, productive and balanced lifestyle for the common good. As an interdisciplinary educational philosophical approach, existential literacy draws its insights from social sciences and humanities. It aims to spread practices and attitudes of SEIM, existential justice and radical transformational intercultural pedagogies that build durable relationships and responsibility in fostering a culture of human dignity (Dewey 1997; Freire 2000; Lobmam and Perone 2018; McLean 2013). For example, Freire (2000) discusses the cultural divide that creates inequity in societies today: 'director culture/society' and 'silence culture/alienated society' (8–9). This dichotomized cultural treatment, according to Freire, disparages cultures assumed to be inferior or with less power. Freire appeals to conscientization to resist or 'demystify' this tendency and equitably treat all cultures with dignity (12). In the same vein, existential literacy theory proposes pedagogies and policies that radically oppose disparaging educational practices to encourage SEIM, behaviours, and skills/competences for sustainable individual and community 'development' (Sachs 2015: 3–4).

## Existential Literacy: A Socio-philosophical Educational Approach to Language Pedagogy

Drawing upon sociological, philosophical and educational linguistic perspectives, the theory of existential literacy fosters the idea of building and rebuilding exemplary individuals and societies in handling intercultural humanity. That is, individuals and societies with an understanding of the imperative of the multiplicities of modern world identities within its interconnectedness and with the virtues of humility, hope and courage try to learn and integrate new experiences from different cultures and environments in order to become exemplary individuals and societies in the processes of building better human relationships and better societies for all (Dewey 1938/1997; Freire 1992; Gordon 1988; Marcel 1967).

As mentioned earlier, Gordon (1988) articulates the attempt 'to use the results of whatever understanding is achieved to improve in substantial fashion the welfare of humankind' (3) as the most significant intellectual and ethical imperative that our species collectively should be engaged in. This sociological perspective is integrative, intercultural and existential because of the interconnectedness of human experiences in today's modern world. No suffering is any more an isolated experience to one sole community or nation. Hence, our common suffering should be addressed by a collective effort and a collective set of strategies for the common good. In a multilingual world, this effort must be considered by implementing multilingual policies that are inclusive or that address 'the political legitimacy of linguistic minority rights' (Balosa 2022a: 148). Human beings use languages 'to bring about a change of reality through words or by the sheer performance of appropriate words by the appropriate person' (Kramsch 2009: 8). They also make 'particular meanings' (Kramsch 1998: 4) proper to their cultural identities to be adopted by the members of their community or their 'speech community' (Ibid.). Hence, refusing to include a given language in a national language policy is tantamount to rejecting the dignity of that language and the capacity of the speakers of that language to bring about a change of reality through words of their language or the specific meanings of their expressions related to their cultural identities. This behaviour does not encourage the intercultural mindset or effort for the welfare of the entire humanity (Gordon 1988). The theory of existential literacy proposes a transformed behaviour from which all cultures are to be subjects of learning or understanding in the effort to improve common existence.

Paulo Freire thought that critical pedagogy must promote hope. He argues: 'Hopelessness paralyzes us, immobilizes us. We succumb to fatalism, and then it becomes impossible to muster the strength we absolutely need for a fierce struggle that will re-create the world' (Freire 1992: 8). Existential literacy helps re-create the world in that it equips its advocates or users with strategies or skills to resist unjust traditions, social injustices, manipulative politics, uncritical pedagogies (uncritical teaching and learning) and destructive and impoverishing illiteracy. It also encourages and inspires intercultural solidarity in building and developing a SEIM.

In discussing experience and education, John Dewey asked a deep question, which significantly inspires the theory of existential literacy. He asks: 'How shall the young man or woman become acquainted with past in such a way that the acquaintance is a potent agent in appreciation of the living present?' (Dewey 1938/1997: 23). Dewey thought that progressive education should not reject knowledge of the past and should emphasize the importance of education only as a means. As shown in the question he asked, Dewey advocated for a model of education or knowledge or literacy that was integrative and intercultural in that learners (youth or adults) would feel being in possession of 'a potent agent in appreciation of the living present' (Ibid.). This is exactly the model of educational experience and intercultural life perspectives that existential literacy proposes, not merely to foreign languages classrooms but to all knowledge or educational setting spaces. It is this literacy that may help renew the reflection about and the appreciation of life within equity, unity and diversity. It is here that literacy plays its true role – the role of helping human beings better their existence. For example, Alfred North Whitehead suggests: 'We have to remember that the valuable intellectual development is self-development' (Whitehead 1929/1967: 1): that is, a development that resists 'inert ideas' – 'ideas that are merely received into the mind without being utilized, or tested, or thrown into fresh combinations' (Ibid.). Here again, the relevance of the theory of existential literacy is demonstrated by supporting knowledge or life experiences that are real, productive and in combination or integration with different knowledge – interculturality.

Since this chapter focuses on the culture of dignity for all languages in modern language classrooms, I cannot close this section without looking at educational linguistics on this proposal.

Hult (2008) defines educational linguistics as 'an area of study that integrates the research tools of linguistics and other related disciplines of the social sciences in order to investigate holistically the broad range of issues related to language and education' (10). Spolsky (2008) proposes that 'questioning language management may seem to move us beyond the sphere of language policy and educational linguistics into fundamental questions of identity and philosophy' (4). He adds that 'it is a reasonable step in a study of both fields and fair to note that most scholars in the field tend toward activist positions, assuming that their expertise in various aspects of educational linguistics gives them responsibility as well as ability to attempt to manage language education' (Ibid.). Existential literacy encourages teachers and learners to engage in dialogue on building durable relationships by embracing all languages existing in the sociolinguistic identity of the classroom. That is, it supports critical pedagogy in enhancing the disposition of valuing all languages and cultures not merely for intercultural communication needs, but also for individual and collective culture of dignity with respect to all languages and all identities (Canclini 2001; Freire 1992; Gouhier 1987; McLean 2013).

## Existential Literacy, Globalization and Critical Pedagogy

Steger (2009) defines globalization as 'a process, a condition, a system, a force, and an age' (8). He adds that 'it is a social condition characterized by tight global economic, political, cultural, and environmental interconnections and flows that make most of the currently existing borders and boundaries irrelevant' (Ibid.). Beck (2000) discusses globalization as a multiple-dimensioned discourse of internationalized life. For example, he argues that regarding communication, 'national states can no longer cut themselves off from one another; their army-patrolled frontiers are full of holes, at least as far as their insertion in the space of global communications is concerned' (17). Beck calls this dimension of globalization 'informational globalization' (Ibid.). He discusses another dimension in which he argues that all social players everywhere in the world, in every domain from consumption through production to architecture, transport, municipal politics and so on are engaged in. He calls this dimension 'ecological globalization' (18). Beck discusses other dimensions of globalization such as 'economic globalization' – the regulation of transnational or global economies, and 'cultural globalization' (Ibid.). He argues: 'globalization does not have to be a one-way street – a regional personality, regional musical, or artistic culture, and/ or a regional dish can acquire world states and a global significance' (18, 19). He concludes his reasoning arguing that globalization has certainly been the most widely used and misused keyword in disputes of recent years and will be in the coming years too. He suggests that globalization is also one of the most rarely defined, the most nebulous and misunderstood, as well as the most politically effective words. That is, everyone can in manipulative ways use globalization to exploit the vulnerable or minority groups. Finally, he proposes that it is necessary to distinguish various dimensions of globalization – any list of these would have to include, without making any claim to completeness or rigour, the dimensions of 'communications technology, ecology, economics, work organization, and culture' (19). This is where critical pedagogy should intervene. That is, adjusting educational practices to the globalization discourses and clarify what needs to be clarified and critique what needs to be criticized.

Appadurai (2001) proposes a deeper consideration of the relationship between the knowledge of globalization and the globalization of knowledge. He affirms that democracy, globalization and pedagogy are intertwined to the extent that globalization is not simply the name for a new epoch in the history of capital or in the biography of the nation. It is, rather, marked by a new role for the imagination in social life – a role that has many contexts (14). Foreign language educators should explore these contexts and address the value of all languages as 'markers of deep identity of a community, individuals, or group of people' (Hagège 2008: 7) and the 'sincerity – the state or the quality of the self' (Trilling 1972: 2) of our cultural identities within the global cultural-ecological landscape. They should also be inspired by the American educator John Erskine (1879–1951) who had discussed '[t]he happy combination of character and intelligence and the recognition of the value of this combination in our neighbors' (Erskine 1915: 13).

## Theoretical Framework

This chapter employs existential sociolinguistics as its theoretical framework. Existential sociolinguistics[1] is a paradigm in analysing language issues based on the matrix of 'the treatment and recognition of existing languages and the value of linguistic and cultural diversity and its impact on equity and human dignity' (Balosa 2022a: 149, 155). It argues that all languages should be inseparably treated from the treatment of human beings or users of these languages. That is, any mistreatment of a language is tantamount to a discriminatory and oppressive behaviour towards human beings, users of these languages or varieties of these languages. Existential sociolinguistics agrees with existing paradigms in contemporary sociolinguistics, linguistic anthropology and intercultural communication studies' focus on 'advancing a moral case for the protection of world's languages' based on 'four broad and mutually reinforcing strands of arguments for maintenance of linguistic and cultural diversity: public good, the world-view, the biodiversity and the rights arguments' (Danesi 2020: 1–2; Orman 2008: 62; Piller 2016: 73). Yet, it proposes a fifth strand of argument to this moral case, that is, the strand of the analysis of language and language speakers' treatment from *a human dignity perspective* (Marcel 1954, 1963). Language issues in Bible studies and religious influences on colonized cultures and people figure among topics of interest to existential sociolinguistics (Fromm 1966; Hobsbawn 1962; Sorrells 2016).

In addition, this paradigm advocates for radical transformation of sociolinguistic injustice. For example, in his article 'Mutual Learning as an Agenda for Social Development' (2007), philosopher Tu Weiming reminds us of 'the emergence of new communal critical self-consciousness among public intellectuals' and how it better facilitates 'individuals' participation in strengthening cooperation for social development through various sources and help realize inspiring leadership on the global scene' (333). The existential sociolinguistic paradigm provides an opportunity for mutual empowerment and unity within diversity for a culture of dignity for all. It also appeals for a 'sustainable existential intercultural mindset (SEIM) – an understanding of human worth within its diversity as a force that sustains our symbolic universal brotherhood and public/community diplomacy' (Balosa 2022a: 151, Banda 2022: 230).

## Critical Pedagogy and Existential Sociolinguistics

Wink (2011) reminds us that 'there is no one critical pedagogy', but definitions 'within the context, within praxis – integration of theory and practice' rather than glossary definitions are encouraged (28). Wink suggests that critical perspectives do not mean bad, nor to criticize; rather, they mean to find 'new ways of seeing and knowing, that is seeing beyond – looking within and without and seeing more deeply the complexities of teaching and learning' (Ibid.). Giroux (2020) suggests that critical pedagogy should help liberate teaching and learning from 'fascist cultures and the dictatorship of ignorance across the world' (195). Indeed, existential sociolinguistics as defined earlier provides critical pedagogy valid arguments to deconstruct established oppressive and discriminatory treatments of minority languages. In the world of complex identities, plural hierarchy of discourses, foreign language educational policies, national language policies and global/international language policies that marginalize minority or non-dominant languages, existential sociolinguistics encourages a critical stance towards language issues which are also life issues. Hence critical pedagogy and existential sociolinguistics foster attitudes and actions that may generate an intercultural awareness in and out of language classrooms for the common good, that is, 'a sense of universality – wisdom and common sense' (Marcel 1954: vii), a responsibility of 'building an environment for learning and development' for individuals and for communities (Lobman and Perone 2018: 5).

## Research Method

This chapter uses philosophical reflection as its research method to articulate the importance of understanding and reflecting on the value of cultural resources to foster a culture of dignity for all languages and cultures in and out of the classrooms (Aiken 1956/1984; McLean 2013; Marcel 1952/2008). In *The Age of Ideology: The 19th Century Philosophers* (1956/1984), the moral philosopher Henry D. Aiken wrote: 'Philosophical reflection is an indispensable adjunct of the conduct of life' (p. viii). He argues that 'it is impossible to adhere to the Socratic dictum, "know thyself (yourself)!" if one knows nothing else' (Ibid.). In today's connected world system, it is appropriate to reflect upon life's issues using philosophical reflections as practical wisdom. Maritain (1940) reminds us that '[f]eeling and acting for justice redress the balance of things – without political justice, there cannot be peace, freedom, and happiness for the peoples' (91–5, 114). Alleviating oppression and discrimination against minority languages and speakers of these languages requires reflections to analyse 'the techniques or strategies', politics and discourses used by these forces (Marcel 1952/2008: 30). The question is: How can philosophical reflections help one conduct research within an existential literacy approach? In his book *The Existential Background of Human Dignity* (1963), the French existential philosopher Gabriel Marcel suggests that the problem of today's world and its spirit of abstraction 'cannot be separated from a certain lack of love, that is, the inability to treat a human being a human being' (123). From this argument, I understand that philosophical reflections entail analysing texts and discourses in various life contexts including historico-religious texts or biblical texts to determine whether human beings of a given society or community are being treated with dignity.

In this chapter, the method of philosophical reflection is deployed by analysing the way in which hegemonic treatment of minority languages in educational practices fails to appreciate the inseparability of the treatment of a given language and its users or speakers, and act accordingly. It is also deployed in analysing the consequences and the harm that minority groups suffer because of the failure of the existential recognition of the dignity of languages, their cultural resources and their cultural identities by the dominant powers within and out of the established traditional educational and pedagogical system. For example, reflecting on the ways that the voice of minority language speakers are heard or rejected in democratic nations' classrooms can tell us about the state of the culture of dignity for all languages and identities. In certain traditional societies, educating girls used to be perceived as a taboo. In some modern societies, qualified men are still being paid more than women with the same qualification and performing the same job. In this context, the philosophical reflection method deconstructs these policies and reveals a new orientation for more humane practices and policies. The French philosopher Jacques Maritain once argued: 'All begins at the spiritual level, and if the transformation is not first a moral one, nothing will really be renewed or transformed' (Maritain 1940: 41). He adds: 'It is this transformation that leads to building just structures for common existence' (42, 43). Furthermore, Maritain discussed how true justice operates. He writes: 'True justice recognizes the varieties of traditions, the diversity of historic conditions, and the treatment of all human beings as beings with the same fundamental dignity and different qualities or characteristics' (95). From this perspective, and in my opinion, philosophical reflection can be perceived as that spiritual place where all begins to achieve any moral transformation that may lead to building just structures for the common existence and the treatment of all human beings with the same fundamental or basic dignity.

For example, in this chapter I demonstrate how I deployed philosophical reflection in my French classroom by judiciously using the learners' home languages in fostering the awareness of languages' equal dignity and consciousness of cultural identities as 'cultural resources' (McLean 2013: 65). I also deployed this method to monitor how a teacher, or an educator, can build a mentorship for durable relationship and creating an environment for learning, self-consciousness and development (Lobman and Perone 2018). The more policymakers and educators can deploy philosophical reflection in their dealing with linguistic and cultural diversity in and out of the classroom, the more they will foster a culture of dignity for all languages, cultures and identities. This behaviour, as encouraged by existential literacy, should promote a SEIM.

## How Can Teachers Determine Language Classroom Strategies That Foster Existential Literacy?

To answer this research question, we need to reflect on how foreign language instructors can engage in 'communal critical self-consciousness' in their teaching practices (Tu 2007: 333). The first evaluative procedure is *existential literacy mentorship for building relationships*. This observational indicator should determine whether there is an 'I will give you a hand!' attitude or practices from teachers' strategies. Hence, their students should be looking at them as *global intercultural mentors*. As I mentioned earlier, Tu (2007) argues that 'the emergence of a new communal critical self-consciousness among public intellectuals will better facilitate American participation in strengthening cooperation for social development' (Ibid.). From this self-consciousness, Tu suggests: 'The American people could benefit from a spirit of distributive justice in economy, an ethic of responsibility in politics, a sense of trust in society, and, above all, a culture of peace' (Ibid.).

Existential literacy encourages these attributes as strategies in building relationships in the classrooms. From an *existential literacy mentorship for relationship-building* perspective, existential literacy provides a framework of a global mutual learning and evaluative *hand-giving* approach to pedagogies in language classrooms. Paul Freire once said: 'There is no possibility for teaching without learning. As well as there is no possibility of learning without teaching' (Wink 2011: 102). Freire's argument and its relationship-rich educational vision is justified by Felten and Lambert (2020) who insist that '[s]tudents' interactions with peers, faculty, and staff positively influence the breadth and depth of student learning, retention, and a wide range of other outcomes, including critical thinking, identity development, communication skills, and leadership abilities' (p. 5). Secondly, Freire (1993) argues that '[w]e want a progressive and truly competent educational system, not a demagogically populist one – one that respects the ways of beings of its students, their class and cultural patterns, their values, their knowledge, and their language' (p. 37). The second evaluative procedure of existential literacy pedagogies is *global intercultural-intellectuality mentorship for existential justice*. This procedure entails the teachers' commitment to exemplary attitudes and practices with respect to intercultural epistemology in promoting intercultural communication reflections and competences and social justice' in their classrooms. Here I define interculturality as a self-conscious commitment to understanding, participating and celebrating humanity in its comprehensive diversity. In this regard, the French philosopher Paul Celier made a claim that humanity should foster global intercultural-intellectuality mentorship for existential justice. He writes: 'We believe in humanity as a universal society of human beings, we believe also in an inalienable identity of all human beings in their ways of observation, ways of judgement and ways of reasoning, we believe in a common reason to all or to a human nature present in all' (Celier 1974: 59). Indeed, in building durable intercultural relations, one must recognize aspects of human diversity in its singularity and universality if we are to communicatively function for peace and freedom for all in this intercultural world.

Dewey (1938/1997) argues that '[t]he only freedom that is of enduring importance is freedom of intelligence – freedom of observation and of judgment exercised on behalf of purposes that are intrinsically worthwhile' (p. 61). From their classrooms, language instructors can operate as transformational intercultural agents as they spread the notion of *existential justice* towards all languages, cultures and humans. That is, the awareness of cultural dependence and interdependence may be a constructive force of solidarity and mutual empowerment if used within existential justice or an equitable recognition of all existing languages, cultures and human beings. Existential justice supports SEIM (Balosa 2022b: 151; Banda 230).

## Decolonization and Existential Literacy

The past and recent research on decolonization, post-decolonization and culturally responsive pedagogy articulates issues related to social and human justice (Fanon 1952/2008; Freire 1975/2005; Macedo 2019; Pirbhai-Illich et al. 2017) and supports the importance of existential literacy in and out of foreign language classrooms. Fanon (1952/2008) has summoned the world to unite their effort for the independence and the dignity of every people across the globe. He writes: 'Striving for a New Humanism – understanding mankind – racial Prejudice – understanding and Loving' (xi). He believed that an individual must endeavour to assume the universalism inherent in the human condition to be successful. Hence, Fanon wrote: 'we urgently need to rid ourselves of a series of defects inherited from childhood' (Ibid.). Here is where critical pedagogies can become an appropriate intervention for radically transforming entrenched practices of humiliation in the politics of languages across language policies and across institutions where the treatment of human and linguistic diversity is oppressive (Schwartz 2019; Urciuoli 1996). That is, the awareness of their responsibility to adjust to life realities and to transform them for their better existence and the existence of their surroundings is denied to them. It is reasonable to describe this behaviour as a colonialist behaviour that must be decolonized if we are to cultivate a SEIM. I hope the insights from this chapter contribute to the cultivation of virtues in and out of language classrooms in promoting the culture of dignity for all language for the common good (Block and Cameron 2002; Fairclough 2006; Gee 2017).

## Decolonization and Existential Literacy in Modern Foreign Language Classrooms

The experience of colonial educational policy is to prevent a certain class or race from acquiring literacy. This dehumanizing and discriminatory politics has generated shame and lack of self-esteem in colonized people to use their languages in encounters with major dominant world languages. For example, in Balosa (2006), I share experiences from my English as Second Language students, who, using their home languages, not only helped them better learn English, but also helped establish durable relationships, 'students' self-esteem, and friendship' (p. 3). It became evident that students felt recognized and dignified as their L1 was treated with respect and dignity. Their participation increased and the atmosphere of trust and mutual empowerment made learning enjoyable. In my French class in South Philadelphia High School, we have multiple languages: Lingala, Mandingo, Swahili, Indonesian, Vietnamese, Spanish and Portuguese. In grammar lessons of conjugation and telling one's age in French, the students find it interesting to notice that while English uses the verb *to be* to talk about one's age, French uses the verb *to have*.

Example 1: English:   I am sixteen years old.   French: *J'ai seize ans.*

English:   How old is Aisha?   French: *Quel âge a Aisha?*

English:   She is sixteen years old. French: *Elle a seize ans.*

To make sure that students remember this grammatical pattern, I use the notion of *linguistic difference*. I insist that using this notion will help them not to fall into the thinking of languages in terms of one given language structure. Each language is its own entity and has its own rule of use and sounds. Certain languages may have similar grammatical patterns and semantic indicators such as cognates but that does not make them the same. One day, as we were reviewing 'talking about one's age in French', we found out that Lingala, Swahili and French use the same pattern. They use '*to have* plus age', contrary to English that uses '*to be* plus age'.

1a. The translation of 'to have' in English, French, Lingala and Swahili:

**English:** 'to have'; **French:** 'avoir'; **Lingala:** 'kozala na'; **Swahili:** 'kukuwa na'

1b. The translation of 'to be' in English, French, Lingala and Swahili:

**English:** 'to be'; **French:** 'être'; **Lingala:** 'kozala'; **Swahili:** 'Kukuwa'

Example 2: English:   *I am sixteen years old.*   French: *J'ai seize ans.*   Lingala: *Nazali na mbula zomi na motoba*

English: *How old is Aisha?*   French: *Quel âge a Aisha?*   Lingala: *Aisha azali na mbula boni?*

English: *She is sixteen years old.*   French: Elle a seize ans.   Lingala: *Azali na mbula zomi na motoba*

Example 3: English: *I am sixteen years old.*   French: *J'ai seize ans.*   Swahili: *Niko na mwaka kumi na sita.*

English: *How old is Aisha?*   French: *Quel âge a Aisha?*   Swahili: *Aisha iko na mwaka ngapi?*

English: *She is sixteen years old.*   French: Elle a seize ans.   Swahili: *Iko na mwaka kumi na sita.*

Using the similarity in French, Swahili and Lingala as regards 'talking about age in French' helps students value all languages as worth of dignity and respect. The students' attention was drawn to the fact that 'kozala' alone without the particle 'na' means 'to be' and is not used to talk about age in Lingala; rather, one uses 'kozala na' to mean 'to have' to talk about one's age. Likewise, 'kukuwa' alone without the particle 'na' means 'to be' and is not used to talk about age in Swahili; rather, one uses 'kukuwa na' to mean 'to have' to talk about one's age. The purpose of this strategy is to decolonize the students' mindset from oppressive linguistic diversity treatment. It also helps them perceive linguistic and cultural difference as a positive sociocultural reality. Mignolo and Walsh (2018) encourage us to walk in the path of decoloniality to be able 'to create the possibilities of building a radically distinct world' (11). Macedo (2019) argues that 'derogatory labels' attributed to languages other than the world major languages are used mainly to categorize linguistic realization and are primarily social labels designed to typecast them so as to devalue their corresponding speakers' cultures, races, ethnicities, and class' (11). In the same vein, Wa Thiong'o (1986/2011) argues that '[l]anguage was the most important vehicle through which the power fascinated and held the soul prisoner. Language was the means of the spiritual subjugation' (27). These arguments should help foreign language teachers apply critical pedagogies to transform the imprisoned minds on language issues into a mind of culture of dignity for all languages.

I found that using students' first languages in teaching French conjugation emboldened them in using their home languages in and out of the classroom and eliminated the perception of using their languages as a taboo or a shameful behaviour (Hult 2014). One day, I said: 'silence, s'il vous plaît!' to the class. Immediately, a student from Guinea Conakry asked me: 'Dr. Balosa, do you know how to say "silence, please!" in Mandingo?' Another student from Indonesia asked: 'What is Mandingo?' The student from Guinea Conakry replied: 'It is my language! In Guinea we speak Mandingo!' After the student instructed me on her language: 'Hei mafa!' means 'Silence, s'il vous plaît!' – I went to the chalk board and wrote the expression in three languages:

> **English**: Silence, please!
> **French**: Silence, s'il vous plaît!
> **Mandingo**: Hei mafa!

Wa Thiong'o (1986, 1993) and Macedo (2019) support this practice in decolonizing the mind on language issues. This small literacy practice fosters the understanding and appreciation of linguistic and cultural diversity and contributes to deconstructing the colonized attitudes on human diversity. Wa Thiong'o (1993) writes: 'Local knowledge is not an island unto itself; it is part of the main, part of the sea. Its limits lie in the boundless universality of our creative potentiality as human beings' (p. 29). This reasoning supports critical pedagogy in foreign language classrooms (Balosa 2006)[2] in that it promotes a culture of dignity for all languages and cultures and creates an environment for intercultural learning, intercultural relations and SEIM.

Bucholtz et al. (2019) present the case of California Latinx youth as agents of sociolinguistic justice. They argue that '[d]ue to political developments in California, many Americans of Latinx heritage have experienced their entire education under draconian and discriminatory policies that ban both their language and their culture. Young people's languages of heritage have been devalued and ignored, despite the established importance of students' home languages for future academic success and social-being' (167). They add that 'in the face of such marginalization, Latinx youth in California have been demanding sociolinguistic justice, or self-determination for linguistically subordinated individuals and groups in sociopolitical struggles over language' (Ibid.). What Bucholtz et al. (2019) call sociolinguistic justice and that I call *existential justice* should be evident in language educators' treatment of other languages in their classrooms (Baugh 2018). Miscommunication can cost one's life. For example, in patient–doctor interaction, or patient–hospital communication, miscommunication can lead to death. Frustration in medical professionals' communication or teaching communication may ensue because language barriers may cause some to favour monolingualism. But how does that do justice to the existence of other languages? Existential literacy suggests that frustration should not push one to adopt the mentality of what Tubino (2015) calls 'homogenization of cultural and linguistic diversity from the language and culture of the hegemonic elite' (259). Rather, it should look upon existential literacy coping strategies such as the awareness and appreciation of cultural and linguistic diversity.

## Deconstructing Cultural and Linguistic Prestige as a Monopoly of Dominant Cultures, Languages and Economic Products

Cultural prestige in the choice of consumptions of various products including languages to learn or to use is a popular practice in life, but it should not operate in the disparagement of other cultures. Students need to be helped to understand this politics of consumption to make judicious decisions on their linguistic consumption if we are to discourage colonized mentalities in today's human affairs or inclusive and participative democracies (Canclini 2001; Pirbhai-Illich et al. 2017; Stolle-McAllister 2019).

Rosenau (1980) shares a preoccupation with the emergence of greater complexity in the affairs of states and the interaction of societies – 'tendencies toward greater interdependence' and the fostering of 'the transnationalization of world affairs' (1). By that Rosenau means 'the process whereby international relations conducted by governments have been supplemented by relations among private individuals, groups, and societies that can and do have important consequences for the course of events' (Ibid.). If we agree with this global social reality, foreign language educators should use their classrooms as a space for deconstruction of colonized and colonizing mentalities in cultural and linguistic use and language policy. In this regard, Rosenau (1980) argues: 'The tasks of educators have undergone change as the world becomes more interdependent' (106). Existential literacy provides a theoretical framework for this change's understanding and adjustment in and out of language classrooms to promote the value and dignity of all languages and cultures.

## Conclusion

This chapter has proposed *existential literacy* as a theoretical framework that supports critical pedagogy in and out of foreign language classrooms. It has demonstrated the ways in which intercultural relations nurture virtues such as love, patience, courage, empathy and existential justice towards learners and users of all languages in fostering 'the culture of peace' (Tu 2007: 333).

This theoretical framework suggests two evaluative procedures from which language educators or policymakers can determine existential literacy strategies in and outside the classrooms: First, *existential literacy mentorship for relationship-building* – dispositions and actions that recognize and demonstrate that all life experiences, all cultures and all languages are worthy of participating in our common humanity. Second, *global intercultural-intellectuality mentorship for existential justice* – an exemplary leadership that emphasizes both individual and collective qualities such as love, wisdom, justice and balanced power in the management of intercultural relations in and out of the classrooms for the achievement of what Jacques Maritain calls 'true justice' and what I call *existential justice* (Maritain 1940: 92). Indeed, these two evaluative procedures by which one can identify existential literacy strategies encourage the moral responsibility of language educators in and out of the classrooms to foster a culture of happiness and dignity for all as guided by the principle of SEIM.

Using existential literacy in critical pedagogy boosts deconstructing colonized dispositions and enhancing intercultural forces to promote linguistic and cultural diversity and build an environment for learning, self-consciousness and development for all (Lobman and Perone 2018; Stolle-McAllister 2019). It encourages *global intercultural-intellectuality mentorship*, that is, an understanding of and the participation in the global textualities of the modern life system and an attitude of fostering intercultural epistemology and radically rejecting traditional hegemonic and elitist epistemology centred in Western or Global North epistemology (Fishman 1989: 20). It finally helps us remember: 'What avail is it to win prescribed amounts of information, to win ability to read and write, if in the process the individual loses his/her soul –loses his/her appreciation of things worthwhile' or life (Dewey 1938/1997: 49). I hope that this chapter contributes to the cultivation of moral obligation, hope and courage conducive to building durable relationships and a culture of dignity for diversity in and out of the language classrooms. Courage and hope should enable us to accept 'who we are' and accept 'who others are' as well, yet build better and durable intercultural relations as we learn from and mutually empower one another. Language educators and policymakers should find here insights that (re)invigorate them in re/constructing possibilities for a happy life for all. Hence, a SEIM will motivate all of us to make efforts towards building and sustaining trust in intercultural relations and understandably and sensitively manage our human, cultural, linguistic, identity and personality diversity for a better existence for all in and out of the language classrooms.

This chapter has also helped us understand in which ways the theory of existential literacy as a socio-philosophical educational approach to language pedagogy fosters hope, courage and integration of experience/diversity 'to appreciate the living present' (Dewey 1938/1997: 23, Freire 1992: 8) and counteracts behaviour that sustains mistrust towards human, linguistic and cultural diversity and discriminatory policies. It has demonstrated how interculturality may encourage and boost the recognition of modern society's interconnectedness and its multilingual and multicultural realities that we should not undermine. Finally, this chapter has encouraged and motivated us to use the understanding of ourselves and other people's multiple knowledge, literacies, life experiences and communication styles to better our common existence. I hope that the reading of this chapter should interpellate not only language educators but also scholars, students, policymakers, institutions and individuals interested in fostering a culture of human dignity for all in and out of the classrooms, and using the insights proposed in the chapter to advocate for a sustainable existential intercultural mindset as the key set of strategies in counteracting anti-intercultural and oppressive literacies.

## Notes

1  'Foundations in Existential Sociolinguistics' – Keynote Speech on 15 March 2021, at the Virtual Biannual Conference of

   IAISLC at the Federal University of Santa Catarina, Brazil; https://www.youtube.com/watch?v=TPOPZTaw6oU

2  https://www.tesol.org/read-and-publish/journals/other-serial-publications/compleat-links/compleat-links-volume-3-issue-1-(march-2006)/three-examples-of-better-english-learning-through-the-l1.

   This chapter shares examples of how the use of students' L1 (Portuguese and Spanish) had built students' self-esteem, confidence and a friendly learning environment. Contrary to the swim or sink model of teaching the target language in the target language, these examples revealed that using students' L1 can disentangle complex grammatical and cultural notions to facilitate learning.

# References

Aiken, H. D. (1956/1984), *The Age of Ideology: The 19th Century Philosophers*, New York: American Book Company.
Appadurai, A., ed. (2001), *Globalization*, Durham, NC: Duke University Press.
Balosa, D. (2006), 'Three examples of better English learning through the L1', *Essential Teacher 3:* Complete Links: http://www.tesol.org/s_tesol/secetdoc.asp?CID=1222&DID=5720.
Balosa, D. (2022a), 'Existential Sociolinguistics: The Fundamentals of the Political Legitimacy of Linguistic Minority Rights', in S. Makoni, C. G. Severo, A. Abdelhay and A. Kaiper-Marquez (eds.), *The Languaging of Higher Education in the Global South: De-Colonizing the Language of Scholarship and Pedagogy*, 147–62, New York: Routledge.
Balosa, D. (2022b), 'Integrationism: Roy Harris Artspeak, Artistic Creativity, and Human Diversity in the Age of Globalization', *Fórum Linguistico* 19: 7280–98.
Banda, F. (2022), 'Concluding Commentary', in S. Makoni, C. G. Severo, A. Abdelhay, and A. Kaiper-Marquez (eds.), *The Languaging of Higher Education in the Global South: De-Colonizing the Language of Scholarship and Pedagogy*, 228–32, New York: Routledge.
Bateson, G. (1980), *Mind and Nature: A Newcessary Unity*, New York: Bantam Books.
Bateson, G. (2000), *Steps to an Ecology of Mind*, Chicago, IL: The University of Chicago Press.
Baugh, J. (2018), *Linguistics in Pursuit of Justice*, New York: Cambridge University Press.
Beck, U. (2000), *What Is Globalization?* Trans. by P. Camiller, Malden, MA: Polity Press.
Block, D. and D. Cameron (2002), *Globalization and Language Teaching*, New York: Routledge.
Brown, R. H. (1987), *Society as Text: Essays on Rhetoric, Reason, and Reality*, Chicago, IL: The University of Chicago Press.
Bucholtz, M., D. I. Casillas and J. S. Lee. (2019), 'California Latinx Youth as Agents of Sociolinguistics', in N. Avineri, L. R. Graham, E. J. Johnson, R. C. Rinner and J. Rosa (eds.), *Language and Social Justice in Practice*, 166–77, New York: Routledge.
Canclini, N. G. (1995), *Hybrid Cultures: Strategies for Entering and Leaving Modernity*, Minneapolis, MN: University of Minnesota Press.
Canclini, N. G. (2001), *Consumers and Citizens: Globalization and Multicultural Conflicts*, Minneapolis, MN: University of Minnesota Press.
Celier, P. (1974), *La Parole et L'Être: Essaia sur le Mystère de la Communication*, Paris: Aubier Montaigne.
Danesi, M. (2004), *Messages, Signs, and Meanings: Basic Textbook in Semiotics and Communication Theory* (3rd ed.), Toronto: Canadian Scholars Press.
Danesi, M. (2020), *Language, Society, and New Media: Sociolinguistics Today* (3rd ed.), New York: Routledge.
Dewey, J. (1938/1997), *Experience & Education*, New York: Touchstone.
Dworkin, R. (2006), *Is Democracy Possible Here? Principles for a New Political Debate*, Princeton, NJ: Princeton University Press.

Erskine, J. (1915), *The Moral Obligation to Be Intelligent and Other Essays*, New York: Duffield & Company.
Fairclough, N. (2006), *Language and Globalization*, New York: Routledge.
Fanon, F. (1952/2008), *Black Skin, White Masks*, Trans. by R. Philcox, New York: Grove Press.
Felten, P. and L. M. Lambert. (2020), *Relationship-Rich Education: How Human Connections Drive Success in College*, Baltimore, MD: Johns Hopkins University Press.
Fishman, J. A. (1989), *Language & Ethnicity in Minority Sociolinguistics Perspective*, Philadelphia, PA: Multilingual Matters.
Freire, P. (1970/2000), *Cultural Action for Freedom* (Revised ed.), Cambridge, MA: Harvard Educational Review.
Freire, P. (1975/2005), *Education for Critical Consciousness*, New York: Continuum.
Freire, P. (1992), *Pedagogy of Hope: Reliving Pedagogy of the Oppressed*, Trans. by R. R. Barr, New York: Continuum.
Freire, P. (1993), *Pedagogy of the City*, New York: Continuum.
Fromm, E. (1966), *You Shall Be as Gods: A Radical Interpretation of the Old Testament and Its Tradition*, New York: Holt Rinehart & Winston.
Gee, J. P. (2017), *Teaching, Learning, Literacy in Our High-Risk High-Tech World: A Framework for Becoming Human*, New York: Teachers College Press.
Giroux, H. A. (2020), *On Critical Pedagogy*, New York: Bloomsbury Publishing.
Gordon, M. M. (1988), *The Scope of Sociology*, New York: Oxford University Press.
Gouhier, H. (1974), 'Préface', in P. Celier (ed.), *La Parole et L'Être: Essaia sur le Mystère de la Communication*, 7–11, Paris: Aubier Montaigne.
Gouhier, H. (1987), *L'Anti-humanism au XVIIe Siècle*, Paris: Librarie Philosophique.
Hegège, C. (2008), *Combat pour le Français au Nom de la Diversité des Langues et des Cultures*, Paris: Odile Jacob.
Hobsbawm, E. (1962), *The Age of Revolution, 1789–1848*, New York: Vantage Books.
Hornberger, N. H., ed. (2003), *Continua of Biliteracy: An Ecological Framework for Educational Policy, Research, and Practice in Multilingual Settings*, Tonawanda, NY: Multilingual Matters.
Hult, F. M. (2008), 'The History and Development of Educational Linguistics', in B. Spolsky and F. M. Hult (eds.), *The Handbook of Educational Linguistics*, 10–24, Malden, MA: Blackwell.
Hult, F. M. (2014), 'How Does Policy Influence Language in Education?', in R. E. Silver and S. M. Lwin (eds.), *Language in Education: Social Implications*, 159–75, London: Bloomsbury.
Lobman, C. and T. Perone, eds. (2018), *Big Ideas and Revolutionary Activity: Selected Essays, Talks and Articles by Lois Holzman*, New York: East Side Institute.
Kramsch, C. (1998), *Language and Culture*, New York: Oxford University Press.
Kramsch, C. (2009), *The Multilingual Subject*, New York: Oxford University Press.
Macedo, D., ed. (2019), *Decolonizing Foreign Language Education: The Misteaching of English and Other Colonial Languages*, New York: Routledge.

Mallon, F. E. (2012), 'Introduction: Decolonizing Knowledge, Language, and Narrative', in F. E. Mallon (ed.), *Decolonizing Native Histories: Collaboration, Knowledge, and Language in the Americas*, 1–19, Durham, NC: Duke University Press.

Marcel, G. (1954), *The Decline of Wisdom*, London: Harvill Press.

Marcel, G. (1963), *The Existential Background of Human Dignity*, Cambridge, MA: Cambridge University Press.

Marcel, G. (1967), *Problematic Man*, Trans. by B. Thompson, New York: Herder & Herder.

Marcel, G. (1952/2008), *Man Against Mass Society*, Trans. by G. S. Fraser, South Bend, IN: St. Augustine's Press.

Maxwell, N. (2014). *Global Philosophy: What Philosophy Ought to Be*, La Vergne, TN: Ingram Book Company.

Maritain, J. (1940), *De La Justice Politique: Notes sur la Présente Guerre*, Paris: Plon.

McLean, C. (2013), 'Literacies, Identities, and Gender: Reframing Girls in Digital Worlds', in B. J. Guzzetti and T. W. Bean (eds.), *Adolescent Literacies and the Gendered Self: (Re)constructing Identities through Multimodal Literacy Practices*, 64–73, New York: Routledge.

Mignolo, W. D. and C. E. Walsh. (2018), *On Decoloniality: Concepts, Analytics, and Praxis*, Durham, NC: Duke University Press.

Miller, D. (2013), *Justice for Earthlings: Essays in Political Philosophy*, New York: Cambridge University Press.

Neuliep, J. W. (2021), *Intercultural Communication: A Contextual Approach* (8th ed.), Los Angeles, CA: Sage.

Orman, J. (2008), *Language Policy and Nation-Building in Post-Apartheid South Africa*, Vienna: Springer.

Piller, I. (2016), *Linguistic Diversity and Social Justice: An Introduction to Applied Sociolinguistics*, New York: Oxford University Press.

Pirbhai-Illich, F., S. Pete and F. Martin (2017), *Culturally Responsive Pedagogy: Working Towards Decolonization, Indigeneity, and Interculturalism*, New York: Palgrave McMillan.

Plummer, K. (2021), *Critical Humanism: A Manifesto for the Twenty-First Century*, Medford, MA: Polity Press.

Rosenau, J. N. (1980), *The Study of Global Interdependence: Essays on the Transnationalization of World Affairs*, New York: Nichols Publishing Company.

Rushkoff, D. (2019), *Team Human*, New York: W. W. Norton & Company.

Sachs, J. D. (2015), *The Age of Sustainable Development*, New York: Columbia Uniuversity Press.

Schwartz, H. L. (2019), *Connected Teaching: Relationship, Power, and Mattering in Higher Education*, Starling, VA: Stylus.

Spolsky, B. (2008), 'Introduction: What is Educational Linguistics?', in B. Spolsky and F. M. Hult (eds.), *The Handbook of Educational Linguistics*, 1–9, Malden, MA: Blackwell.

Sorrells, K. (2016), *Intercultural Communication: Globalization and Social Justice* (2nd ed.), Los Angeles, CA: Sage.

Steger, M. B. (2009), *Globalization: A Very Short Introduction*, New York: Oxford University Press.

Stolle-McAllister, J. (2019), *Intercultural Interventions: Politics, Community, and Environment in the Otavalo Valley*, Amherst, NY: Cambria Press.

Taylor, C. (1995), *Philosophical Arguments*, Cambridge, MA: Harvard University Press.

Tillich, P. (1952/2014), *The Courage to Be* (3rd ed.), New Haven, CT: Yale University Press.

Trilling, L. (1972). *Sincerity and Authenticity*. Cambridge, MA: Harvard University Press.

Tu, W. (2007), 'Mutual Learning as an Agenda for Social Development', in M. K. Asante, Y. Miike and J. Ying (eds.), *The Global Intercultural Communication Reader* (1st ed.), 329–34, New York: Routledge.

Tubino, F. (2015), *La Interculturalidad en Cuestión*, Lima, Perú: Pontificia Universidad Católica del Perú, Fondo Editorial.

Urciuoli, B. (1996), *Exposing Prejudice: Puerto Rican Experiences of Language, Race, and Class*, Boulder, CO: Westview Press.

Wa Thiong'o, N. (1986), *Decolonizing the Mind: The Politics of Language in African Literature*, Portsmouth, NH: James Currey.

Wa Thiong'o, N. (1993), *Moving the Center: The Struggle for Cultural Freedom*, Portsmouth, NH: Heinemann.

Whitehead, A. N. (1929/1967), *The Aims of Education and Other Essays*, New York: The Free Press.

Wink, J. (2011), *Critical Pedagogy: Notes from the Real World* (4th ed.), New York: Pearson.

# CHAPTER 2

# English Teaching in the Global South

# Interculturality, Postcoloniality and Critical Pedagogy

*Hamza R'boul*

## Introduction

The global spread of English has brought about several changes that have influenced the linguistic diversity and cultural plurality of many southern contexts (R'boul 2022a). In particular, the Global South is a state of being that refers to a situation of dependency and dispossession (Shome 2019). The postcolonial condition of the Global South renders English highly appealing in terms of its status-bearing significance, cultural superiority and neoliberal attitudes (Belhiah 2020; Jaafari 2019). Postcolonial contexts are characterized by complex social formations, cultural infrastructures and power inequities where teachers are required to consider their positionality and exert agency in their classroom decisions and practices. This has made interculturality[1] imbalanced due to the lack of reciprocal influence with postcolonial contexts having to speak English in order to be visible (Warriner 2016).

Morocco is a multilingual country that can be situated within the Global South and the expanding circle of English-speaking countries since English does not have special administrative status in the country, but it is widely studied as a foreign language (Belhiah 2022; Benzehaf 2021). Morocco is characterized by linguistic hybridity due to the presence of local languages which are Arabic and Tamazight in addition to several foreign languages including French, English and Spanish (Belhiah et al. 2020). Morocco has been struggling with linguistic dependency on the French since the end of the colonial policy in the twentieth century. French has been dominating domains of higher education, business and diplomacy although local languages have the status of official languages of the country as indicated in the constitution (Ennaji 2009).

The boundaries between the personal, the social, the political and the pedagogic are not rigid; instead, their intersections among these elements are substantial and ubiquitous. That is why locating the global growth of English within the framework of coloniality is useful in understanding how power relations are maintained. The intersections of language, education and political power offer some reflections on north–south relationships (Dervin and Simpson 2021; R'boul 2021). These assumptions entail ethical dilemmas in English language teaching (ELT) within the historical perspectives of postcolonial contexts. A pertinent question here is whether English would be a language that speaks for the subaltern or perpetuates their subordination. With the increasing spread of English, it seems important to examine how English influences local culture, language and identity from the perspectives of teachers, especially since multiple scholars have argued that English is likely to replace French in Morocco in the future (Marley 2004).

This chapter argues that ELT has to consider the specificities of the Global South in order to use English for southern spaces' benefit rather than as a tool to maintain colonial-like relations. This chapter aims to amalgamate theoretical arguments and empirical evidence to (i) clarify the type of influences exerted by the spread of English in the Global South, and (ii) discuss teachers' understandings of the intersection of English language, coloniality and imbalanced interculturality. Data was collected using focus group discussions with teachers to provide meaningful evidence for the theoretical arguments advanced throughout the chapter.

# Theoretical Framework

## *Power Imbalances between the Global North and South*

To better understand how the spread of English is informed by colonial differences, it is necessary to zoom outward to consider larger forces that have established a persistent ideology around the position of English (Vafai 2017). Colonial differences have been manifested in the non-balance of knowledge production, as southern epistemologies are limited to the status of subaltern perspectives (Sousa Santos 2018) while western–northern ecologies and epistemologies are historically dominant and superior (Mignolo and Walsh 2018; Garcia and Baca 2019). Anglo-Atlantic leadership places politically–economically distal spaces in 'the sociology of absences' (Sousa Santos, 2018) by rendering their languages and epistemologies subaltern and derivative. The geopolitics of knowledge (Mignolo 2018) is important here because it can be directly linked to the geopolitics of language and how this latter informs its trajectories in a linear narrative. The skewed geopolitics of knowledge has created circumstances where the colonized speaks 'the language of the colonizer in order to exist in the colonizer's eyes, not his own' (Tolman 2006: 192).

Postcolonial theory emphasizes that the current power imbalances between the Global North and South are largely created by colonial differences. To maintain these inequalities, language is an integral part of how the lingering structures of coloniality exert their power. Critical perspectives argue that the global spread of English is grounded on structural systems, for example, globalization and coloniality (Hsu 2017). These structural systems further clarify the position of the global spread of English within the current colonial differences. Power imbalances between the Global North and South are, therefore, maintained through the domination of a particular linguistic pattern. The construction of linguistic hierarchies that employ English as discursive power would entail the ascendency of Anglophone perspectives, as the skewed geopolitics of knowledge are a reflection of the inequalities between the Global North and South.

## *The Global Spread of English in the Global South: Cultural Superiority of Anglophone Perspectives in ELT*

Critical applied linguistics literature has criticized ideological issues and imperialistic tendencies in foreign and second language theories and praxis (Macedo 2017; Mirhosseini 2018). Critical scholarship has challenged the traditional understandings of ELT by examining the representations of neoliberalism in English teaching materials and methods (Babaii and Sheikhi 2018; Daghigh and Rahim 2021). This is particularly relevant in the current circumstances as the global spread of English has shaped the sociolinguistic situation of a lot of postcolonial contexts, resulting in the relegation of the local languages and identities of non-Western speakers (Hsu 2015). The contemporary accounts of the historicity of colonial English in the Global South argue that the authority of native speakers and their cultures reflects 'the long-standing assumption that the White community can "save" peoples of color by teaching them English' (Jenks and Lee 2020: 186).

Multiple studies have investigated teachers' beliefs and practices regarding teaching culture with a special emphasis on how participants come to perceive the status of Anglophone and local cultures. Tajeddin and Pakzadian (2020) concluded that the representation of Inner-Circle varieties[2] and their associated cultural contents are dominant in global ELT textbooks. Liu (2018) clarified that teachers in China granted a prestigious status to native English speaker teachers (NESTs), particularly Anglo-American Caucasians, and Inner-Circle English and culture. Also, participants held Inner-Circle English as the learning/teaching target. Although teachers expressed a desire to include the Outer and Expanding Circle cultures, it was merely a supplement to Inner-Circle culture.

As a response to the results, some voices have argued that the 'threat' of English might be balanced by the promotion of local language and culture (Pan and Seargeant 2012). However, a more important aspect to note, which this paper is trying to reflect, is that the concern is not about the inclusion of local perspectives; it is about the possible preferential representations of Anglophone perceptions that would entail the subalternity of local cultures. Due to the privilege–subordination dynamics that imbue Global North and South relations, the inclusion of local perspectives does not ensure equal appreciation of local and Anglophone knowledge, ontologies and perceptions. Taking these ideas into account, the main aim is to explore teachers' and students' perspectives related to the privileged status of Anglophone spaces; the rationale for conducting this study is that due to power imbalances, students might be (explicitly or not) encouraged to distance themselves from their local ontologies and embrace modern and Western perspectives (R'boul 2022a).

## *Critical Pedagogy and Teaching English in the Global South*

Building on the range of insights discussed in the previous sections, it is important to anchor our understanding of critical pedagogy in the very attempt of disrupting the colonial structures that might have been maintained (either inadvertently or otherwise) through English education. The previous sections have established the warrants for a nuanced understanding of critical pedagogy that foregrounds (i) a critical perception of power inequalities, (ii) imbalanced intercultural relations, (iii) colonial attitudes of the global spread of English and (iv) teachers' agency in resisting hegemonic linguistic and cultural discourses.

This chapter defines 'critical pedagogy' as the teaching practices that (i) are informed by critical understandings of linguistic, cultural and sociopolitical issues, (ii) endeavour to undermine the reproduction of inequalities, and (iii) take into consideration the specificities of the context where the teaching is taking place including the positionality of learners and the wider sociocultural and linguistic milieu. That is why this chapter builds its theoretical premises and empirical research on the linguistic dependency of Morocco and its postcolonial positionality. It also centres the place of

English in Morocco with regards to the country's local languages, cultures and perspectives.

The rationale for conducting this research is to underline the importance of teachers' and students' perspectives in dismantling the reproduction of hegemonic discourses in English teaching classrooms. Conducting this study in Morocco would allow pinpointing the type of complexities entailed in teaching English in the Global South as well as the difficulties that may thwart the very process of reclaiming their identity, culture and knowledge. Therefore, the main purpose here is to discuss the possibility of enabling southern individuals to have access to English, but at the same time, how they have come to develop a critical appraisal of the role of English and how it can be used for their own benefit. English teaching should be oriented towards balancing the global implications of English and local specificities.

The Global South has been making enormous efforts to assume more visibility in global affairs. English, as the linguistic medium of modernity and globalization, has been understandably presented as a necessity for development and keeping abreast of contemporary advancements. While these assumptions have been internalized, this chapter opens the floor for a critical consideration of English teaching within the particularities of the Global South, especially its postcolonial malaise and its inability to realize a true 'post'-colony era. Within these conditions, critical pedagogy has even more legitimacy; however, while its interpretation may be commonly agreed upon, its implementation should be primarily based on the nature of the context and its complexities. That is why this chapter does not claim a consensus on the theorization and implementation of critical pedagogy, but it, rather, calls educators to adapt its principles in a way that takes into account the cultural, linguistic and sociopolitical circumstances of their context. Critical pedagogy should be understood as the pedagogical framing of the critical insights on society that considers education to be a key element in undermining the possible manifestations of coloniality, power inequalities and imbalanced interculturality.

## *English Language in Morocco*

Morocco's official languages are Arabic and Tamazight while French is the nation's second language and English is used as a foreign language. The Moroccan linguistic situation has been characterized by the historical power struggle between local and foreign languages. While local languages are internalized as the languages of local identity and traditions, French and English are seen as high-prestige languages which represent modernity and status-bearing significance (Chakrani and Huang 2014). In recent years, English has gained more recognition and greater status as a global language in Morocco due to the strong demand for a lingua franca (Jebbour 2021; R'boul 2022b). This spread was ascribed, by Moroccan scholars, to the impact of the ideology of modernity on language attitudes (Chakrani and Huang 2014). This spread has promoted the belief that English may replace French as the country's second language in the future (Jaafari 2019; Zouhir 2013).

In a country that has been struggling with linguistic dependency on French due to its postcolonial positionality, the overwhelming spread of English may further aggravate Morocco's linguistic dependency and its attempt to recover from its postcolonial malaise. Moreover, the historical position of Morocco within the Global South may entail the entanglement of various marginalizing factors that render the country's languages and cultures less appealing compared to Anglophone spaces. For instance, R'boul (2022a) explored the language ontology of EFL Moroccan university students; findings revealed that students used English as an analogy to living another reality that is similar to the lives of Americans and the British. Also, their attitudes favoured Anglophone cultures over Moroccan ones because they are perceived as more modern and liberal.

Kumaravadivelu (2016) argues, in his analysis of the decolonial option in English teaching, that subaltern subjectivities are arguably created by power structures through 'an ensemble of political, social, cultural, [and] economic relations that weaken [subalterns'] will to exercise their agency' (p. 76). Therefore, it is important to investigate (i) how EFL teachers received and internalized English and its possible supremacy including their awareness of its potential role in maintaining power relations and the superiority of Anglophone contexts and (ii) whether their beliefs are underpinned by critical pedagogies that undermine any manifestations of privilege – marginalization dynamics including unequal representation of Anglophone and Moroccan cultures. The main objective of the study is to check whether Moroccan pre-service and in-service teachers are critical of or reinforce discourses that support the superiority of the English language.

## Methodology

### *Research Context and Participants*

This qualitative study is based in Morocco, where English is used as a foreign language that is increasingly spreading and gaining greater status. A total of thirty participants took part in the study. The participants were fifteen EFL pre-service teachers (nine male, six female) and fifteen in-service teachers (eleven male and four female) of English in Morocco – all participants were high school teachers. A total of ten teachers had a university degree for EFL teaching while other teachers had a BA or master's degree in either English linguistics or literary studies. Their teaching experience ranged from one to fifteen years and their native languages were Arabic and/or Tamazight.

Teachers participated in this study voluntarily upon invitation. Pre-service teachers were participating at the time of the study in the teacher training programme administrated by the Ministry of Education.

The pre-service teacher training programme takes place in different major regional centres. The programme includes two semesters over a period of seven months; each semester involves a one-month professional internship in a high school. The focus is mainly on teaching methodology including learning theories, teaching practices and classroom management. Therefore, input on the cultural politics of English is lacking in pre-service training programmes in Morocco. The two semesters consist of the following modules:

- Semester 1: 'Teaching Skills'; 'Approaches and Methods'; 'Classroom Management'; 'Planning'; 'Action research'; 'School life'; 'Education sciences'.

- Semester 2: 'Managing the Learning Situation'; 'Professional Development/Reflective Teaching'; 'ICTs'; 'Testing and Evaluation'; 'Material Evaluation and Adaptation'; 'Legislation and Ethics'; 'Didactic Production and Workshops'; 'Micro Teaching and Analysis of Professional Situations'.

## *Data Collection and Analysis*

Data was collected using focus group discussions in order to (i) allow participants to elaborate on their ideas and interact/react to other participants' views, and (ii) continuously modify prompts during the discussions according to participants' responses and beliefs. Due to the imposed pandemic restrictions, group discussions were held using the video communications platform 'ZOOM'. There were a total of six group discussions (three for pre-service and three for in-service teachers); each one involved five participants and they all lasted for approximately forty-five minutes up to one hour. All group discussions were conducted in English.

Focus group discussions were conducted in English due to two main reasons. First, conducting critical discussions about the impact of English in English may help make participants more aware of their agency in speaking and teaching English. This would prompt teachers to rethink how English influences their identities, cultures and beliefs. Second, since the mother tongues may not provide equivalents to many academic concepts and constructs, it was necessary to conduct focus group discussions in English.

The discussions were mediated through the use of particular questions. The prompts were informed by relevant critical applied linguistics literature and involved references that were designed to prompt teachers to explore the hegemonic understandings of English promoted by English language education. Questions were mainly used to guide the discussion towards specific topics including the supremacy of English, the dominance of US and UK resources on English language teaching theory and praxis, marginalization of local languages and cultures, power relations, American expansionism and their awareness of the potential colonial-like effects of the global spread of English. Importantly, discussions were not only guided by the researcher's pre-constructed questions; some questions were also raised during the discussions as reactions to the research participants' responses.

Three important ethical concerns were taken into account: anonymity, confidentiality and informed consent. Participants' identity was protected throughout the recruitment and dissemination process. Two documents were used to ensure the informed consent of the research participants. The 'Information Sheet' explained all the steps of the research process. The 'Consent Form' clarified the decisions made by the participants if they agreed to participate in the study as well as the university's Data Protection Policy. Both participants and the researcher had to sign the 'Consent Form'. 'Revocation of Consent' was available for participants in case they decided to withdraw their consent to participate in the research at any stage of the study.

The discussions were audio-recorded. On completing the group discussions, the audio files were transcribed verbatim to form the data. Thematic analysis was used to code and group responses into recurring themes. Numerous pages of written data were at hand after all transcripts were made. The qualitative analysis of interview data was conducted using QDA Miner software. The transcripts were entered into the software, then the relevant pieces were highlighted under different labels to create codes. Then, categories were created by bringing several codes together. Categories were labelled accordingly to develop themes and subthemes. The themes are presented in a hierarchy in terms of importance, recurrence and relevance to the research objectives.

## Results

Selected extracts from group discussion data have been included for illustration. Two main criteria have underpinned the selection of the extracts. The statements included in the text are (i) the most prominent and pronounced in terms of their clarity and relevance to the aims of the study, and (ii) the most representative of the identified themes and subthemes. Pre-service teachers are named PT1 to PT15 while in-service teachers are named IT1 to IT15.

Based on the analysis of the data collected, teachers' responses did not distinctly feature critical understandings of the global spread of English and its potential implications for local cultures and languages. Most teachers indicated that they tried to actively include local culture while their main aim was to develop students' communicative competence. Teachers' beliefs did not reflect the ideas, assumptions and recommendations made in the critical literature on the global spread of English, the cultural politics of English language teaching and decoloniality. Teachers continued to perceive that English was not a threat to local languages and cultures. In particular, teachers displayed an unclear attitude towards English teaching's assimilationist tendencies. Importantly, there were not any major discernible differences between pre-service and in-service teachers. That is why the results are presented as inclusive of all participants.

It is important to acknowledge that since questions were framed within the academic discourses the researcher was familiar with, research participants' responses and the study's outcomes may have been influenced by the type of questions asked. The following sections present the four main themes of the study's findings.

## *The Inclusion of Local Culture: Comparison as a Teaching Approach*

In response to the prompt 'Anglophone cultures are dominant worldwide; so how do you account for students' local culture?', all teachers maintained that they actively included local culture and traditions in their teachings. They noted that they were using locally produced materials which feature frequent references to Moroccan cultures including food, traditions celebrations and suchlike:

> 'I am in favour of including local culture; I appreciate the fact that all books have a unit on culture; these units usually have references to Moroccan culture like names and traditions.' (IT5)

> 'When we teach English, we automatically teach its embedded culture. You can't separate culture and language. For example, I think it is very important that we not only teach about supermarkets and malls but also Souk [marketplace or street where goods are sold, especially greengrocery].' (PT12)

> 'I always make sure that I use Moroccan names and give examples that are related to Moroccan culture.' (IT11)

Although teachers emphasized the usefulness of including Moroccan culture, they reported that their practices would be/were based on a comparison between Moroccan and Anglophone cultures. Teachers noted that in order to understand the target culture and communicate interculturally, students need to understand their native culture first. In particular, several teachers (IT1, IT14, IT6, IT13, PT6, PT11 and PT8) indicated that they compared Moroccan culture either with Anglophone or international cultures in terms of norms, values and practices. However, only two teachers (IT3 and IT13) were doubtful of the implications of using comparison in teaching, especially between Moroccan and, for instance, American culture.

> 'I know that a lot of teachers compare Moroccan culture to American or British culture. I know they do it innocently, but it is obvious that the Anglophone culture will look better in many aspects while I know Moroccan culture will be better in other aspects.' (IT3)

> 'Comparison will just make our culture look traditional and old-fashioned.' (IT13)

## *Unclear Attitude Towards English Teaching's Assimilationist Tendencies*

Assimilationist tendencies refer to the processes whereby non-natives assume and resemble the understandings, cultural ideas and languaging associated with the dominant Anglophone countries. The most important prompt during the discussion was 'Do you think there are assimilationist attitudes in English teaching because many studies have argued that English represents a case of linguistic imperialism and modern coloniality?' Teachers' responses were not clear in terms of either agreeing or disagreeing with the prompt. Teachers did not use the specific concepts or ideas that are often employed in the scholarship. Most teachers emphasized that it was not necessary to induce students to behave and talk like native speakers, but they regarded speaking and languaging in a similar way to native speakers as a desirable quality. In particular, IT3 mentioned the idea of 'world Englishes' and how English is used worldwide, but American and British English were still the benchmarks that they still aspired to and tried to develop their students' abilities to match. However, the other teachers expressed neutral opinions that did not provide a clear stance on whether English teaching involved assimilationist attitudes.

> 'I have limited knowledge about "linguistic imperialism"; In Morocco, I do not see that English teaching entails assimilationist practices. A lot of my students are typical Moroccans although they are good in English.' (IT7)

> 'I think I remember my professor in a cultural studies course mentioning something about linguistic imperialism and coloniality. This may be the case in countries that were colonized by the British but I do not think it is the case here in Morocco. English teaching here is only to develop students' level in the English language.' (PT5)

Another prompt was 'Do you practise any caution with regards to assimilation in your practices?' Teachers replied that assimilation would require a long time. They further clarified that assimilation does not happen due to English teaching, but, rather, through students' exposure to other cultures, especially American culture, through music and movies. One important remark was that teachers noted that it was up to the teacher to either encourage students to embrace other cultures or strike a balance between foreign and local culture. PT1, IT5 and IT14 explained that it was, indeed, difficult to speak English and not reflect its cultures in one's behaviours and mindset.

## *Focus on Developing Students' Linguistic Competence*

Teachers were asked about their readings in relation to English language teaching. The majority of participants explained that their readings were mainly for professional development while few participants noted that they read only for pleasure (PT5 and PT13). Their readings included major books on teaching the four skills: reading, writing, speaking and listening. Teachers were then asked whether they had read anything related to the cultural politics of English language education. While some participants were unsure about the exact significance of the concept, other teachers indicated that they were more interested in practical applications rather than theory.

> 'I know there are so many things about English language teaching, but I feel that I need to read things that will help me improve my teaching.' (IT15)

> 'Since we are currently in a training program, I prefer to read books or articles that provide me with clear guidelines on how to teach.' (PT4)

It was clear that teachers are more concerned about their practices rather than the theoretical discussion of the orientations embedded in English language teaching. It seemed that reading about the cultural politics of English language education did not serve the ultimate aim of their classes. Given their emphasis on teaching the four skills, it can be inferred that teachers were keen on developing students' linguistic competence rather than other critical aspects which would supposedly require more effort and attention. Moreover, concepts of neoliberalism and hegemony were not discussed extensively by teachers due to either their unfamiliarity with these conceptions or their conviction of their irrelevance to the Moroccan context.

## *The Spread of English and the Status of Local Cultures and Languages*

All teachers viewed the increasing spread of English positively. They noted that because English is currently the most important and useful language in the world, Morocco would benefit from embracing English rather than

French. They further explained that English is the language of science, technology and business, so its spread is quite expected. Importantly, when teachers were asked whether English may pose a threat to local languages and cultures, they maintained that it was not the case for the time being. Almost all teachers clarified how French has gained its current status due to the colonial legacy in Morocco, but English was not associated with colonialism. Moreover, teachers noted that many countries were using English as a second language, but local languages and cultures were still respected and appreciated; examples included countries such as Malaysia and Scandinavian countries.

'Using English will grant Morocco more recognition.' (IT4)

'If you write in Arabic or French, only a few people will read it.' (PT9)

English was not seen as a threat to local languages and cultures by any teacher. This could be attributed to the ongoing debate on using French rather than Arabic in teaching science subjects and the attendant concerns about relinquishing local languages. Teachers further explained that English would offer students more job prospects and a better future since they would be able to work internationally. Although the researcher asked again about the possibility of English threatening the status of local languages and cultures, teachers did not seem to be concerned about it. It was clear at that point that English was generally perceived positively because of its role in world dynamics and the opportunities it offers. Furthermore, teachers were asked about how textbooks produced by Anglophone institutions may be encouraging students to abandon their cultures and languages; teachers explained that they did not notice any clear sign of such a claim. They argued that those textbooks were developed to be used internationally. For instance, PT5 indicated that 'even if textbooks favour Anglophone cultures, it is the teacher's task to make sure that does not happen'.

## Discussion

Drawing on the results, teachers' beliefs and teachers' responses did not feature critical attitudes towards the global spread of English or how English teaching might be contributing to the maintenance of power imbalances. However, it is important to note that teachers are not to be blamed. Several factors may have contributed to this sentiment, especially considering English's lack of colonial connotation in Morocco. Teachers did not express any concern about the greater status of English in Morocco; this might be due to (i) teacher education programmes' lack of input informed by scholarship on the cultural politics of English language education and (ii) the absence of English's association with colonial legacy. This could imply that teachers' practices prioritize developing students' linguistic competence first before seeking to promote students' critical understanding of English and its global spread. For instance, only two teachers (IT3 and IT13) were sceptical about the usefulness of using comparison as a teaching approach. They noted that comparison would not help present Moroccan culture in a desirable way, especially when it was compared to Anglophone cultures (the US and/or the UK). Since power imbalances situate southern postcolonial spaces within the margins of modernity (Mignolo and Walsh 2018), teachers' reliance on comparison in English teaching as a way of introducing culture or interculturality may further highlight the differences between Morocco and developed countries such the United States and the United Kingdom.

Given teachers' unclear attitude towards English teaching with regards to coloniality and its global spread, it can be safe to argue that they might be unaware of how their beliefs and possibly practices may be perpetuating the subalternity of Moroccan languages, cultures and perspectives. English was generally regarded positively by all participants, evidenced by their emphasis on the range of opportunities it offers. While this remains credible to a great extent, teachers viewed the global spread of English and its teaching as entirely benevolent; this is particularly an assumption that is not congruent with the body of scholarship offered. Also, these understandings are not aligned with the principles of critical pedagogy. Teachers were convinced that English did not present a threat to local languages and cultures, at least for the time being. Furthermore, participants' input on the themes of neoliberalism and hegemony were limited. This can be attributed to the lack of Moroccan-focused scholarship on these concepts; there are limited studies on textbook analysis or teachers' attitudes in Morocco.

Teachers' beliefs were not anchored in the current scholarship on English teaching which calls for more critical attitudes (Siqueira 2020; R'boul 2020). Teachers focused mainly on the positive aspects of the global spread of English; therefore, it can be argued that their teachings may not include explicit practices that encourage reconsideration of the global spread of English and its possible association with power imbalances and privilege-marginalization dynamics. This means that while the main aim is to develop learners' linguistic competence, there is some possibility that students could perceive speaking English and embracing its cultures as standards that they should be striving to meet. Considering these results, the continuation in delivering English learning classes without using critical approaches is likely to complicate the country's linguistic dependency in the future.

## Conclusion

Hegemonic understandings of English will continue to control southern institutions, curricula and pedagogy unless teachers consciously seek to counteract their overwhelming influence. Teachers are asked to embrace and reflect decolonial thinking in their beliefs and practices; this necessitates decentring the hegemony of UK and US domination of ELT theory and praxis. While teacher training programmes lack critical input on the cultural politics of English, teachers are tasked with the mission of exhibiting a higher level of agency that is built on their awareness of their societies' status within global affairs. Teacher education programmes are advised to prepare language educators to teach for critical and reflexive interculturality (Dervin and Jacobsson 2021). This may also include embracing postmodern theorizations of the intersection of English and interculturality, for example, transcultural communication through global Englishes (Baker and Ishikawa 2021).

Also, teachers need to be supported to recognize that ELT is more than teaching English; it is a delicate practice that requires a nuanced understanding of the positionality of English in their societies as well as power imbalances between their contexts and Anglophone spaces. Teachers' critical awareness of power imbalances should be underpinned by an understanding of how the global spread of English is both a manifestation and mechanism for maintaining colonial-like relations between the Global South and Anglophone spaces. Indeed, this awareness would not be fully realized without a nuanced consideration of Morocco's linguistic dependency and its attempts to further promote the presence of English. Linguistic dependency could be critically dealt with as a condition of current power imbalances which requires a locally sensitive vision that considers local specificities with regards to language, culture and identity. It is a mission of striking a balance between what is global and necessary and what is local and essential to the development of a local context.

Overall, English teaching training programmes have to consider preparing teachers for the new challenges of the global spread of English. The domination of a particular linguistic pattern is often an indicator of power imbalances. This could be relevant not only to Morocco but also to other postcolonial spaces that have been struggling with linguistic dependency. Teachers should seek to prepare students to use English for their own benefit and develop critical insights into how English might pose a threat to the local identities, cultures and languages. In particular, English language teachers should anchor their practices in the current scholarship on the cultural politics of English language teaching.

## Notes

1 While this chapter recognizes that interculturality is polysemic and it is more of a point of view depending on how one defines it (Dervin 2016), this chapter defines this contested concept as the dynamics and processes involved in the co-construction of meanings, identity and culture during intercultural interactions.

2   The Inner Circle refers to the traditional bases of English where it acts as a first language. The countries involved in the Inner Circle are the United States of America, the United Kingdom, Canada, Australia and New Zealand. The Outer Circle refers to the non-native contexts where English is part of a country's chief institutions, and it is an important second language. The Outer Circle consists of countries that are former colonies of the United Kingdom or the United States of America including Kenya, Malaysia, Singapore and so on. The Expanding Circle refers to the countries where English is learnt as a foreign language.

# References

Babaii, E. and M. Sheikhi. (2018), 'Traces of Neoliberalism in English Teaching Materials: A Critical Discourse Analysis', *Critical Discourse Studies*, 15 (3): 247–64. https://doi.org/10.1080/17405904.2017.1398671.

Baker, W. and T. Ishikawa. (2021), *Transcultural Communication Through Global Englishes: An Advanced Textbook for Students* (1st ed.), Routledge. https://doi.org/10.4324/9780367809973.

Belhiah, H. (2020), 'English as a Global Language in Morocco: A Qualitative Study of Students' Motivations for Studying English', in H. Belhiah, I. Zeddari, N. Amrous, J. Bahmad and N. Bejjit (eds.), *English Language Teaching in Moroccan Higher Education*, 33–48, Singapore: Springer. https://doi.org/10.1007/978-981-15-3805-6_3.

Belhiah, H. (2022), 'EMI in Morocco: Attitudes, Merits, Challenges, Strategies, and Implementation', in S. Curle, H. Holi, A. Alhassan and S. Scatolini (eds.), *English-Medium Instruction in Higher Education in the Middle East and North Africa: Policy, Research and Pedagogy*, 147–66, London: Bloomsbury Academic. http://dx.doi.org/10.5040/9781350238572.0015.

Belhiah, H., M. Majdoubi and M. Safwate. (2020), 'Language Revitalization through the Media: A Case Study of Amazigh in Morocco', *International Journal of the Sociology of Language*, 2020 (266): 121–41. https://doi.org/10.1515/ijsl-2020-2114.

Benzehaf, B. (2021), 'Multilingualism and its Role in Identity Construction: A Study of English Students' Perceptions', *International Journal of Multilingualism*. http://doi.org/10.1080/14790718.2021.2003369.

Chakrani, B. and J. L. Huang. (2014), 'The Work of Ideology: Examining Class, Language Use, and Attitudes Among Moroccan University Students', *International Journal of Bilingual Education and Bilingualism*, 17 (1): 1–14. http://doi.org/10.1080/13670050.2012.718319.

Daghigh, A. and H. Rahim. (2021), 'Neoliberalism in ELT Textbooks: An Analysis of Locally Developed and Imported Textbooks Used in Malaysia', *Pedagogy, Culture & Society*, 29 (3): 493–512. http://doi.org/10.1080/14681366.2020.1755888.

de Sousa Santos, S. (2018), *The End of the Cognitive Empire: The Coming of Age of Epistemologies of the South*, Durham, NC and London: Duke University Press.

Dervin, F. (2016), *Interculturality in Education: A Theoretical and Methodological Toolbox*, Palgrave Macmillan. https://doi.org/10.1057/978-1-137-54544-2.

Dervin, F. and A. Jacobsson, eds. (2021), *Teacher Education for Critical and Reflexive Interculturality*, Cham: Palgrave Macmillan. https://doi.org/10.1007/978-3-030-66337-7.

Dervin, F. and A. Simpson. (2021), *Interculturality and the Political within Education* (1st ed.), Routledge. https://doi.org/10.4324/9780429471155.

Ennaji, M. (2009), 'Multiculturalism, Citizenship, and Education in Morocco', *Mediterranean Journal of Educational Studies*, 14 (1): 5–26.

Garcia, R. and D. Baca, eds. (2019), *Rhetorics Elsewhere and Otherwise: Contested Modernities and Decolonial Visions*. Champaign, IL: National Council of Teachers of English.

Hsu, F. (2015), 'The Coloniality of Neoliberal English: The Enduring Structures of American Colonial English Instruction in the Philippines and Puerto Rico', *L2 Journal*, 7 (3), 123–45. https://doi.org/10.5070/L27323549.

Hsu, F. (2017), 'Resisting the Coloniality of English: A Research Review of Strategies', *The CATESOL Journal*, 29 (1): 111–32.

Jaafari, T. (2019), 'Language Debates and the Changing Context of Educational Policy in Morocco', *Journal of Global Initiatives: Policy, Pedagogy, Perspective*, 14 (2): Article 9. https://digitalcommons.kennesaw.edu/jgi/vol14/iss2/9.

Jebbour, M. (2021), 'English Language Teaching in Morocco: A Focus on the English Department', *The Journal of North African Studies*, 26 (1): 103–15. https://doi.org/10.1080/13629387.2019.1681267.

Jenks, C. and J. Lee. (2020), 'Native Speaker Saviorism: A Racialized Teaching Ideology', *Critical Inquiry in Language Studies*, 17 (3): 186–205. https://doi.org/10.1080/15427587.2019.1664904.

Kumaravadivelu, B. (2016), 'The Decolonial Option in English Teaching: Can the Subaltern Act?', *TESOL Quarterly*, 50: 66–85. https://doi.org/10.1002/tesq.202.

Liu, J. (2018), 'Native-Speakerism in ELT: A Case Study of English Language Education in China', Doctoral Dissertation. The University of Liverpool.

Macedo, D. (2017), 'Imperialist Desires in English-Only Language Policy', *The CATESOL Journal*, 29 (1): 81–110.

Marley, D. (2004), 'Language Attitudes in Morocco Following Recent Changes in Language Policy', *Language Policy*, 3: 25–46. https://doi.org/10.1023/b:lpol.0000017724.16833.66.

Mignolo, W. (2018), 'Foreword: On Pluriversality and Multipolarity', in B. Reiter (ed.), *Constructing the Pluriverse: The Geopolitics of Knowledge*, ix–xvi, Durham, NC: Duke University Press.

Mignolo, W. and C. Walsh. (2018), *On Decoloniality: Concepts, Analytics, Praxis*, Durham, NC: Duke University Press.

Mirhosseini, S. (2018), 'Issues of Ideology in English Language Education Worldwide: An Overview', *Pedagogy, Culture & Society*, 26 (1): 19–33. https://doi.org/10.1080/14681366.2017.1318415.

Pan, L. and P. Seargeant. (2012), 'Is English a Threat to Chinese Language and Culture? The "Threat" of English in China Might Be Balanced by the Promotion of Chinese Language and Culture', *English Today*, 28 (3): 60–6. https://doi.org/10.1017/s0266078412000302.

R'boul, H. (2020), 'Re-imagining Intercultural Communication Dynamics in TESOL: Culture/Interculturality', *Journal for Multicultural Education*, 14 (2): 177–88. https://doi.org/10.1108/jme-03-2020-0016.

R'boul, H. (2021), 'North/South Imbalances in Intercultural Communication Education', *Language and Intercultural Communication*, 21 (2): 144–57. https://doi.org/10.1080/14708477.2020.1866593.

R'boul, H. (2022a), 'The Spread of English in Morocco: Examining University Students' Language Ontologies', *English Today*, 38 (2): 72–9. https://doi.org/10.1017/S0266078420000449.

R'boul, H. (2022b), 'English Medium Instruction in Moroccan Universities: Implications for Multilingualism, Linguistic Dependency and Epistemic Justice', *Journal of Multilingual and Multicultural Development*. https://doi.org/10.1080/01434632.2022.2069250.

Shome, R. (2019), 'Thinking Culture and Cultural Studies – From/of the Global South', *Communication and Critical/Cultural Studies*, 16 (3): 196–218. https://doi.org/10.1080/14791420.2019.1648841.

Siqueira, S. (2020), 'ELF with EFL: What Is Still Needed for This Integration to Happen?', *ELT Journal*, 74 (4): 377–86. https://doi.org/10.1093/elt/ccaa038.

Tajeddin, Z. and M. Pakzadian. (2020), 'Representation of Inner, Outer and Expanding Circle Varieties and Cultures in Global ELT Textbooks', *Asia-Pacific Journal of Second and Foreign Language Education*, 5: 10. https://doi.org/10.1186/s40862-020-00089-9.

Tolman, J. (2006), 'Learning, Unlearning, and the Teaching of Writing: Educational Turns in Postcoloniality', *Critical Inquiry in Language Studies*, 3 (2–3): 191–202. https://doi.org/10.1080/15427587.2006.9650846.

Vafai, M. (2017), 'Introduction to the Theme Section: Language, Identity, and the Legacy of Colonialism', *The CATESOL Journal*, 29 (1): 75–9.

Warriner, D. S. (2016), '"Here, Without English, You Are Dead": Ideologies of Language and Discourses of Neoliberalism in Adult English Language Learning', *Journal of Multilingual and Multicultural Development*, 37 (5): 495–508. https://doi.org/10.1080/01434632.2015.1071827.

Zouhir, A. (2013), 'Language Situation and Conflict in Morocco', Conference paper presented at the 43rd Annual Conference on African Linguistics. Somerville, MA: Cascadilla Proceedings Project.

# CHAPTER 3

# Pedagogical Stylistics and World Literature in Upper Secondary Schools

*Isabella Marinaro*

## Introduction

The aim of this chapter is to trigger a reflection on the English literature pedagogy applied in those upper secondary schools where history of English literature is a subject that mainly focuses on the 'British canon' and where students' linguistic awareness of the literary text is poor (e.g. in Italian upper secondary schools). In this chapter, we will deal with World Literature in English (WLE), a literary phenomenon that is sometimes ignored in upper secondary schools, in particular in those upper secondary schools where the English syllabus is mainly British-centred, on both a linguistic and literary level. We might say that such an English literature pedagogy is anachronistic mainly because the number of non-British authors writing in English has largely exceeded the number of British writers. Moreover, such a practice runs the risk of aligning these school systems with the conservative approach typical of the legacy of the British Empire, and the subliminal message that 'British' literature seems to be the only literature which is worth the name 'English literature'. Since the number of WLE writers has so greatly exceeded that of British (and American) authors, it is ethically correct that school syllabi reflect the reality of our globalized world. Tackling WLE at school encourages teenagers to open up to the ideas of pluralism, polycentrism and cosmopolitanism, and leads them towards a broader culture of inclusiveness. The objective of this chapter is to introduce a method whose aim is to widen teenage students' knowledge of English literature and raise their critical awareness, also from a linguistic point of view. This can be accomplished through

(1) enriching the traditional English literature syllabus with new *content*, namely introducing WLE authors and passages;
(2) using a stylistic approach as a possible *method* of textual analysis.

This chapter will also propose a case study, and concrete suggestions for classroom follow-up activities will be provided.

## A Brief Theoretical Frame of Pedagogical Stylistics

Before tackling the reasons why a stylistic approach should be considered essential when dealing with WLE as well as with 'traditional' English literature, it is necessary to explain what stylistics, and pedagogical stylistics in particular, is.

Contemporary stylistics focuses on the style of writers, their special manner of expression in terms of clarity and effectiveness (Verdonk 2006: 196). The aim of stylistics is not to merely describe the formal features of a text in itself, but also to 'show their functional significance for the interpretation of the text; or in order to relate literary effects or themes to linguistic "triggers" where these are felt to be relevant' (Wales 2016 [1990]: 400). Two of the main key ideas of this discipline are 'defamiliarization' and 'foregrounding'. In other words, what 'deviates' in a text is actually the main focus of stylistics as this discipline aims to identify those linguistic features of a text that somehow deviate from the norm and, above all, become strategic in the communication of meaning. Literary language, in particular, is suited for a stylistic approach since it presents features that can be considered as 'deviations' from the norm. Not only do such features add aesthetic value to the text, but they are also essential with regards to meaning-making. Stylistics helps understand these deviations with reference to a linguistic system and the context in which they appear.

For the reasons mentioned previously, we may say that pedagogy should be considered as one of the most appropriate applications of stylistics since, in this discipline, the investigators, in our case students, are put at the very centre of their investigation. Consequently, thanks to a stylistic approach to literary texts in the classroom, teenage students become active observers and critics of the analysed texts. The stylistic process of interpretation is never based on personal impressions as one of the tenets of this discipline is that it is firmly text-grounded and that the analysis must be carried out similarly to a scientific inquiry. When following a stylistic approach to the literary text in the classroom, students should not be asked to express their 'subjective impressions' since their observations must remain text-grounded. Instead, students should be encouraged to focus their attention on the function and effects of language features, that is, on the words employed in the text under investigation and their effects as opposed to other possible choices.

## World Literature in English in the Classroom: 'Comparative Intertextuality'

Before tackling the topic of WLE in the classroom, we should define precisely what we understand by the term 'World Literature'. This is a very hard task since there are many interpretations that cannot all be summarized in this chapter. The term 'World Literature' was coined by Goethe in 1827. According to Goethe, as Damrosch quotes, national literature had become an 'unmeaning' expression (Damrosch 2003: 1). For Goethe, WL offered a new literary perspective and a new cultural awareness, even though his frame of reference was still strictly European. Today some scholars claim that WL is the best literature that every single nation produces, while others believe that it is, rather, a 'process' (Moretti 2000, Damrosch 2003). In his attempt to define WL, W. Cohen states that a new 'attention to the world' seems to make us look beyond the idea of a 'continuing mistreatment of the poor nations by the rich' (Cohen 2017) simply because the world itself has changed: it has become 'globalized', this term comprising both its positive and negative connotations.

Cheah perceives Goethe's idea of WL as a dynamic process of literary exchange which also entails the ethical aim of fostering mutual understanding and tolerance between countries through the revelation of universal humanity despite natural differences, as well as the assessment of such differences, which naturally leads to gaining insight into human nature.

Expanding on Goethe's idea of *Weltliteratur*, E. Sturm-Trigonakis (2013) asserts that we are witnessing a deep change in process, content and linguistic practice in literature due to globalization. Sturm-Trigonakis points out that globalization is not a phenomenon that simply affects literature, but that literature is actually one of the many forces behind globalization that interact 'with other cultural expressions, policies, technologies and communication networks across national borders and oceans' (Sturm-Trigonakis 2013: 5). Such a new WL is an attempt to manage the heterogeneity of WL itself.

No other language, apart from English, offers the opportunity to combine the study of foreign canonical literature with the study of WL as WLE texts are originally written in English. The upper secondary school provides the right environment to begin an effective work of opening young people's minds to further dimensions offered by WLE not only to read 'the Other', but also to 'read otherwise' (Cooppan, in Damrosch 2009: 34). Thus, in current upper secondary school syllabi, WLE should be given the same level of importance as the so-called 'canonical' texts. A methodological problem might arise, namely how to tackle both literary productions.

In this chapter, we propose a stimulating way to tackle both traditional English literature and WLE using a 'comparative intertextuality' approach. The term 'intertextuality' denotes 'the relationship between texts, especially literary texts',[1] or, referring to literature, it is 'the ways in which texts are interrelated and meanings that arise out of this'.[2] It is evident that both these descriptions emphasize the idea of *relationship* between texts. Such a relationship can be either intentional or unintentional. In literature, intertextuality means that any book leads to another book, or other books (Bernardelli 2018 [2013]: 7). All literary works are interconnected somehow. Thus, it is possible to put different texts 'into dialogue' with one another once a shared feature has been identified. Different and culturally distant texts can be compared and contrasted on the basis of, for example, similarities in the topics covered since writers who belong to disparate cultures and ages may tackle similar topics or use similar rhetorical devices. It could be useful and stimulating to analyse these factors and focus on the linguistic tools that different authors employ to express their own perceptions and visions of the world. Moreover, comparing 'canonical' authors with contemporary writers from the four corners of the world might reveal how much our culture today relies on the past and that there are similar topics and problems among cultures in our globalized reality.

J. O. Newman claims that there are three ways of dealing with texts:

**(1)** Intertextuality: 'texts in dialogue with other texts, belonging to different cultures and periods';
**(2)** Comparatively, according to a historical focus;
**(3)** Using the lens of the genre. (Newman, in Damrosch 2009: 122)

These three methods of approaching diverse texts offer interesting possibilities to tackle WL. Since providing upper secondary school students with the historical display of English literature is a starting point, the most suitable way to enrich the traditional syllabus with WLE seems to be the methodological approach of putting texts into dialogue with each other. This chapter offers an example of intentional comparative intertextuality approach between a 'canonical' excerpt from English literature textbooks in use in Italian *liceo*[3] and an example of non-canonical English literatures, or a 'culturally other' example (Newman, in Damrosch 2009: 132). The comparative analysis of the texts will be carried out using a stylistic approach and examples of classroom activities will be provided. EFL upper secondary school teachers will not have to avoid a traditional

English literature programme and its chronological order of authors, and they will also be able to deal with new and unconventional topics and authors. Exploring new cultural perspectives, experiences of distant people, unknown frames of mind and new linguistic shades of English, not only gives new English literatures their dignity, but it is also an ethical action of teaching tolerance and respect. English literature teachers could adopt the comparative intertextuality method and carry out a comparative stylistic analysis of two excerpts confronting a 'canonical' English literary text with a WLE text. Such texts can be put into conversation with each other on the basis of, for example, a shared topic, the rhetorical devices employed, the narrative focus and the narrative structure. It is crucial to shift from 'Oxbridge' centrality[4] to the pluricentrism of today's world. Teenagers should be introduced to the plurality of English-speaking voices and cultures across the world, their 'authenticity' and newness. WLE passages can be selected on the basis of

- Their linguistic peculiarity;
- Cultural factors;
- The choice of interesting topics for teenage students;
- The variety of genres;
- The integration of 'other' cultures;
- Their length;
- The fact that their authors are contemporaneous.

Rather than forcing their students to agree with other cultures, teachers should help them accept the viewpoints and opinions of other people. According to Hall, teachers should not encourage students'

> 'passive reception and acceptance, but rather broaden the horizons of all, to the benefit of all. (. . .) Culture is a real issue for learners' identities, not a straightforward 'subject' to be 'taught'. (Hall 2005: 119–120)

Enriching the traditional syllabus of English with passages from WLE also implies a cultural challenge and stimulates students' creativity, especially when the text is approached using stylistics. Moreover, students are placed at the very centre of the learning process.

The following is a case study involving a comparative stylistic analysis of two texts and suggestions for class activities.

When dealing with 'canonical' writers, teachers could introduce the authors and excerpts included in English literature textbooks in use. What is new is the combination of the canon and the 'Others' and the stylistic exploration of the language employed in these texts so as to broaden the pedagogical perspective of English literature.

## Case Study: Daniel Defoe and Bidisha: The 'Other's' Gaze

What the eighteenth-century Defoe and the contemporary broadcaster, film-maker and writer of Indian origin share is the observation capacity shown in their journals, that is, in *Robinson Crusoe* and *Venetian Masters: Under the Skin of the City of Love* (2008), respectively. The two novels can be categorized as travelogues inasmuch as one relates the fictitious version of a shipwrecked man, and the other narrates the impressions and real experiences of the writer during her stay in Venice. In this chapter, we will focus on a single episode of Robinson's adventures, that is to say, his meeting with Friday, the 'Other' on the island, in which we are offered a very stereotypical portrait of him. Throughout all her novel, instead, while referring to the people she meets and their habits, Bidisha's impressions shift constantly: at times she is fascinated and often astonished.

The fictitious Robinson and the real Bidisha are interesting observers of what surrounds them. Through the comparative analysis of the two extracts, students are able to identify the tools and style, thus the strategies of description, and to reflect on the way the 'Other' may appear from the observer's perspective.

*Robinson Crusoe* is considered a cornerstone of the colonial novel and the relationship between Robinson and Friday has been revisited and interpreted many times in the twentieth century in a postcolonial view, as Walcott (1980) and Coetzee (1986) show, to quote two of the most relevant examples.

The reason why the novel has become so important, not only in the field of English literature, is probably the wide range of possible symbolical interpretations of Robinson's diary and of his relationship with Friday. Bidisha's novel, instead, is a real travelogue which presents the impressions of the writer during her stay in a real place, Venice. *Venetian Masters* is a poignant picture of a city and, above all, of the people living in Venice, their habits and frame of mind. Despite their deep differences in settings, types of characters, situations and, surely, writers' intentions, both novels share some features, such as the type of language that is used in personal journals. Therefore, students are also able to familiarize themselves with the language style mainly used in travelogues, understand its main features and, consequently, put their findings into practice applying a critical approach to the text. In our analysis, we will focus our attention on a famous passage of *Robinson Crusoe*, an excerpt that is very easy to find in many English literature textbooks in use at present.

Defoe, D. (1719/1981), *The Life and Strange Surprizing Adventures of Robinson Crusoe: of York, Mariner: Who Lived Eight and Twenty Years, all Alone in an Un-inhabited Island on the Coast of America, Near the Mouth of the Great River of Oroonoque; . . . Written by Himself*, London, Melbourne and Toronto: Dent, Everyman's Library, 149–50.

1  He was a comely, handsome fellow, perfectly well made, with straight, strong
2  limbs, not too large: tall and well-shaped; and, as I reckon, about twenty-six years of
3  age. He had very good countenance, not a fierce and surely aspect, but seemed to have
4  something very manly in his face; and yet he had all the sweetness and softness os a
5  European in his countenance, too, especially when he smiled. His hair was long and
6  black, not curled like wool; his forehead very high and large; and a great vivacity and
7  sparkling sharpness in his eyes. The colour of his skin was not quite black, but very
8  tawny; and yet not an ugly, yellow, nauseous tawny, as the Brazilians and Virginians,
9  and other natives of America are, but of a bright kind of a dun olive-colour, that had in
10  it something very agreeable, thought not very easy to describe. His face was round and
11  plump; his nose was small, not flat, like the negroes; a very good mouth, thin lips, and
12  his fine teeth well set, and as white as ivory.
13  After he had slumbered, rather than slept, about half-an-hour, he awoke again,
14  and came out of the cave to me: for I had been milking my goats which I had in the
15  enclosure just by: when he espied me he came running to me, laying himself down
16  again upon the ground, with all the possible signs of an humble, thankful disposition,
17  making a great many antic gestures to show it. At last he lays his head flat upon the
18  ground, close to my foot, and sets my other foot upon his head, as he had done before;
19  and after this made all signs to me of subjection, servitude, and submission imaginable,
20  to let me know how he would serve me so long as he lived. I understood him in many
21  things, and let him know I was very well pleased with him. In a little time I began to
22  speak to him; and teach him to speak to me: and first, I let him know his name should be
23  Friday, which was the day I saved his life: I called him so for the memory of the time. I
24  likewise taught him to say Master; and then let him know that was to be my name: I
25  likewise taught him to say Yes and No and to know the meaning of them. I gave him
26  some milk in an earthen pot, and let him see me drink it before him, and sop my bread
27  in it; and gave him a cake of bread to do the like, which he quickly complied with, and
28  made signs that it was very good for him.
29  I kept there with him all that night; but as soon as it was day I beckoned to him
30  to come with me, and let him know I would give him some clothes; at which he seemed
31  very glad, for he was stark naked. As we went by the place where he had buried the two
32  men, he pointed exactly to the place, and showed me the marks that he had made to find
33  them again, making signs to me that we should dig them up again and eat them. At this,
34  I appeared very angry, expressed my abhorrence of it, made as if I would vomit at the
35  thoughts of if, and beckoned with my hand to him to come away, which he did
36  immediately, with great submission.

This excerpt narrates Robinson's description of Friday, an indigenous man whom he has just met on the island. Robinson is trying to establish a contact with 'the Other', but the differences between them remain significant and contribute to Robinson's assumption of superiority. Students should be informed that there are two objectives of the stylistic analysis of the extract, that is, (i) to explore the linguistic traits which prove the strongly unbalanced and asymmetric relationship between the two men, and (ii) the exploration of Robinson's point of view regarding Friday. The interaction between Robinson and Friday occurs according to Robinson's terms and reveals Robinson's scrutinizing gaze at the 'Other'.

The passage is written using the technique of narrative report of speech/ thought acts (NRS/TA, Leech and Short 2007 [1981]), which immediately contributes to establishing Robinson as the 'controlling narrator' (G. D. Fulton 1994: 5), implying that Robinson guides the conversation with Friday for his own benefit. The first contacts with Friday are based on gestures for the lack of a common language, but immediately these basic gestures represent a way for Robinson to establish a relationship of domination over Friday (J. S. Farr 2017: 555).

As G. D. Fulton claims, with reference to Gadamer's paradigm on dialogue, the conversation between Robinson and Friday cannot be defined as a 'dialogue' since there is no mutuality, personal opening, sharing differences and, above all, there is no 'transformation into a communion, in which we do not remain what we were' (Fulton 1994: 6). Robinson, rather, educates Friday with the ultimate desire to convert him into a good Christian and he also teaches him Western rationality and self-restraint.[5] Appearing as 'not totally black' and willing to learn, Friday proves to be a good potential disciple. Robinson's behaviour and descriptions reveal his patronizing attitude, which underscores Friday's spiritual weakness and justifies the fact that Robinson converts the submitted Friday to Christianity. Moreover, becoming a teacher also reinforces Robinson's convictions of justness and rightfulness of his own beliefs and habits. Following Todorov's line of thought, to Robinson, Friday immediately appears as the 'innocent, potentially Christian Indian[s]',[6] or, as E. W. Said asserts, Robinson inevitably feels his 'fateful superiority' to Friday (Said 1989: 215). Robinson desperately needs Friday, not only to put an end to his loneliness, but, strategically, also as the figure of a good Indian who, once 'civilized', can help his master as a negotiator with those natives who refuse the 'blessing of civilization' and the 'true faith' (Todd 2018: 150). What is more, after so much time spent on the island, Friday's presence in Robinson's life is fundamental just like for a 'king' who has been 'without subjects' so far.[7]

The prevalent use of NRS/TA (narrative report of speech/thought acts) pinpoints the only point of view of the narration, that is to say Robinson's, and connotes reliability which is essential since the novel is written in the form of a diary. At first sight, we may observe that the story is narrated exclusively through Robinson's eyes. There is a prevalence of the first-person singular pronoun 'I', expressed or implied, with a total absence of direct speech. Robinson, the narrator, is 'I', thus the subject, while Friday is nearly always 'him', therefore the object. This linguistic feature emphasizes that the absence of dialogue is not simply due to the fact that Friday cannot speak Robinson's language, but, rather, because the centre of the action is Robinson. The absence of dialogic reciprocity and the implied superiority felt by Robinson is also communicated through the fact that he does not make any attempt to learn Friday's language. Throughout the novel Robinson refers to Friday using the expression 'savage', or other distancing associations.

In order to analyse the passage in a more detailed way, it can be divided into three main paragraphs, more specifically (i) from line 1 to line 12, (ii) from line 13 to line 28 and (iii) from line 29 to line 36, where each part presents peculiar characteristics.

(1) The first twelve lines foreground the abundance of adjectives referring to Friday's physical descriptions: his height, age, character. The narrator's attempt is to depict the indigenous man emphasizing his non-African and non-Amerindian features, and, rather, his 'European' features, and omit a detailed description of his skin colour. The difficulty of bestowing Western traits on an American Indian is conveyed by the non-definitions, or definitions by contrast, expressed through the use of the negation:

- 'Not too large', line 2;
- 'Not a fierce and surly aspect', line 3;
- 'Not curled', line 6;
- 'Not quite black', line 7;
- 'Not an ugly yellow', line 8;
- 'Not very easy to describe', line 10;
- 'Not flat', line 11.

What further foregrounds the narrative is the high occurrence of adjectives in general to depict the unknown 'Other': thirty-seven adjectives in twelve lines. Defoe employs a nominalization of adjectives, thus a reinforcement of adjectives, in only two cases, namely with the words 'sweet' (becoming 'sweetness') and 'soft' (becoming 'softness'), when referring to 'a European in his countenance' (lines 4–5).

Friday's body is, therefore, objectified and his description resembles the one of 'a beloved lady of a Renaissance sonnet'[8] and makes him more acceptable as Robinson's 'companion' for a WASP reading public. These descriptions also aim to transmit an image of a 'good savage', harbinger to Friday's future conversion into a Christian West-like and well-mannered 'creature' on the island. As Fulton underlines, the use of non-finite, dependent clauses and nominal groups 'disposes the readers less to question what Crusoe narrates', thus to believe those descriptions, and it also grants Robinson the 'control of monologic narrative' (Fulton 1994: 16). Leech and Short specify that the NRS/TA is a form of narration which is even more indirect than the indirect speech and readers automatically see the events entirely from the narrator's perspective (Leech and Short 2007 [1981]: 259–60).

The use of descriptions is a constant trait of the novel and this is because it is a diary of an adventurous life. Nevertheless, this feature is in line with one basic trope in the literature of colonialism, as Todd remarks, the 'surveying of territory from a high vantage point' (Todd 2018: 142) even though, this time, the subject of the description is a human being. Not only does this paragraph present the situation and Robinson's first perceptions of Friday, but it also paves the way for the following actions, that is to say, the definition of the hierarchy between the two men, with the consequent 'taming' of the 'savage' which culminates in Friday's conversion to Christianity. As Wheeler puts it,

> [*i*]f cannibalism is the more important practice signifying savagery, then Christianity is the most significant feature constituting European identity in *Robinson Crusoe*. (Wheeler 1995: 836)

In *Robinson Crusoe*, the descriptions not only aim to illustrate the New World to English readers, but they also mainly show how challenging the New World is. In this way, Defoe underscores both Robinson's ability to cope with all the difficulties of the savage place and his success in imposing his Western superiority on the island.

(2) Lines 13–28 shift the reader's attention from the descriptions of the 'savage' to the relationship between the two men. Here, Robinson establishes his dominion over the indigenous man, teaches him to speak as well as how to eat, and, finally, 'baptises' him with a new name, thus prefiguring Friday's future conversion to Christianity and imposing the Western 'importance of time' on him. Robinson's complete and absolute superiority over Friday is figuratively conveyed by the gesture of the submission which Friday makes as well as by the acceptance of some basic rules which are typical of servants: saying 'yes'/'no' and calling Robinson 'master'. It is the language of the colonizer which is imposed, a further way to underline Robinson's sense of domination. Robinson's position of superiority over Friday is also transmitted linguistically. This is the section where we can observe the highest occurrence (thirteen times) of the object pronoun 'him' which foregrounds Friday's passive behaviour:

- Line 21, twice;
- Line 22, three times;
- Line 23, once;
- Line 24, twice;
- Line 25, once;
- Line 26, twice;
- Line 27, once;
- Line 28, once.

(3) In the third paragraph (lines 29–36), we can observe that Robinson continues educating Friday by trying to instil some social rules, such as wearing clothes, which implies Friday's renouncing his cultural traditions. As Wheeler puts it, the most visible difference between savages and Christians is the absence of clothing for the

first as well as skin colour. It is worth noticing that Robinson's action of discouraging Friday's habit of eating human flesh occurs immediately after the indigenous man's acceptance of wearing clothes (Wheeler 1995: 840–1).

The digital processing of the passage (Figure 3.1) reveals that despite the fact that the narrator's point of view, expressed through the first-person singular pronouns 'I' and 'me', is dominant, the third-person singular pronouns 'him', 'he', and 'his' occur the most frequently. This explains that the focus of Robinson's narration is Friday, the 'Other', through the narrator's perspective. This is also proved by the higher occurrence of the third-person subject pronoun 'he' (nineteen times) as opposed to Robinson's 'I' (seventeen times), as shown in Figure 3.1.

Another trait that reveals Robinson's centrality as a narrator and his scrutinizing gaze to gather information about the 'Other' is provided by the deictic function of the third-person singular subject pronoun 'he' at the beginning of the passage referring to Friday. This pronoun shifts the reader's attention to the subject of Robinson's description. It therefore works as a cataphoric element in the discourse. The initial 'he', followed by the long list of descriptive adjectives and nominal sentences, conveys a sense of climax which culminates in Robinson's naming the 'Other'. This happens in the second paragraph, where the name 'Friday' conflates with the third-person object pronoun 'him'. 'He', together with the descriptions and references to 'him', stimulate the reader's imagination and participation in the portraying

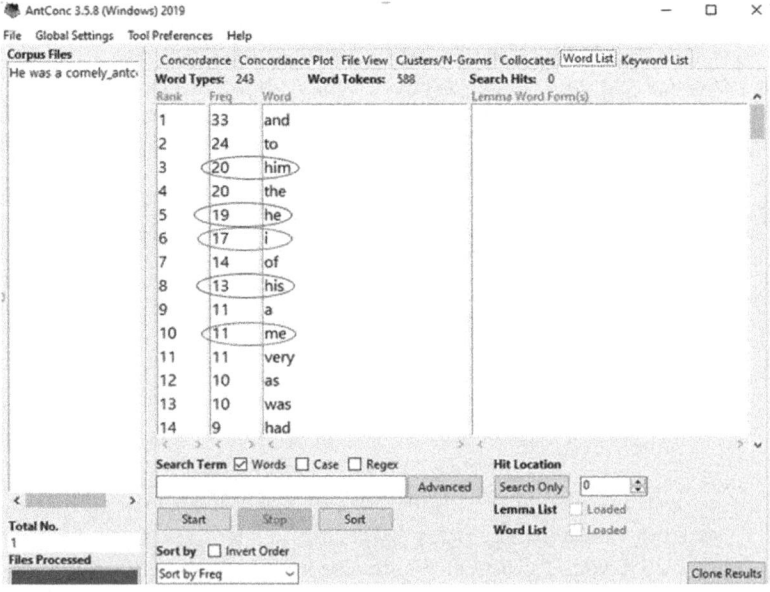

**FIGURE 3.1** *Frequency of the third-person and of the first-person pronouns.*

of the 'Other', whose complete picture is given with the attribution of the personal name, *naturally* in compliance with the Western colonizer's perspective. Moreover, Robinson's centrality is also reinforced by the choice of transitive verbs when referring to the English shipwrecked man. These verbs are associated with the first-person subject pronoun 'I', while the use of intransitive verbs is referred to Friday, as Tables 3.1 and 3.2 show:

**TABLE 3.1** First-person Subject Pronoun 'I' and Transitive Use of Verbs

| | |
|---|---|
| beckoned to him to come with me/with my hand to come away | line 35 |
| began to speak to him | line 22 |
| called him | line 23 |
| gave him some milk/a cake of bread | lines 26, 27 |
| let him know | lines 21, 22, 24 |
| let him see drink | line 26 |
| teach him | line 22 |
| taught him | lines 24, 25 |
| saved his life | line 23 |
| understood him | lines 20–21 |
| would give him some clothes | line 30 |

**TABLE 3.2** Intransitive Verbs Referred to 'He'/Friday

| | |
|---|---|
| awoke again | line 13 |
| came out | line 14 |
| came running | line 15 |
| had slumbered | line 13 |
| lived | line 20 |
| laying himself down | line 15 |
| seemed very glad | lines 30–31 |
| smiled | line 5 |
| was a comely | line 1 |
| was stark naked | Line 31 |

Once having explored Defoe's passage, the students can appreciate another kind of travelogue, that is, Bidisha's diary written during her stay in Venice. In 2004, Bidisha had the opportunity to stay at a noble's *palazzo* owned by her Italian friend's family. Then she moved to a small flat in order to experience living in Venice in a more independent way.

The extract is drawn from one of the last sections of the diary when Bidisha evaluates her whole experience.

Bidisha, (2008), *Venetian Masters. Under the Skin of the City of Love,* Chichester: Summersdale. Chapter 12, pages 237–8.

```
1    I'm exactly halfway through my stay and I've enjoyed my time here. I love the
2    beauty around me. I don't see it merely as a false mask hiding some 'real' crumbling
3    face, nor are the churches nothing more than dusty museums of forgotten relics. The
4    beauty here is real; even a builder's boat loaded with shovels and hammers looks dainty
5    as it bobs stiffly around a corner. An immense and blissful calm has descended since I
6    moved into my studio in the campiello and I love living alone. The weekends bring
7    packages of goodies from home so the postman, a friendly, comfortable-looking man
8    in his forties – perhaps a bit simple? – raps on the door and shouts 'Posta! Miss
9    Bidisha? A package for you! I think it's from your mother!' up at my window. He can
10   be heard doing this for lucky recipients all over San Polo, a sort of mobile personal
11   information service. I've turned out to be good with money, which is something I never
12   expected, having frittered away nearly every penny I made when I was younger. I've
13   discovered the ascetic inner me: frugal of food and finance, disciplined in work and
14   exercise – and clean! Astounding. I certainly set no precedent for it before. I love
15   having no television and find that not only do I not miss it, but that the new films I see
16   outside I experience with greater attention, sensitivity and patience than before. I am
17   never lonely. It is refreshing too to be in a place where people are not afraid of the
18   streets or the darkness and don't live their lives crippled with the imagined terrors that
19   re so common in a larger city. And thanks to the patronage of Stef's family I can see
20   that there is a certain (narrow) stream of Venetian society which, as the cliché goes, is
21   truly serene, civilised, unsleazy, intelligent, polished and composed.

22       Underneath the cordiality, however, there is a crabbed conservatism which is
23   dismaying in its obviousness, its hypocrisy and in the speed with which Venetians can
24   switch from the former mode to the latter. And so much of the pleasantness of daily
25   life here is linguistic: it's to be found in the easily flowing orders, questions enquiries,
26   purchases pleases, thank yous, remonstrations and avowals that form part of any
27   person's rota of quotidian errands and arrangements. These are hard to adopt with any
28   naturalness if you're a stranger, no matter how good your Italian is especially from
29   someone who so obviously – racially – has no claim to familiarity with Italian culture.
```

Bidisha's travelogue is actually a sharp criticism of Venetians. The title is split into two phrases (i) *Venetian Masters* and (ii) *Under the Skin of the City of Love,* and the effect is a kind of oxymoron as the writer offers two contrasting visions of this Italian city. The first part conveys a positive image of Venice by recalling the supreme artists who lived in and were inspired by this city for its beauty. The preposition 'under' at the beginning of the second part, instead, insinuates that the beauty of this city, world-famous as the 'city of love', is actually spoilt by something slyly hidden and the author is about to explain in detail in her account what it is. The objective of students' stylistic analysis is to explore the strategies employed by Bidisha to depict Venice as a double-faced place, the most beautiful and romantic city in the world, but also the most untrustworthy place she has ever visited.

Since this book is written in the form of a diary, the passage is narrated in the first-person singular, and it is therefore focused on Bidisha's point of view. Bidisha immediately concentrates on the 'beauty' around her. This quality is depicted as intrinsic to Venice. Beauty is thus present in every single detail, no matter if it is a piece of art, or a postman's behaviour. The writer believes that living immersed in beauty inevitably triggers a virtuous cycle which makes every single detail beautiful and, consequently, the writer also feels permeated by this beauty. This idea is conveyed through a series of examples abounding with positive descriptive adjectives. Bidisha's observations are outlined in Figure 3.2.

The outline reveals that the writer's definition of beauty, ('the beauty around me', line 2), is the starting point for a long series of positive observations about Venice and Venetians, first expressed through negations of bad aspects, thus through litotes: 'beauty is not' followed by negative

"the **beauty** around me" (l. 2)

| is **not**: | |
|---|---|
| *negative images / adjectives* | A **false** mask hiding some **crumbling** face (ls. 2 –3) |
| | In the churches which are not **dusty** museums of **forgotten** relics (l. 3) |

| is **real** and visible in: | |
|---|---|
| *positive images / adjectives* | The **daintiness** of a builder's boat loaded with shovels and hammers (l. 4) |
| | The writer's **blissful** calm descended since she moved to her flat (ls. 5 –6) |
| | The writer's **love** for living alone (l. 6) |
| | The writer's **joy when receiving packages** from her family in the weekends (ls. 6 - 7) |
| | The **friendly, comfortable-looking** postman (l. 7) |
| | The **lucky** recipients all over San Polo (l. 10) |
| | The writer's turning out to be **good** with money (l. 11) |
| | The writer's discovering of her **ascetic** inner self (l. 13) |
| | The writer's **disciplined** work (l. 13) |
| | The writer's becoming **clean** (l. 14) |
| | The writer's **love** for having no television (l. 14 –15) |
| | The writer's major experiencing of films watched outside, with **greater attention, sensitivity** and **patience** (ls. 15 –16) |
| | The people's **lack of fear** of streets and darkness as Venice is not a large town (ls 17 –19) |
| | The Venetian society which is **serene, civilised, unsleazy, intelligent, polished** and **composed** (ls. 20 –21) |

**FIGURE 3.2** *'The beauty around me.'*

adjectives 'false/crumbling/dusty/forgotten'. Then, Bidisha provides a long list of examples depicting positive qualities of the city and the positive impact that its beauty has had on her. In this second section, the writer concentrates on positive images and adjectives, as emphasized in my bolding.

Notwithstanding all the positivity towards the effects of Venetian beauty, at the end of the first part there is a seemingly meaningless adjective that works as a turning point in the discourse. Its apparently minor importance is communicated by the fact that it appears within brackets as though it were not really important in the celebration of all that beauty. The adjective is 'narrow' (line 20) and resembles a small *crack* in the description of Venice's magnificence. It brings readers straight to the second part of the excerpt which, just like the title of the novel, reveals the untrustworthiness of the Italian city.

The *crack* is introduced by the preposition 'underneath' (line 22) and is further reinforced by the adverb 'however', in the same line, which, by definition, can be used to add a comment that contrasts with what has just been asserted.[9] In this second part, the author does not spare Venetians a sharp criticism and, eventually, she criticizes Italian culture in general. In this section, the word that counterbalances the initial 'beauty' is 'conservatism' (line 22), reinforced by the adjective 'crabbed' which precedes it. 'Crabbed conservatism' is the other face of 'cordiality' (line 22), the word that summarizes the manners of Venetians. 'Cordiality' matches 'hypocrisy' (line 23), and, eventually, 'pleasantness' (line 24). Bidisha explains that the pleasantness of Venetians is a quality that is just linguistic (lines 24–5). She feels that the kind of politeness which Venetians resort to when dealing with others is only a formality and, thus, it is not sincere. Venetian 'crabbed conservatism', therefore, works like the aforementioned 'the beauty', that is to say, it precedes a list of examples, which now creates negative connotations. According to Bidisha, Venetians are hypocritical as they quickly shift from their natural beauty and elegance to their crabbed conservatism, therefore their pleasant manners are only a surface 'underneath' which hides their real hypocritical nature. What dismays Bidisha even more is the presumed inability of any non-Venetian and, in a broader sense, non-Italian, to understand and adopt those complex manners with 'naturalness' (line 28). Thus, in the opinion of Bidisha, it is virtually impossible for strangers to establish any 'cooperative principle' when communicating with Venetians.[10] This bitter conclusion also contains a more serious implication expressed through the adverb 'racially' (line 29), according to which Venetians, and Italians in general, consider themselves as a 'race' apart, capable of excluding any stranger (line 28) from their circle of alleged superiority. The second part of the excerpt can be outlined as illustrated in Figure 3.3.

Students' attention should be drawn to the structure of the passage, which is clearly divided into two separate parts. The first part is 'positive'

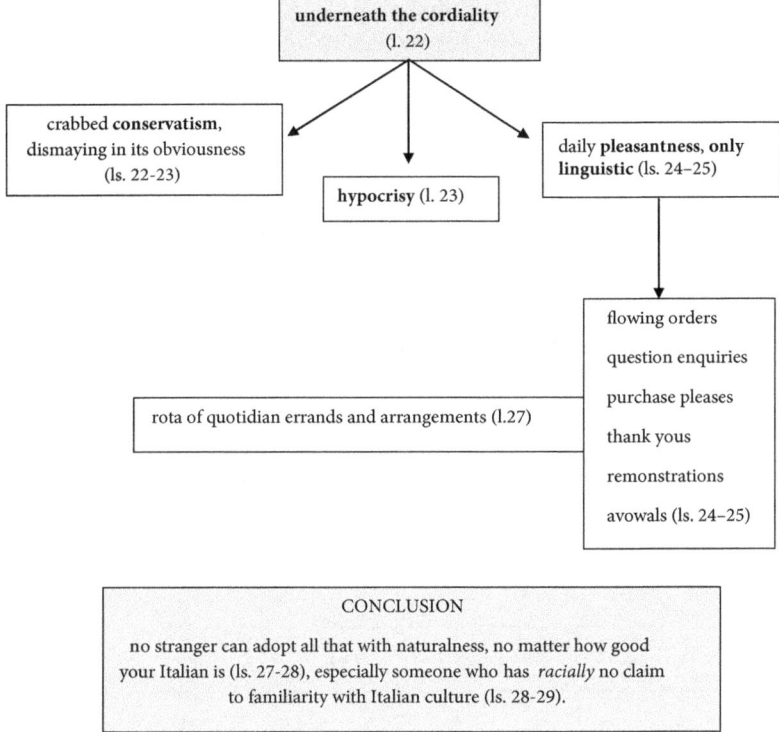

**FIGURE 3.3** *'Underneath the cordiality.'*

with variations of Venetian beauty, the second is definitely 'negative', and reveals the real face of conservatism and hypocrisy 'under the skin' of Venetian cordiality. The moral of the story is that it is impossible for any stranger to understand Venetians, and Italians in general. The 'city of love' is an uneasy experience for foreigners, no matter how good their Italian is. The conclusion is painful and unappealing: it is a matter of 'race'.

Bidisha's talking at length of 'the beauty' around her in the first part is functional for the bitter considerations in the second section and, above all, for the unflattering conclusion. The writer has adopted a well-known communication strategy known as a *captatio benevolentiae*,[11] that is, she first introduces the positive aspects of the matter to ingratiate herself with the reader. In this way, the readers receive the 'bad piece of news' with greater openness. It is clear that Bidisha's conclusions are unpleasant for Venetians, but, through the initial exaltation of Venetian beauty, she has undoubtedly found an effective way to voice her bitter conclusions without hurting people's feelings too much. In this way, the author succeeds in writing all her reflections about Venetians without running the risk of having a 'racist' attitude towards Italians.

The stylistic exploration of Bidisha's gaze at the 'Other' is quite complex because, differently from Robinson's vision of Friday, it is not 'black and white', but full of shades and contrasts.

Bidisha, just like Defoe, adopts the NRS/TA strategy, which is mainly concentrated between lines 25–7, where she lists the linguistic speech acts observed in Venice. Adopting this strategy, the writer confirms her total control of the narration. This strategy, as already mentioned, is suitable for the diary as a literary genre, and thus, by extension, for a travelogue.

## Follow-up Classroom Activities

After the stylistic appreciation of the two excerpts, students should be involved in follow-up activities. Students' linguistic choices should be in compliance with the linguistic strategies shared by Defoe and Bidisha and explored in the two excerpts, scilicet (i) first-person narration, (ii) 'not' descriptions followed by actual descriptions and (iii) narrative report of speech/act strategy to reinforce the narrator's centrality.

> Aim: To Focus on the Linguistic Devices to Describe the 'Other'

### *Activity 1.*

Write an anecdote about one of your trips. Using no more than 300 words, write in the form of a diary entry or a blog post. Describe the place you visited and the local customs that struck you the most. Explain why you were so struck. Write your narration in the first-person singular.

### *Activity 2.*

Using no more than 300 words, write in the form of a travelogue about some unusual or negative event in your life that happened to you on one of your trips. Use the first-person narration. Use the 'not' description form, or the litotes, so as to avoid being too direct, negative and impolite.

### *Activity 3.*

In no more than 300 words, write a blog post about an event that happened on one of your trips focusing on the local habits that struck you as different from yours. Use the first-person narration.

## Conclusion

This chapter has aimed to provide a reflection on the pedagogy of English literature in those upper secondary schools where history of English literature is mainly taught following a timeline of 'canonical' British writers. Such a traditional approach is too teacher-centred and teenage students are rarely engaged in activities that stimulate their active participation in the text analysis. Through the presentation of a case study, we have attempted to show how it is possible to enrich the traditional English literature syllabi with new content, namely WLE, using a stylistic approach to the text. Before presenting the case study that contrasts a passage from Defoe's *Robinson Crusoe* with an excerpt from Bidisha's *Venetian Masters*, we briefly illustrated a theoretical frame for understanding what stylistics is and why its pedagogical application might be useful to enrich the traditional English literature syllabi, especially when WLE is introduced. We firmly believe that following a British-centred English literature syllabus is anachronistic and that it aligns those school systems that still employ this practice with a conservative approach typical of the legacy of the British Empire. No longer is 'English literature' exclusively British. It is rather the expression of the numberless voices of writers worldwide whose cultures and language are valuable in that they reflect the true reality of our globalized world. The practice of what we have called 'comparative intertextuality' might encourage teenagers to open up to the ideas of pluralism, polycentrism and cosmopolitanism and, more importantly, helps them attain the target of a broader culture of inclusiveness.

## Notes

1  See entry 'intertextuality' at: https://www.oxfordlearnersdictionaries.com/definition/english/intertextuality.

2  See entry 'intertextuality' at: https://www.collinsdictionary.com/dictionary/english/intertextuality.

3  'liceo' (*lyceum*) is a five-year upper secondary school type where students are especially offered academic education emphasizing Italian literature, Latin or Ancient Greek, together with all the scientific subjects. English literature is studied during the last three years of the course.

4  As G. Hall states, '[*t*]he strict "Beowulf to Virginia Woolf" approach of old-style Oxbridge English study was uncritically exported to the colonies and beyond. Colleagues from (say) Egypt or the West Bank often display detailed knowledge of literary history of this kind, literature as subject of study for its own sake. Their scholarly erudition is admirable, but is it what their students need?' (Hall 2005: 146).

5  See Dennis Todd, (2018), '*Robinson Crusoe* and Colonialism', in Richetti J., *The Cambridge Companion to 'Robinson Crusoe'*, Cambridge University Press; p. 154.

6  See Tzvetan Todorov, (1984), *The Conquest of America: The Question of the Other,* New York: Harper & Row; page 46, quoted in Jason S. Farr, (2017), 'Colonizing Gestures: Crusoe, the Signing Sovereign', in *Eighteenth Century Fiction* Volume 29, No. 4, Summer 2017; p. 557.

7  See Eric Jager, (1988), 'The Parrot's Voice: Language and the Self in *Robinson Crusoe*', in *Eighteenth Century Studies* 21, no. 3: 317, DOI: https://doi.org/10.2307/2738687, quoted in Jason S. Farr, (2017), 'Colonizing Gestures: Crusoe, the Signing Sovereign', in *Eighteenth Century Fiction,* Vol. 29, No. 4, Summer 2017, p. 545.

8  See Rivka Swenson, (2018), '*Robinson Crusoe* and the Form of the New Novel' in John Richetti (ed), *The Cambridge Companion to 'Robinson Crusoe',* Cambridge University Press; p. 19.

9  See entry 'however', Collins Online Dictionary, at: https://www.collinsdictionary.com/dictionary/english/however.

10  For a short definition of 'cooperative principles', see Nørgaard, N., Montoro, R., Busse, B., (2010), *Key Terms in Stylistics*, Continuum: London, New York; pp. 67–9.

11  As Katie Wales maintains in her *A Dictionary of Stylistics*, the *captatio benevolentiae* is present at the beginning of an oration (= exordium or premium) and one of its functions is 'to put the listener in the right frame of mind by the "capturing of good will"'; (Wales, 2016 [1990]: 150).

# References

Bernardelli, A. (2018/2013), *Che cos'è l'intertestualità*, Roma: Carocci ed. (Le Bussole).
Bidisha. (2008), *Venetian Masters. Under the Skin of the City of Love*, Chichester: Summersdale.
Coetzee, J. M. (1986), *Foe*, New York: Viking Press.
Cohen, W. (2017), 'World Literature: What's in a Name?', *OUPblog*. Available online: https://blog.oup.com/2017/10/world-literature-definition/ (accessed 30 September 2020).
Damrosch, D. (2003), *What is World Literature?* Princeton, NJ and Oxford: Princeton University Press.
Damrosch, D. (2009), *Teaching World Literature*, New York: The Modern Language Association of America.
Farr, J. S. (2017), 'Colonizing Gestures: Crusoe, the Signing Sovereign', *Eighteenth-Century Fiction*, 29 (4): 537–62.
Fulton, G. D. (1994), 'Dialogue With the Other as Potential and Peril in *Robinson Crusoe*', *Language and Literature*, 3 (1): 1–20.
Hall, G. (2005), *Literature in Language Education*, London: Palgrave Macmillan.
'However', *Collins Dictionary of English*. Available online: https://www.collinsdictionary.com/dictionary/english/however (accessed 28 May 2020).
'Intertextuality', *Collins Dictionary of English*. Available online: https://www.collinsdictionary.com/dictionary/english/ (accessed 23 January 2020).

'Intertextuality', *Oxford Learner's Dictionary*. Available online: https://www.oxfordlearnersdictionaries.com (accessed 23 January 2020).

Leech, G. and M. Short. (2007/1981), *Style in Fiction*, Harlow: Pearson Education Ltd.

Moretti, F. (2000), 'Conjectures on World Literature', *New Left Review*, II (1). Available online: https://newleftreview.org/issues/II1/articles/franco-moretti-conjectures-on-world-literature (accessed 20 May 2020).

Nørgaard, N., R. Montoro and B. Busse. (2010), *Key Terms in Stylistics*, London and New York: Continuum.

Richetti, J., ed. (2018), *The Cambridge Companion to 'Robinson Crusoe'*, Cambridge: Cambridge University Press.

Said, E. W. (1989), 'Representing the Colonized: Anthropology's Interlocutors', *Critical Inquiry*, 15 (2): 205–25.

Sturm-Trigonakis, E. (2013), *Comparative Cultural Studies and the New Weltliteratur*, West Lafayette, IN: Purdue University Press.

Todd, D. (2018), '*Robinson Crusoe* and Colonialism', in J. Richetti (ed.), *The Cambridge Companion to 'Robinson Crusoe'*, Cambridege: Cambridge University Press.

Verdonk, P. (2006), 'Style', in K. Brown (eds.), *Encyclopedia of Language and Linguistics* (2nd ed., Vol. 12), 196–210. Oxford: Elsevier.

Walcott, D. (1980), *Remembrance and Pantomime*, New York: Farrar, Strauss and Giroux.

Wales, K. (2016/1990), *A Dictionary of Stylistics*, London and New York: Routledge.

Wheeler, R. (1995),'"My Savage", "My Man": Racial Multiplicity in *Robinson Crusoe*', *ELH*, 62 (4): 821–61.

# Part II
# Multilingualism, Translingualism and Linguistic Diversity

# CHAPTER 4

# From Babble to *Babel*

# Engaging Linguistic Diversity in the College Classroom at Home and Abroad

*Lucile Duperron*

## Introduction

Sociolinguistic scholarship about the Ancient World reminds us that globalization and multilingualism are ongoing phenomena (e.g., Adams et al. 2002). For example, in first-century Palestine, Ong (2016) argues, a social justice advocate, Jesus, 'as a member of that ancient society, must have been a multilingual speaker' (193) who probably code-switched between Hebrew, Aramaic, Greek and Latin, depending on the social domains in which he needed to communicate. In contemporary globalized societies and multicultural classrooms, modern language critical pedagogy underscores the benefits of leveraging learners' language repertoires to level the language playing field and counteract monolingual rules of academic success as part of its social justice agenda.

As a French-born-and-raised language educator who pursues her academic career in the dominant US English-speaking collegiate environment, I have framed my educational *persona* as that of an intercultural mediator between languages and cultures. However, how does that professorial role translate on the ground? Specifically, how does the content of my courses, my pedagogical approaches to language teaching and my mentoring relationship with my students critically reflect the dynamic processes that inform the multiethnic and multilingual cultures and societies of my home and my host countries? And how do my own linguistic and cultural heritages participate in shaping my understanding and practice of my profession, given that they belong to a long history of colonial legacies?

Kramsch and Zhang (2018) underscore the paradox that native instructors teaching their first language abroad bear the burden and responsibility of negotiating differing epistemological concepts of language mediation that they must reconcile in their daily practices. In the case of Metropolitan French educators' perceptions of their national language as a mediating tool to teach their culture at home, Kramsch and Zhang (2018) contend that they tend to conceive of it as 'mediat[ing] access to and integration into French society and the international community through intellectual rigor, critical reading of texts, precise and coherent writing . . . appreciation of beauty, felicitous pronunciation, and morally acceptable norms of behaviors such as discipline and respect of institutional authority' (6). In contrast, the US-based view of language mediation focuses on 'access to the global economy by stressing individual autonomy, creativity, negotiation, and teamwork' (Kramsch and Zhang 2018: 6). It is important to recognize these divergent frameworks as they can cause native instructors to resort to self-censorship in order to adapt to the dominant pedagogical practices in their host culture (Kramsch and Zhang 2018).

In response to this cultural and ethical dilemma, they proposed a bias-reducing paradigm, that of the 'multilingual instructor', to frame and support the work of language learning and teaching. According to Kramsch and Zhang (2018), the special ability of multilingual instructors to 'manage the use of [linguistic] codes in various cultural contexts' (5) is what can transcend the binary roadblocks of language as symbolic power, such as the relationships between dominant versus minority languages, or perceptions of native versus non-native speakers in the language classroom. In this chapter, I describe a curricular initiative developed with Kramsch and Zhang's 'multilingual instructor' stance in mind for the purpose of (i) raising US-based students' awareness of the symbolic power of language embedded in the experience of linguistic diversity at home and abroad and (ii) reconciling the epistemological differences within the concept of mediation, that is, between US-acquired and French-based intellectual traditions in the teaching of French language and culture in the US collegiate environment. Before I move on to describe the two courses that address these issues and the educational theories behind them, I will unpack the important distinctions, proposed by Piller's (2016) critical sociolinguistic framework, between 'multilingualism', 'linguistic diversity' and 'intercultural mediation', all of which undergird my teaching practices and course development.

## A Clarification of Terms

'Multilingualism' is a commonly used term to describe communities' and individuals' ability to converse daily in more than one language. In framing the role of the 'multilingual instructor' as an intercultural mediator, Kramsch and Zhang (2018) argue that the adjective has undergone a critical turn in educational and scholarly circles. This includes a shift towards education for social justice through (i) the development of 'intercultural communicative competence' – a critical skill advanced by Byram (1997) that views the capacity to communicate effectively and ethically beyond one's own cultural frame of reference as a dialogical enterprise and as an instrument for social change (Byram, 2008) – and (ii) the broadening of the term 'multilingual' in applied linguistics circles to mean the concept of translanguaging, that is, the 'flexible reliance on two languages to serve one's immediate needs' (Kwon and Schallert 2016: 138) including its recognition in multicultural educational spaces (Canagarajah 2002).

Piller (2016) points out that from a critical sociolinguistic perspective, the vernacular use of the term 'multilingualism' (i) assumes too much of a consensual and neat separation between language varieties across communities and (ii) reduces the use of two or multiple languages to a socially neutral fact. In response to these theoretical inaccuracies, Piller coins the phrase 'linguistic diversity' as a critically inclusive concept that recognizes, in response to (i), that language boundaries are more blended and shifting when language communities come into contact with one another, and, in response to (ii), that inequalities can develop in linguistically diverse communities because of the hierarchical position of some languages over others in 'local language pyramids' (Piller 2016: 14). Although multilingualism is, indeed, a universal and historically ubiquitous phenomenon, the concept of linguistic diversity captures both this dimension and the role of 'stratification' among languages that leads to issues of social justice since 'the language practices of those who are disadvantaged in other ways – because of their legal status, their gender, their race, or their class – are usually the ways of speaking that are the least valued, and language thus becomes one aspect of cumulative disadvantage in diverse societies' (Piller 2016: 14).

As a further terminological distinction, because it is influenced by sociological theories of power through language (e.g., Bourdieu 1982), French sociolinguistic scholarship has focused 'on the individual as the locus and actor of contact [and] has encouraged a shift of terminology from multilingualism (the study of societal contact) to plurilingualism (the study of individual's repertoires and agency in several languages)' (Moore and Gajo 2009: 138). The concept of linguistic diversity has focused primarily on societal contact and how it impacts communities and individuals. However, the notion of linguistic diversity combines both multilingualism and plurilingualism – a topic for another time and place.

Circling back to Kramsch and Zhang's (2018) paradigm of the role of the multilingual instructor as an intercultural mediator, Piller (2017: 4) also provides the useful clarification that intercultural communication has gradually become an 'umbrella term' to describe and analyse from various theoretical vantage points the multitude of 'mundane and ubiquitous' interconnected practices that occur with the spread of globalization. She thus charges scholars and educators alike to remember that 'the fundamental research question of the field of intercultural communication [is] to ask who makes culture relevant to whom in which context for which purposes' (Piller 2017: 7).

This set of critical research goals combined with the theoretical developments in applied linguistics have led multiple practitioners and researchers to re-articulate the legitimacy of language teaching and learning from a transdisciplinary perspective that visibly connects the study of world languages with larger issues of social justice (e.g., Reagan and Osborn 2021). This shift matters even more because race, class and gender identity make up the bulk of social justice discourses on US-based college campuses, while language is rarely recognized as an equally significant marker of social identity. According to Piller (2016: 5), 'if we do not understand how linguistic diversity intersects with social justice . . . we will not be able to work toward positive change'. In this chapter, I thus argue that world language and culture departments that include the experiences of multilingual speakers from their local and overseas communities and who address positionalities in their curriculum are well equipped to effect that change through critical pedagogy (CP). The next section briefly articulates theoretical aspects of CP, which are applied in the form of two teaching models that connect language diversity to a social justice agenda: (i) Culturally Sustaining Pedagogies (CSP), and (ii) Academic Service Learning (ASL).

## Critical Pedagogy in the Modern Language Classroom

An educational approach that 'aims at blending a "language of critique" with a "language of possibility" in education' (Guilherme 2002: 34), CP is rooted in democratic principles of access and representation as well as in the postmodern critical awareness that cultures and identities in contact are fluid and relational rather than fixed and reified. Nurturing this critical awareness through education is key because it engages students and teachers in co-constructed dialogues that may free up one another from essentializing perspectives of culture and identity, which are unfit to capture the elusive complexities of globalized multicultural societies.

When applied to modern language education, CP is thus well suited to train the 'critical intercultural speaker [to be] aware of the multiple, ambivalent, resourceful, and elastic nature of cultural identities in an intercultural encounter' (Guilherme 2002: 126). This includes the possibility of transforming the modern language classroom into a space where intercultural speakers are not limited to learning languages as linguistic codes, but, rather, can engage with the political dimension of linguistic diversity. This is because CP principles not only rest on the recognition that mutual negotiations of identity and culture shape intercultural encounters, but they also articulate the inherent political and ethical nature of education through curriculum building (Guilherme 2002). Teaching methods that enact these principles in the classroom tend to converge on issues of social justice. For the purposes of this chapter and its focus on linguistic diversity, I will discuss the two pedagogical models, CSP and ASL, the combination of which felicitously embeds critical language education in diverse multilingual contexts.

CSP bridges critical theory and pedagogy to override assimilationist teaching practices and redirect them into asset-based pedagogies, that is, additive pedagogies that harness the knowledge and language of all members of diverse societies and benefit them equally: 'the future is a multilingual and multiethnic one, regardless of attempts to suppress that reality. For too long we have taught our youth (and our teachers) that Dominant American English (DAE) and other White middle-class normed practices and ways of being alone are the key to power, while denying the languages and other cultural practices that students of color bring to the classroom' (Paris and Alim 2017: 6). Responding to the negative impact of language ideologies in the classroom, an insight of CSP, and central to my project, is to legitimize communicative practices that shuttle between prestige and non-prestige language varieties as evidence of complementary skills, instead of stigmatizing the latter and idealizing the former (Rosa and Flores 2017).

This shift in language attitudes is the first step to level the language playing field by recognizing the contributions of multilingual minoritized speakers in multicultural societies, instead of labelling them as so-called 'long-term English learners' or 'heritage speakers' whose ability to navigate multilingual spaces will never match monolingual standards of appropriateness. To clarify their position, Rosa and Flores (2017) add that they 'are not suggesting that people from racialized or language-minoritized communities should not seek to engage in linguistic practices deemed appropriate . . . [or] that advocates of asset-based approaches to language education should abandon all their efforts to legitimize the linguistic practices of their language-minoritized . . . students' (185–6). Rather, the goal of CSP is to reframe models of language education that reach beyond ideological divides regarding the legitimacy of linguistic and cultural appropriateness (Flint and Jaggers 2021).

Another teaching method that reflects critically on issues of access in diverse societies is ASL, 'a comprehensive pedagogical model that enhances learning through engagement with the community' (Purmensky 2009: 3). The course design is built on five interrelated elements: (i) reciprocity of goals between local communities and students; (ii) service that promotes civic engagement; (iii) reflection that taps into students' critical awareness about their experience; (iv) development of leadership skills; and (v) diversity that reflects intersectionality among students and communities (Purmensky 2009: 4–16). Although these specifications are not initially designed to articulate how language ideologies might impact educational access and academic success, their combined imperatives of useful reciprocity, civic engagement through service and critical reflection about diversity do contribute to raising critical awareness about linguistic diversity in the language classroom: Because ASL grounds intercultural encounters in a mutually beneficial experiential project, world language curricula that harness the translingual skills of their local community members are well positioned to transform modern language pedagogy by shifting dominant monolingual discourses of appropriateness to a critical understanding of language acquisition and usage in multilingual and multicultural societies.

In their overview of Community-Based Service Learning (CBSL) and its application to language education, Palpacuer Lee, Curtis and Curran (2018) describe this combination as being an 'experiential paradigm in the United States and in international settings over the past 20 years, with the goal of enhancing the linguistic and communicative competence of language learners and advancing the intercultural competence that is necessary for global citizens to engage with a diverse world' (169). Through their extensive survey of the secondary literature on the benefits of CBSL in language education, they report that this teaching method enhances confidence and motivation to learn languages by providing authentic communicative opportunities that expand learners' linguistic and intercultural development (e.g., Pelletieri 2011; Hummel 2013). Moreover, in the case of CBSL research with bilingual speakers of Spanish and English in the US-based classroom (e.g., DuBord and Kimball 2016; Pascual y Cabo, Prada, and Louther Pereira 2017), Palpacuer Lee, Curtis and Curran (2018) highlight the findings that the community piece embedded in service-learning pedagogy is an effective and beneficial practice that 'creates a social space in which bilingualism can be practiced and consolidate participants' positive views on language activism, bilingualism, and biculturalism' (174). The authors conclude that the language profession is stepping into 'a new frontier, where language, culture, and social action intersect through CBSL' (171), and they call for a new era of 'research and practice by considering specifically what service-learning affords with . . . linguistic and cultural development for language students and pre-service teachers and . . . social action that emphasizes the common ground where languages and communities intersect' (172).

Responding to this call for action, the next section describes a curricular initiative in the First-Year writing programme and in French and Francophone Studies at a US-based undergraduate liberal-arts college that (i) articulates the study of world languages and language education through the prism of translingualism, (ii) harnesses linguistic diversity as an equally foundational component of the curricular commitment to social justice and inclusion in higher education, along with race, class, gender, religion and national origins, and (iii) enacts CP through civic engagement projects that leverage linguistic diversity at home and abroad.

## An Implementation Model in the Collegiate Context

The touchstones of a US-based collegiate liberal-arts education are the first-year seminar (FYS) and the Senior Seminar. Both are crucial curricular opportunities for world language and culture departments to highlight the relevancy of learning languages, and to reflect critically about linguistic diversity. Through its writing programme, the FYS, taught in English, is the initial course in which undergraduates practise academic discourse and are challenged by expectations of language appropriateness, among other college-level writing goals. From a critical pedagogy perspective, it makes sense to design the FYS as a teaching and learning space that discusses the factors behind language choices rather than only presenting rules about written academic discourse. This pedagogical strategy does not dismiss the value of communicative effectiveness, but it aims to convey that for every language variety and register speakers use in their daily interactions, language choices are the complex, conscious and unconscious results of explicit and implicit negotiations of meaning situated at the crossroads of speakers' cognitive processes, language attitudes and social positioning.

Moreover, it opens the academic discussion about effective writing to students' lived experiences and their corresponding language repertoires, instead of limiting classroom discourse to writing conventions from a monolingual perspective. As such, it contributes to asset-based pedagogies, the teaching philosophy of which includes the recognition that multicultural classrooms are composed of students with a wide range of linguistic backgrounds, who effectively shuttle between language varieties and registers. As a case in point, the seventeen students enrolled in the FYS described in this chapter encompassed White domestic speakers of English who were at various acquisitional levels of classroom-instructed languages; White domestic speakers of English with previous long-term immersion in another language and culture; simultaneously bilingual domestic minority speakers of English of immigrant parents who spoke another language at home; domestic minority speakers of English adopted from another country by White domestic and international speakers of English and other languages, and who were learners of their birthplace's languages or their adoptive parents' languages other than English; and international bilingual minority speakers of English who spoke their home language from birth while learning English as part of their educational journey. These domestic and international students interacted in turn with adult immigrants who spanned nine different languages and countries of origin through three English Language Learning (ELL) classes taught by a local non-profit organization, the Employment Skills Center (ESC). The pairing was designed to raise awareness about the cognitive costs and social factors involved in any language learning experience – including the FYS students' – which in turn aimed to generate critical discussions of the various obstacles, especially linguistic discrimination, which minoritized communities experience daily at home and abroad.

At the opposite end of the collegiate curriculum, the Senior Seminar is the institutional culmination and recognition of students' achievement in their major. Modern language majors are expected to demonstrate their linguistic proficiency and intercultural competence as foundational elements of their undergraduate education. Since the 2007 publication of the MLA (Modern Languages Association) Ad Hoc Committee on Foreign Languages Report, world language and culture departments have attempted to reverse the monolingual habitus of the native speaker that is inculcated in language education:

> The language major should be structured to produce a specific outcome: educated speakers who have deep translingual and transcultural competence. Advanced language training often seeks to replicate the competence of an educated native speaker, a goal that post adolescent learners rarely reach. The idea of translingual and transcultural competence, in contrast, places value on the ability to operate between languages. Students are educated to function as informed and capable interlocutors with educated native speakers in the target language. They are also trained to reflect on the world and themselves through the lens of another language and culture. They learn to comprehend speakers of the target language as members of foreign societies and to grasp themselves as Americans – that is, as members of a society that is foreign to others. They also learn to relate to fellow members of their own society who speak languages other than English. (n.p.)

Surprisingly, the report's language about translingual learners' effective communication with 'educated native speakers in the target language' carries a monolingual assumption regarding the speakers of the said target language. This unreciprocated relationship is troubling for French since the latter is used internationally in both first- and second-language contexts. Moreover, any scholarly and educational foray in *Francophonie* undermines the very notion of 'educated native speakers', a choice of words that is reminiscent of the monolingual ideology in support of the French State's colonial project. Even though it does espouse a CP perspective, the MLA language and recommendations simultaneously reinforce the very hierarchies CP and the overall MLA report endeavour to reassess regarding language 'nativeness'.

This internal contradiction underscores how strong the bias of the superiority of the native speaker remains. It is especially the case for

Metropolitan French – the variety of French spoken within the political borders of France – because of its history as the 'standard' employed by the French State to represent its power at home and abroad. Uncovering the pervasive monolingual discourses in educational and institutional spaces was thus decisive in constructing a French seminar for graduating majors with an asset-based pedagogical design that brings 'ideological clarity' (Lin 2020: 205) about the tacitly monolingual assumption that French is a homogeneous language variety, specifically within France.

Consequently, in their French seminar, students were invited to decentre the hegemonic position of Metropolitan French through engaging with the intersections between language, identity and politics thanks to legal, scholarly and artistic works spanning the sixteenth to the twenty-first century, which traced how the rise of monolingual ideologies gradually impacted multilingual communities and minorities in France. In other words, the seminar was designed to highlight the issues of linguistic diversity in French society that result from the special political status of standardized French in the national language pyramid.

Moreover, the course harnessed its institutional connection to a study-abroad site located in the city of Toulouse, in Southwestern France, with a goal of reaching a more nuanced understanding of the ways in which linguistic diversity is the situated outcome of the complex interactions between international, national and local histories and places. This aspect of the course focused on political, educational and professional contexts: (i) Occitan activism to reclaim a gradually minoritized regional language in France; ii) public schools' French language learning programmes for immigrant minors; and (iii) language policies at the Toulouse headquarters of the multinational aeronautic company, *Airbus*.

The FYS and Senior Seminar are thus two sides of the same coin. The former aims to build intercultural competencies that are supported by critical (CP) and experiential (ASL) pedagogies to engage the challenges of linguistic diversity in and out of the dominant English composition classroom. The latter shares similar goals of critical awareness through an in-depth linguistic, historical and cultural analysis that harnesses students' advanced proficiency in French to challenge hexagonal views of language and culture in France and explore the situated complexities of language diversity. The next section delves into the syllabus design underpinning the goals of each course.

## Syllabus Design

### *First-Year Seminar*

The FYS initiative greatly benefitted from a national Mellon grant for civic engagement that was sponsored institutionally by the Center for Civic

Learning and Action at Dickinson College, USA. Access to such grants is seminal to bridge critical theory into practice, as they help to recognize the work done on the ground by educators and volunteer organizations. The first order (and challenge) of syllabus design was to combine equitably the critical goals and learning components of the writing programme with ASL pedagogy in order to sustain students' confidence in their academic progress and frame concurrently their commitment to volunteer work according to the ASL specifications described in the previous section of this chapter: The minute service-learning programming feels like an added burden to their academics, and students might lose the impetus to serve, a form of demotivation under stress that would defeat the very philosophy of civic engagement which inspires ASL pedagogies. Similarly, there is significant logistical work that is initially required on the part of partnering organizations' staff and educators (Purmensky 2009). Therefore, it is especially important to connect regularly with all stakeholders and align activities according to the schedule and habits of each organization. This attention to pace prevents volunteer enthusiasm from devolving into fatigue and manages potential tensions that naturally arise from the differential goals and functions of the partnering organizations.

Moreover, striving for a balanced approach spoke to the expectation of reciprocity between local communities and students – another specification of ASL course design – because meeting the needs of the community matters as much as supporting students' ability to succeed academically. In the case of the FYS described in this chapter, both FYS students and ELL students were engaged in learning how to communicate effectively in a high-stakes environment. FYS students had to pass the course to continue their studies, and ELL students sought job opportunities and learnt how to navigate the ins and outs of their host community. Reciprocity was also defined through the civic engagement purpose of the course: FYS students provided an opportunity for ELL students to access the rich resources of their local academic community while ELL students enabled FYS students to access the educational and social opportunities afforded by linguistic diversity through their mutual relationship.

Finally, the diverse languages, religions, countries of origins, socioeconomic statuses, gender, ethnicities and age groups garnered through the ASL collaboration between the FYS and the ELL programmes reflected the intersectionality that is also a feature of ASL course design to develop intercultural competence (IC). The FYS emphasis on the role of language as an identity marker acted as a useful reminder that IC also depends on language proficiency for individuals' capacity to interact and respond appropriately and ethically to cultural differences, especially since this component is strikingly absent from major IC frameworks and constructs (Garrett-Rucks 2016).

Managing an equitable, reciprocal and diverse collaboration among partners opened the space and time for reflection that can promote critical awareness through ASL experiences, a fourth feature of the ASL pedagogical model. To that end, the writing programme embedded the ASL experiential component of the course in a critical investigation of the cognitive, psychological and sociolinguistic dimensions of bilingualism and biculturality and their connection with linguistic diversity in multicultural societies. Writing assignments were designed sequentially to critically reflect on issues of (i) language identity, (ii) language development, (iii) language ideologies, and (iv) language education. Correspondingly, students drafted a series of writing assignments that scaffolded the writing goals of the FYS program: (i) A language autobiography was modelled after Cathy Park Hong's critically engaged essay 'Bad English' from her book *Minor Feelings* (2020) to challenge assumptions of appropriateness in language use. (ii) The classic FYS compare-and-contrast paper was dedicated to adult versus child language development in a second language and examined the latest cognitive research on bilingualism to sensitize FYS students to the fact that the adult learners of the ESC often

> face a formidable task. They have to fashion a new communicative system while they are struggling to communicate, using whatever information they can glean from their TL [target language] interlocutors. Those interlocutors are not likely to be patient and supportive . . . . At the same time, the communicative tasks are often vitally important: the learner seeks employment, social services, refuge – and strives to maintain face under conditions of unavoidable asymmetry and inequality. The capacity of human beings to learn under such circumstances is impressive. (Slobin 1993: 239)

(iii) The simulation of a local school district debate about financing a bilingual education programme enabled students to reach beyond political divides, interrogate their own language attitudes and analyse how language ideologies and economics shape the educational landscape. Students read anti- and pro-bilingual education journalistic articles, gathered information about the cognitive and social benefits of bilingualism, investigated local educational budget expenses and read about perceptions regarding bilingualism to prepare their arguments. The debate was modelled after the successful Proposition 227 campaign of 1998, which made California schools limit bilingual education and mainstream Spanish-speaking students to English classrooms (Legislative Analyst's Office). (iv) Finally, students wrote and adapted a final research paper into a scientific poster, the topic of which reflected the interests they developed through their ASL experience. Projects ranged from cognitive to psychological and educational aspects of language learning.

Throughout the semester, students charted their reflections about their service-learning experience by writing weekly field notes, which in turn provided qualitative research data for their research topic. The final goal of ASL pedagogy, to develop leadership skills, was enacted through the official

**FIGURE 4.1** *Poster exhibition opening event. Reproduced with the permission of Rick Coplen.*

opening of a month-long poster exhibit at the college library in lieu of the traditional final exam, which allowed students to take responsibility for their work and articulate in their own words the critical role of language as a social and cognitive marker of identity in their local community and beyond. The event brought together a mix of fellow students, college professors, librarians and administrators, as well as local political figures, and Employment Skills Centre teachers, staff and students (Figure 4.1). The public nature of the exhibit was explicitly designed to make language diversity and multilingual speakers in the community not only visible but also heard, instead of confining discussions to the FYS classroom. Finally, it created an approachable and casual opportunity for language education for all library patrons on their way to the circulation desk. Librarians spontaneously reported that many strolled through the exhibit and asked them questions about the FYS and most importantly, the ESC.

## *French Senior-Year Seminar*

As Byram and Wagner (2018) remind us, 'intercultural competence is not an automatic byproduct of language teaching' (147). Therefore, they recommend that language educators devise teaching pedagogies that foster relationships among language speakers in and out of the classroom environment to develop deeper intercultural skills. The concept of the French Senior-Year Seminar outlined in this chapter originated from a desire to make world language and culture curricula prominent intercultural contact zones in which language learners and educators map out their language proficiency onto critical competencies with goals of cultivating awareness about linguistic diversity at home and abroad and becoming agents of social change. In other words,

> [a]re we teaching students to interact with idealized native standard language speakers only? Or are we helping students to become critical

> linguistic ethnographers (Van Viegen and Lau 2022) who have developed critical language awareness and do not subscribe to the hierarchy of languages while at the same time being able to access the dominant linguistic resources in the institution and society? (Lin 2020: 204)

In terms of syllabus design, the course started with a critical examination of everyday language attitudes (everyone has an opinion about language and languages) as well as of the main language ideologies that are associated with language planning, that is, the development of bottom-up or top-down policies that informally or formally aim to change language practices in a community (Stamper and King 2017). The initial focus on language ideologies provided tangible CP connections with the effects of language policies on minoritized communities in France. Interestingly, language policies are concerned with achieving changes that are not necessarily linguistic in nature (Piller 2016). In the case of language planning in France, the dominant ideology of linguistic assimilation sanctioned by the French State promotes the exclusive use of French in the name of national integration and linguistic integrity (Boyer 2012).

Therefore, the course focused on the unique historical equation between language and political power in France that, *inter alia,* gradually gave prominence to *francien,* that is, the northern dialect spoken by the educated upper classes; the role of the French Academy in institutionalizing this connection; and the impact of the French Revolution on the radical promotion of French as a political tool to unite under one language and one nation the citizens of the new Republic against the divisive power of the former Monarchy. As Article 2 of the French Constitution states: *La langue de la République est le français* (The language of the Republic is French) (Hornsby 2009). The process of tracing the political landmarks of language planning in France simultaneously uncovered the diverse language landscape of the country, with its territory housing the largest number of language varieties in Europe (Cerquiglini 1999). Students' reports on regional languages were the first stepping stone in the seminar to question standardized French as the only language variety in France.

Not only did students become more aware of the diverse regional languages rooted in French soil, but they also discovered how language variation is inextricably bound to geographical and political factors. As a case in point, once they were exposed to the typological and geographical distribution of regional languages in France, students compared the fate of Catalan on each side of the French–Spanish border – where it is an official language – to study the minorization of regional languages under the monolingual spell of the French Republic. Moreover, to make the French major's study-abroad site directly relevant to students' academic experience and by connecting with local interlocutors, the course syllabus included a case study about the status of Occitan, the regional language spoken in the area of Toulouse, France. In contrast to the concept of linguistic assimilation, activities were geared to analyse concurrent language ideologies: Linguistic pluralism supports the coexistence of languages within a community while vernacularizing promotes indigenous languages. Therefore, students reflected on the dynamics between top-down policies such as the European Charter for Regional or Minority Languages (Council of Europe) regarding their preservation in contrast to the French constitution, and bottom-up local language policies aimed at revitalizing Occitan in the region of Toulouse, which was named in 2001 by local politicians the capital of *Occitania* (Amos 2017).

This exploration enabled students to apply CP to a new area of language planning research focused on linguistic landscape. Stamper and King (2017) define the latter as an exciting subfield that 'seek[s] to understand the motives, uses, ideologies, varieties, and contestations of "language" (defined broadly) as displayed in public spaces through, for example, signage and advertising as well as public announcements and currency. This research often seeks to uncover inequities and injustices that are largely invisible, routine, accepted, and taken for granted' (666). In the case of Toulouse, the bilingual French–Occitan signage of streets, although it acknowledges the hegemony of French by placing the official language on top of the regional language, covertly affirms the local primacy of Occitan through translation and adaptation techniques (Amos 2017).

Contrasting the territorial multilingual diversity of regional languages with the top-down political history of language planning in France that made French a national language before it became the majority language it is today paved the way for the next phase of the course: the critical examination of regional French versus standard French, and the extent to which the expression of French language identities became tied to sociolinguistic divisions between Paris and *la province*. Standardization forces have undeniably levelled many distinctions between regional varieties of French, besides accelerating the near extinction of regional languages (Hornsby 2009). However, enduring language attitudes and ideologies towards regional French remain significant. A striking example is the 2008 box office success of the classic French comedy *Bienvenue chez les Ch'tis* (Welcome to the Sticks), which tells the story of a postal worker who gets demoted from his position in the south of France to the less desirable northern region. The plot relies on the stereotype of backwardness enacted by the marked pronunciation of regional French from Northern France and the use of regionalisms, among other comic strategies. Incidentally, this stereotype connects back to the original stigmatization of regional languages in the wake of the French Revolution, as signalled in the very title of the republican Abbé Grégoire's 1794 report, *Sur la nécessité et les moyens d'anéantir les patois et d'universaliser l'usage de la langue française* (On the necessity and means to eradicate patois and universalize use of the French language). The film thus provided an approachable CP point of entry that exposed students to the issue of linguistic discrimination, a theme that was expanded upon to explore the potentially toxic relationship between race and language in postcolonial contemporary France. Specifically, attitudes towards pronunciation were applied to media representations of the so-called *français de banlieue* (inner-city French), which is primarily associated with urban youth descending from immigrants from the former French colonies in the Maghreb and West Africa. Research suggests that the unrealistic portrayal of *français de banlieue* that is supposedly designed to sound authentic pathologizes urban ethnic youth as violent or exoticizes it (Hammoud 2012). Moreover, speakers of so-called *français de banlieue* internalize their own idiolect as disrespectful and as such, distance themselves even further from it. Meanwhile, they are more likely to experience discrimination on the job market based on their pronunciation and their readily identifiable names (Guehria 2020).

Finally, as a counterpoint to the effects of official monolingualism described thus far, the course shifted its focus onto emerging multilingual trends in the context of globalization. On the one hand, students examined top-down French educational policies and immigration laws as implementations of language planning. According to Filhon and Paulin (2015), the main immigrant languages of France are Arabic, Berber, English, German, Italian, Polish, Portuguese, Spanish, Turkish and Vietnamese. This part of the course focused on French-as-a-foreign-language programmes and how they mainstream migrant minors and adults into educational pathways. The goal was to discuss issues of linguistic insecurity and phenomena of intergenerational language shifts by harnessing the study-abroad site of Toulouse again as a case study, thanks to an educational partnership with the University of Toulouse, which created in 2017 the DILAMI (*Dispositif d'Accueil des Immigrés* – reception system for migrants). Because of the pandemic, the course refocused on the CASNAV (*centre académique pour la scolarisation des enfants allophones nouvellement arrivés et des enfants issus de familles itinérantes et de voyageurs*), a public-school administration that manages migrant students' placements in local establishments, which students discussed thanks to a documentary about a migrant ninth-graders' French class, *La Cour de Babel* (Babel's school yard).

On the other hand, students examined the diminishing status of French as an international professional language given the rise of Global English as the new *Lingua Franca*. This was the occasion for the third and final place-based case study, which was devoted to bottom-up internal language policies by *Airbus*, a multinational aeronautic company whose worldwide headquarters are based in Toulouse. All employees are expected to speak English in the workplace, officially as a means of neutralizing language hierarchies within the original consortium of French, German and Spanish companies (Truchot 2013). The international business context uncovered language attitudes and policies that favour English as a medium of supranational excellence in contrast to the home language (Truchot 2013). Three interviews with *Airbus* employees highlighted the role of foreign language proficiency and intercultural skills in managing successful business relations with clients. Both case studies thus raised further critical awareness about the changing linguistic landscape of France on the cusp of three centuries of *unilinguisme* (Boyer 2012: 93).

## Conclusion

This chapter aimed to describe the engaging ways in which world language and culture curricula are organically positioned to contribute to a social justice agenda in higher education in and out of the traditional boundaries of their institutional roles. First, world language and culture departments routinely develop intercultural skills and multilingual writing competencies that can transform English-dominant approaches to academic writing into asset-based pedagogies of translingualism. US-based writing programmes themselves are increasingly gaining awareness of the multilingual turn in composition studies and note that teaching writing 'often (re)creates an uneven linguistic playing field, where some forms of speaking and writing are more valued than others . . . [as] writing instruction has traditionally upheld the linguistic status quo, which is disempowering to particular groups of students, including multilingual and multidialectal writers' (Shapiro 2022: 3).

Moreover, world language and culture programmes must harness their teaching of advanced language proficiency skills to engage in local and international connections that nurture intercultural encounters thanks to a critical examination of linguistic diversity at home and abroad. The most recent study-abroad research suggests that place-based ASL opportunities and programmatic online interactions before, during and after study abroad, as is the case-study programme described in the French seminar, foster deeper intercultural dialogues along with superior language learning opportunities (Marijuan and Sanz 2018). Finally, besides being critically equipped to make language identity-focused contributions to a social justice agenda in higher education, world language and culture programmes must seek further interdisciplinary collaborations to remain both vibrant and indispensable agents of social change. This is a particularly timely opportunity for US liberal-arts colleges to respond to language and culture programmatic needs related to social justice, thanks to their relatable scale and residential commitment to an ethical education.

## Acknowledgements

The writing of this chapter is indebted to the generosity of the Employment Skills Center's ESL team, in Carlisle, Pennsylvania, the funding support of the Center for Civic Learning and Action at Dickinson College, USA, and the engagement of my first-year seminar students and French majors.

# References

Adams, J., M. Janse and S. Swain, eds. (2002), *Bilingualism in Ancient Society: Language Contact and the Written Text*, Oxford: Oxford University Press.

Amos, H. W. (2017), 'Regional Language Vitality in the Linguistic Landscape: Hidden Hierarchies on Street Signs in Toulouse,' *International Journal of Multilingualism*, 14 (1): 93–108.

*Bienvenue chez les Ch'tis*. (2008), [Film] Dir. Danny Boon, France: Pathé.

Boyer, H. (2012), 'Idéologies sociolinguistiques et politique «intérieure» de la France', *Synergies*, 5: 93–105.

Byram, M. (1997), *Teaching and Assessing Intercultural Communicative Competence*, Clevedon: Multilingual Matters.

Byram, M. (2008), *From Foreign Language Education to Education for Intercultural Citizenship: Essays and Reflections*, Clevedon: Multilingual Matters.

Byram, M. and M. Wagner. (2018)', 'Making a Difference: Language Teaching for Intercultural and International Dialogue,' *Foreign Language Annals*, 51 (1): 140–51.

Bourdieu, P. (1982), *Ce que parler veut dire. L'économie des échanges linguistiques*, Paris: Fayard.

DuBord, E. and E. Kimball. (2016), 'Cross-Language Community Engagement: Assessing the Strengths of Heritage Learners', *Heritage Language Journal*, 13: 298–330.

Canagarajah, A. S. (2002), 'Multilingual Writers and the Academic Community: Towards a Critical Relationship', *Journal of English for Academic Purposes*, 1 (1): 29–44.

Cerquiglini, B. (1999), *Les Langues de France: Rapport au ministre de l'éducation nationale, de la recherche et de la technologie et à la ministre de la culture et de la communication*. Available online: https://www.vie-publique.fr/rapport/24941-les-langues-de-france-rapport-au-ministre-de-leducation-nationale-de (accessed 30 March 2022).

Council of Europe, (1992), *European Charter for Regional or Minority Languages*. Available online: https://www.coe.int/en/web/european-charter-regional-or-minority-languages (accessed 30 March 2022).

Filhon, A. and M. Paulin. (2015), *Migrer d'une langue à l'autre*, Paris: La Découverte.

Flint, A. S. and W. Jaggers. (2021), 'You Matter Here: The Impact of Asset-Based Pedagogies on Learning,' *Theory Into Practice*, 60 (3): 254–64.

Garrett-Rucks, P. (2016), *Intercultural Competence in Instructed Language Learning: Bridging Theory and Practice*, Charlotte, NC: Information Age Publishing.

Guehria, W. (2020), 'Français des banlieues-arabe maghrébin, *wèsh–wallah*, déconstruisons un mythe', in K. Gauvin and I. Violette (eds.), *Minorisation linguistique et inégalités sociales. Rapports complexes aux langues dans l'espace francophone*, 105–25, Bern: Peter Lang.

Guilherme, M. M. (2002), *Critical Citizens for an Intercultural World: Foreign Language Education as Cultural Politics*, Clevedon: Multilingual Matters.

Hammou, K. (2012), *De l'histoire du rap en France*, Paris: La Découverte.

Hong, C. P. (2020), *Minor Feelings: An Asian American Reckoning*, New York: One World.

Hornsby, D. (2009), 'Dedialectalization in France: Convergence and Divergence', *International Journal of the Sociology of Language*, 196–7: 157–80.
Hummel, K. M. (2013), 'Target Language Community Involvement: Second-Language Linguistic Self-Confidence and Other Perceived Benefits', *The Canadian Modern Language Review/La Revue canadienne des langues vivantes*, 69: 65–90.
Kramsch, C., and L. Zhang. (2018), 'From the Native and Non-Native to the Multilingual Instructor', in *The Multilingual Instructor*, 1–29, Oxford and New York: Oxford University Press.
Kwon, H. and D. Schallert. (2016), 'Understanding Translanguaging Practices Through a Biliteracy Continua Framework: Adult Biliterates Reading Academic Texts in Their Two Languages', *Bilingual Research Journal*, 39 (2): 138–51.
*La Cour de Babel.* (2014), [Film] Dir. Julie Bertucelli, France: Arte Cinéma.
Lin, A. M. Y. (2020), 'From Deficit-Based Teaching to Asset-Based Teaching in Higher Education in BANA Countries: Cutting Through "Either-Or" Binaries with a Heteroglossic Plurilingual Lens', *Language, Culture and Curriculum*, 33 (2): 203–12.
Marijuan, S. and C. Sanz. (2018), 'Expanding Boundaries: Current and New Directions in Study Abroad Research and Practice', *Foreign Language Annals*, 51 (1): 185–204.
MLA Ad Hoc Report. (2007), *Foreign Languages and Higher Education: New Structures for a Changed World*. Available online: https://www.mla.org/Resources/Research/Surveys-Reports-and-Other-Documents/Teaching-Enrollments-and-Programs/Foreign-Languages-and-Higher-Education-New-Structures-for-a-Changed-World (accessed 15 March 2022).
Moore, D. and L. Gajo. (2009), 'Introduction: French Voices on Plurilingualism and Pluriculturalism: Theory, Significance and Perspectives', *International Journal of Multilingualism*, 6 (2): 137–53.
Ong, H. T. (2016), 'Sociolinguistics and the New Testament', in *The Multilingual Jesus and the Sociolinguistic World of the New Testament*, 69–130, Leiden: Brill.
Palpacuer Lee, C., J. H. Curyis and M. E. Curan. (2018), 'Shaping the Vision for Service Learning in Education', *Foreign Language Annals*, 51 (1): 169–84.
Paris, D. and H. S. Alim. (2017), *Culturally Sustaining Pedagogies: Teaching and Learning for Justice in a Changing World*, New York: Columbia University Teachers College Press.
Pascual y Cabo, D., J. Prada and K. Lowther Pereira. (2017), 'Effects of Community Service Learning on Heritage Language Learners' Attitudes Toward Their Language and Culture', *Foreign Language Annals*, 50 (1): 71–83.
Pellettieri, J. L. (2011), 'Measuring Language-Related Outcomes of Community-Based Learning in Intermediate Spanish Courses', *Hispania*, 94: 285–302.
Piller, I. (2016), *Linguistic Diversity and Social Justice: An Introduction to Applied Sociolinguistics*, New York: Oxford University Press.
Piller, I. (2017), *Intercultural Communication: A Critical Introduction* (2nd ed.), Edinburgh: Edinburgh University Press.
*Proposition 227.* (1998), Legislative Analyst's Office. Available online: https://lao.ca.gov/ballot/1998/227_06_1998.htm (accessed 10 April 2022).
Purmensky, K. L. (2009), *Service-Learning for Diverse Communities: Critical Pedagogy and Mentoring English Language Learners*, Charlotte, NC: Information Age Publishing.

Reagan T. G. and T. A. Osborn. (2021), *World Language Education as Critical Pedagogy*, New York: Routledge.

Rosa, J. and N. Flores. (2017), 'Do You Hear What I Hear? Raciolinguistic Ideologies and Culturally Sustaining Pedagogies', in D. Paris and H. S. Alim (eds.), *Culturally Sustaining Pedagogies: Teaching and Learning for Justice in a Changing World*, 175–90, New York: Columbia University Teachers College Press.

Shapiro, S. (2022), *Cultivating Critical Language Awareness in the Writing Classroom*, New York: Routledge.

Slobin, D. I. (1993), 'Adult Language Acquisition: A View from Child Language Study', in C. Perdue (ed.), *Adult Language Acquisition: Cross-Linguistic Perspectives*, 239–52, Cambridge: Cambridge University Press.

Stamper, K. D. and K. A. King. (2017), 'Language Planning and Policy', in M. Aronoff and J. Rees-Miller (eds.), *The Handbook of Linguistics* (2nd ed.), 655–91, Malden, MA: John Wiley and Sons.

Truchot, C. (2013), 'Internationalisation et choix linguistiques dans les entreprises françaises: Entre « tout anglais » et pratiques plurilingues', *Synergies Italie*, 9: 75–90.

Viegen, S. V., and S. M. C. Lau. (2022), 'Becoming Critical Sociolinguists in TESOL Through Translanguaging and Embodied Practice', *TESL Canada journal*, 38 (2): 199–213.

# CHAPTER 5

# Bridging Languages, Bridging Cultures

# AFL Learners' Translingual Journeys

*Sahar Alshobaki*

## Introduction

This chapter is part of my doctoral research which explores learners' visions of themselves as users of Arabic, their use of motivational strategies to achieve their visions, their attitudes and motivation towards vision-personalized activities added to an existing course, Online Arabic from Palestine (OAfP). OAfP is a beginner course aimed at learners with no Arabic linguistic background; the language of the added activities was English.

The participants of this study are eight female beginner AFL learners with no or little background knowledge of Arabic. All learners were bi/multilingual and had learned at least one language other than their native tongue. The course was delivered to them based on one-to-one teaching to facilitate tailoring the materials according to their visions and reflections. Learners' reflections were mainly in English (the unifying/shared/bridge language between my learners and myself, the teacher/researcher). Learners, however, were encouraged to reflect on the activities using their entire linguistic repertoires. This was mentioned in the instructions I gave for the tasks and orally while giving the classes. For example, the following paragraph is the instructions of the first task which was used as a prompt for the pre-course interview.

> The first task is L2 identity tree (mp3 file). Listen to the audio. Reflect on your previous learning experiences, your current and future image of yourself speaking Arabic. This task will be followed by an interview (WhatsApp or Skype whatever you prefer). You can use any language (Arabic, English, your native language) whatever words that come up to your mind, write it down. The idea is to express your flow of thoughts without interruptions (language obstruction).

As shown earlier, the language of the added activities and the language of giving instructions (especially at the very beginning of the course) were in English, yet other languages from learners' resources were welcomed. Regarding Arabic varieties, I introduced and discussed the language varieties with the participants in the first lesson. I mentioned that I could expand on the Palestinian dialect (which is embedded slightly in the course and my native tongue) if they require and if they see it as part of their visions.

## Scope and Objectives of This Chapter

The chapter is structured into two main sections. The first section briefly reviews the literature related to Arabic multiglossia, translanguaging and translanguaging in Arabic. The second section presents learners' reflections on their multilingual and multidialectal realities as well as elaborating the linguacultural discussions between learners/participants and the teacher/researcher. By linguacultural discussions, I refer to the discussions about both language and culture during the lessons, and thus developing 'linguacultural mobility' which enables learners 'to "move between" linguistic systems and cultural practices' while learning languages, including one's primary language and culture (Leung and Scarino 2016: 91).

## Literature Review

### *Understanding the Multiglossic Nature of Arabic*

Many terms are used to express the complex sociolinguistic phenomenon related to Arabic varieties. One of the earliest terms is 'diglossia' (Ferguson 1959). Ferguson states that diglossia is the coexistence of two or more varieties in a speech community that complement each other; each variety is used to achieve different sociolinguistic functions in that community. The varieties are classified into high and low varieties. The high variety is the conservative form of the language and used for written forms and formal situations while the low varieties are used for informal conversations.

In Arabic, the high/formal variety corresponds to *Fusha*, which includes both Classical Arabic and Modern Standard Arabic (MSA). Classical Arabic (CA) is the language of the Quraan and ancient poetry and texts; MSA is a descendant of CA and is the official language of all Arab countries. MSA is used in formal contexts, literacy, media, political speeches, and religious sermons; it is the language of instruction in schools and universities and the language of the mainstream literature. MSA is perceived as more valued and prestigious than all other colloquial varieties because it is rooted in classical Arabic while colloquial Arabic varieties are seen as corruptions of MSA or CA (Bassiouney 2009; Holes 2004). The low or non-formal variety *Ammiyyah* (colloquial Arabic) is a set of different varieties such as Egyptian, Levantine and Moroccan, to name but a few. These varieties are used in everyday spoken interactions and vary widely among Arab countries and can be different from one another but not strictly separated (Nassif and Al Masaeed 2020; Al Masaeed 2020; Al-Batal 2018; Shiri 2013; Bassiouney 2009; Holes 2004).

Having different varieties, dialects and registers in Arabic could be better described under the term of 'multiglossia' than 'diglossia' (Badawi 1973). Ferguson's higher/lower dichotomy (of *Fusha* and *Ammiyyah*) was criticized by a number of linguists (e.g., Holes 2004; Blanc 1960). These linguists identified several levels of Arabic along a linguistic continuum that extends from colloquial Arabic to classical Arabic. Blanc (1960) mentions that native speakers[1] tend to move from one variety to another even at the sentence level. Moving from one variety to another depends on the situation, the interlocutors and the topic that is being discussed. The more formal the topic is, the more CA variety is being used (Younes 1990). This way, native speakers converse using different levels of varieties in the same conversation (Bassiouney 2009). This continuum led scholars to view Arabic varieties as one communication system and as 'two sides of the same coin' (Younes 2006: 150). They are not separate systems, nor are they different languages, but they are all related to one language system; thus, all varieties go under one language system, 'Arabic as one' (Al-Batal 2018). The 'Arabic as one' vision takes advantage of Arabic mutual intelligibility among the varieties because of the vocabulary and structure similarities (Younes 2015).

## Arabic Pedagogy

Traditionally, AFL programmes have focused on teaching MSA. Teaching colloquial Arabic has been an exception in L2 Arabic curricula (Al-Batal 2018). Some even consider teaching colloquial Arabic to be an 'ideologically and logistically controversial rival to MSA' (Shiri 2013: 17). Teaching MSA only, however, does not prepare learners to have authentic intercultural interactions with native speakers of Arabic. Learners who study only MSA cannot be expected to deal with everyday language use in the Arab world as MSA is not used for this function (Parkinson 1985). Ryding refers to this practice of focusing exclusively on MSA by the term 'reverse privileging' as it focuses on the secondary formal variety rather than the primary colloquial varieties that are used in day-to-day conversations (2006: 16). Similarly, focusing only on a spoken dialect deprives learners from having access to the written language and many other sources that use MSA.

Younes (1990, 2015) states that incorporating colloquial Arabic alongside MSA in teaching AFL may enhance learners' linguistic competence and improve their sociolinguistic repertoire to use Arabic in the same way that it is used by its native speakers. To match learners' expectations of learning Arabic, there has been a rising interest in applying the integrated approach in the last two decades in a few universities, particularly in the United States, showing that learning both MSA and colloquial Arabic is important and 'empowering' (Al-Batal and Glakas 2018: 268). Shiri (2013) and Al Masaeed (2020) also found that equipping learners with spoken varieties helps them understand and access local cultures.

Similary, Nassif and Al Masaeed (2020) investigated how the integrated approach and the usage of multidialects (MSA and Levantine) support L2 learners' sociolinguistic repertoire in their speech production. At the end of the semester, the twenty-eight learners were expected to give a formal presentation using MSA and an informal skit using Levantine Arabic. Data revealed that the participants were aware of the sociologistic expectations and were able to meet them by making predominant use of the expected variety in each task. Thus, not only is the integrative approach important to communicate with native speakers, but it is also a way to get access to native speakers' local cultures as well as enhancing learners' sociolinguistic repertoire and using Arabic authentically.

## *Translanguaging*

In a globalized world, learners come to the classroom with dynamic, vibrant life experiences and rich linguistic trajectories that influence their language learning. This multilingual reality, however, has been ignored in Second Language Acquisition (SLA) for a long time. Historically, monolingual ideologies were dominated, manifested and reinforced by the European nation-state where national boundaries and languages were perceived as separated and distinct (Cenoz and Gorter 2015; May 2014). These ideologies impacted research in applied linguistics causing a monolingual bias that focuses only on the target language and ignores learners' knowledge of other languages (Cenoz and Gorter 2019; Canagarajah and Liyanage 2012; Makalela 2015).

Many scholars (e.g., Makoni and Pennycook 2007; Otheguy et al. 2015) have critiqued viewing languages as distinct linguistic objects. First, monolingual ideologies do not reflect the fluidity and dynamism in real communicative interactions which have long existed in the pre- and postcolonial contexts (Canagarajah and Liyanage 2012; Makalela 2015). Integrating languages and dialects among societies has always been the case for centuries (Blommaert 2010). In addition to the already existing multilingual reality, globalization, increasing migration, mobility and virtual realities have created more diverse linguistic realities in many societies around the world. Monolingual ideologies, however, entail unrealistic representations of how languages are used outside academic settings.

Another point of criticism is that monolingual ideologies perceive native speakers as ideal references in learning a foreign language, which is still common in many parts of the world (Wei 2018; Cenoz and Gorter 2019). This native-speaker bias as referred to by Ortega (2019: 24) 'holds that owning a language from birth results in a form of linguistic competence superior to the competencies that may develop through any other means over the life trajectory'. In other words, comparing learners' efforts of acquiring a language to a native-speaker level might lead to viewing learners as deficient speakers of the target language. Cenoz and Gorter (2014) proposed a shift from imagining ideal monolingual learners to seeing them as multilingual speakers and acknowledging their experiences of other languages. Rather than seeking an idealized image of a native speaker, multilingual learners can be viewed holistically as learners of rich linguistic and semiotic resources who explore and add to their already existing repertoire and use it for different purposes (Cenoz and Gorter 2019).

Eventually, the field of applied linguistics has caught up with these multilingual realities and moved towards advocating shifting from monolingual to plurilingual/multilingual and translanguaging ideologies and practices (Canagarajah and Lyianage 2012). Translanguaging generally 'refers to the reality of bi/multilingual usage in naturally occurring contexts where boundaries between languages are fluid and constantly shifting' (Cenoz 2017: 904) inside and outside educational contexts. Originally, the term was used to explore the intricacies of linguistic communication in a bilingual setting. It was coined by Cen Williams (1994) to refer to a pedagogical strategy that makes use of the flexible and fluid transition from one language to another in a bilingual Welsh/English classroom to enhance learning both languages.

Translanguaging has been used in different language teaching and learning studies (e.g., Cenoz 2019; Galante 2020; García 2009) as a pedagogical concept that grasps the benefits of multilingual/plurilingual practices in teaching and learning a foreign language. These practices utilize learners' entire linguistic repertoires as a great resource to help them learn the target language. This way, translanguaging 'helps to disrupt the socially constructed language hierarchies that are responsible for the suppression of the languages of many minoritized peoples' (Otheguy et al. 2015: 283). It deconstructs language hierarchies inside the classroom that favour certain languages over another (García 2009). From this perspective, the aim of learning languages shifts from attaining the native speaker's level to developing translingual and transcultural competence(s) to operate within different languages and cultures (Ushioda 2017).

## *Translanguaging in Arabic*

In the Arabic context, a few studies (e.g., Abourehab and Azaz 2021, 2020; Al Masaeed 2020; Al Masaeed and Nassif 2020; Trentman 2021) examined the translanguaging perspective within its multiglossic nature. Translanguaging in these studies refers to using all linguistic resources (including English as a global language, learners' native languages and Arabic dialects).

These studies have mainly capitalized on teachers' and learners' ideologies. From teachers' perspectives, Abourehab and Azaz (2021) examined ten AFL teachers' ideologies and beliefs about translanguaging practices (mixing multiple languages and Arabic varieties) and their own classroom practices. The teachers were already using the integrated approach (MSA and at least one dialect). Examining the semi-structured interviews of three teachers, Abourehab and Azaz (2021) found inconsistency between ideology and practice. They found that even though teachers were initially hesitant to accept translanguaging as a pedagogy, their practices were inconsistent with their ideologies. From learners' perspectives, Trentman (2021) investigated the role of language ideologies in shaping sixty-five US AFL learners' experiences in study abroad and in telecollaborations in Egypt and Jordan. She found that monolingual ideologies influenced learners' expectations even though they were using multiple languages in social settings and using English to learn Arabic. Their monolingual expectations left them with a feeling of regret and failure of not using Arabic. Trentman concluded that monolingual ideologies could constrain learning and called for plurilingual-informed pedagogies and ideologies.

Additionally, translanguaging practices were discussed inside and outside the classroom. For instance, Abourehab and Azaz (2020) examined teacher–learner and learner–learner translanguaging practices (different Arabic dialects and English) among heritage language learners in the United States and in the context of a monolingual policy where the standard variety (MSA) is the medium of instruction. They found that translanguaging practices were utilized in discussing linguistic knowledge (e.g., vocabulary and structure) and gave legitimacy to learners' own dialects and thus celebrating their own identities. Similarly, Al Masaeed and Nassif (2020) investigated the multidialectal practices in speech productions of learners who went through training using the integrated approach, learning MSA and Levantine at the same time. They found that learners were able to engage properly according to the sociolinguistic expectations of each variety. They called for more research in understanding and exploring the multidialectal practices among L2 Arabic learners and the benefits of training learners in more than one variety. Regarding outside-the-classroom setting, Al Masaeed (2020) examined the multidialectal and multilingual practices in a study abroad in Morocco. He looked at the interactions between L2 learners and their native-speaker conversation partners. He found these interactions involved translanguaging practices to make meaning and to construct knowledge. He also confirmed the importance of multidialectal practices in enhancing learners' pragmatic competence.

Abourehab and Azaz (2021) argue that translanguaging should be one of the main Arabic pedagogy outcomes, and that teachers could be more open to this pedagogy, considering multidialectalism as an integral part of Arabic. They mention that legitimizing translanguaging in Arabic contexts is a long journey and needs future classroom-based research to investigate learners' and teachers' ideologies and its addition to the language learning. There is also a paucity of studies examining the link between translanguaging and exchanging cultures in a multiglossic language like Arabic (Galante 2020). This chapter extends the current research by presenting learners' translanguaging interactions to reflect on the multilingual/multidialectal realities and experiences as well as illustrating the linguacultural dynamics to explain one's worldview and maintain relationships as discussed in what follows.

## Learners' Translanguaging Journeys

This study takes a reflexive, interpretive exploratory practice approach to data collection. The data collection methods include semi-structured interviews, journal writing, class observation and visual materials. This chapter draws on both pre- and post-semi-structured interviews. The interviews were transcribed (names are pseudonymous) and analysed using a reflexive thematic analysis approach. Throughout the interviews, learners used their entire linguistic resources (mainly English, their native language, and basic MSA/dialect words) to reflect on the multilingual and multidialectal practices as well as linguacultural dynamics with the teacher/researcher.

### Dealing with Multilingual Realities

All learners of this study have mentioned situations where they utilized different languages to communicate in their environment with speakers of other languages (who do not always share the same language). Translanguaging appeared to be used as a means of eluding misunderstanding, gaining power, conveying the message and adding playfulness to conversations. In what follows, some representative excerpts of each sub-theme are provided.

## Translanguaging to 'Bond Over' with People

Describing how she sees herself as an Arabic user, Alaa (a bilingual learner in English and Gujarati) thinks she will be 'serious', for she will be conscious about her words when she speaks and wary of being misunderstood due to her lack of cultural knowledge. Comparing that to Gujarati, she views herself as 'funny' and that she can easily translanguage to fill in her lack of knowledge of a certain word. The following excerpt shows the dynamic nature of Alaa's multilingual trajectories. She mentions:

> In majority sometimes when I don't know a word [in Gujarati], I just say it half in English and then just laugh off but then in Arabic and it's actually like know what I'm saying and also, when you're not from that culture, like misinterpretation is a lot like you can say something but like someone can read it different way. (pre-interview)

Surprisingly, Alaa finds translanguaging using her semiotic resources (English and Gujarati) as a powerful act that she simply and joyfully uses to communicate her message. This view of translanguaging contrasts with what Trentman (2021) found in her research that learners felt a sense of regret and failure when they do not use the target language (Arabic) due to their monolingual ideology. Alaa, on the other hand, mentioned several times that being in a 'multilingual environment' (London) shaped her views and interest in other languages and cultures.

Alaa's fear of misinterpretation can be related to her past experiences with Gujarati. Alaa describes her multilingual/multidialectal experience at school and how translanguaging using English was a way to overcome misunderstanding caused by different meanings of varieties in her own native language, Gujarati. Translanguaging seems to be an act that brings people together again as she explains,

> In Gujarati in school, I speak a different part whereas my friends they're Hindu but they speak Gujarati, so it's weird for me because I'm Muslim, but I'm Indian at same time, so there's a lot of times that I say a word, but they say it different spelling or a different community like different sort of words for the same thing, and I'm just saying that like no, I mean that. then like what's that? . . . Yeah, then that's why I like it because English is like the common sort of language where everyone could, just like say no, this is what I meant. This is what I meant and then you just bond over that. (pre-interview)

Alaa reflected on her ability to translanguage in Gujarati at a sentence/word level or in situations where she was misunderstood during the conversations. When it comes to Arabic, however, she viewed herself as 'serious' and someone who would be cautious with her words. She did not mention translanguaging as a mix of her linguistic repertoire to communicate, but, rather, as a one-language-at-a-time as she could communicate in English in the Arab world. This could be due to her beginner level, so she has not had enough linguistic background and situations with the language yet to use and mix with her other resources. She indicates that translanguaging in the Arab world is an acceptable behaviour when she travelled to a few Arab countries in the Middle East.

> They are very like warm people you can have a conversation with them and also, they don't look down on you if you if you don't speak like Arabic they do. They are like do you speak English and stuff. (pre-interview)

In the above quote, Alaa indicates that the lack of linguistic competence could marginalize the person and leave him/her in an inferior position. This aligns with what Ortega (2019) referred to as native-speaker bias and viewing learners as deficient. For Alaa, the experience of translanguaging using English with Arabic-speaking natives who are 'warm' and welcoming to her eliminates her feeling of incompetence.

## Translanguaging to 'Understand'

Living in multilingual realities, the need to communicate and connect with people exceeds the constraints of languages. Conveying the message seems to be the ultimate target in conversations. It could even exceed the multilingual practices themselves to include multimodal interactions including the entire linguistic and gestural repertoires. This is indicated in the following dialogue with Nowara:

> **Teacher/Researcher:** Yeah, we don't have enough words, but you use your body language, your smile and your words and all hand gestures to express what you want to say.
> **Nowara:** Yeah, it's funny because I'm living with people from all over the world and we have very little native English speakers. So a lot of times we start like I'm talking about something and we don't know the word for that and we start to describing it. And one of us would say I know what you're talking about, but I don't know the word, so everyone like understands, but we don't know the word.
> **Teacher/Researcher:** Exactly that's the point is if you get your message conveyed by your audience, then that's it.
> **Nowara:** . . . Amazing body language says everything. (pre-interview)

The goal is to connect and understand each other. Each one of Nowara's flatmates understands the meaning in his/her own language even though he/she could not figure out what the exact word is in the shared language (English), giving power to maximize understanding above word limits and language barriers. Using different linguistic and cultural repertoires within an intercultural orientation to operate between languages and cultures should thus be the focus for a language learner rather than seeking a native speaker's level of competence (Scarino 2014).

## Translanguaging to Have 'Fun' Interactions

Playfully using the new added linguistic words to her own knowledge, Nowara uses these words to communicate with her Arab flatmates. She says in Levantine dialect 'انا جوا يا تمارا' – (I am inside, Tamara). Nowara narrates,

> I think it's really nice to have my Arabic speaking flatmates that I can practice and they get so happy when I say really stupid word for that. Well, they said like they both like they were talking outside. And then I said انا جوا يا تمارا and she started to scream like oh, this is everything you need to learn! It's really fun. (post-interview)

Translanguaging in this case is a fun experience for Nowara to keep her interactions with her flatmates exciting, light and joyful.

## Translanguaging to Navigate a Certain Meaning among Languages

One of Emy's reasons for learning Arabic is that it distinguishes her from most of the people who would choose to learn more common languages. Emy chooses a Spanish word (her native language) to describe her reason as she feels the meaning could not be fulfilled by using a word from the shared language, English. She says:

> I feel enthusiastic about the language and now and then I wrote in Spanish interessanti . . . I couldn't find the English for that is different in Spanish . . .

> . . . It's not like interesting person, but it's more than like if a person that would be that has something rich to you know, like you're discovering something rich about the person or something interesting about that person.

The above excerpt indicates that translanguaging opens a door for Emy to flexibly choose the best word from her own range of semiotic resources, including her native language, to better convey what she feels.

## Dealing with Multidialectal Realities

### 'We Don't Speak Arabic; We Speak Egyptian'

Nowara reflects on her own experience living in Egypt and dealing with native speakers of Arabic from different countries. Her interactions with them have raised her awareness of the different varieties. She compliments adding the dialect to the course to 'deepen' her awareness and explains:

> I was aware that the dialects are very different, and I remember when I was in Egypt like lots of people used to say we don't speak Arabic; we speak Egyptian and our languages and It's our own language and it's really different from Arabic . . . I also look like met Tunisian people and from Algeria . . . And everyone say I would speak really different and Like people say, we cannot understand Morocco and we cannot understand Tunisians. (post-interview)

The quote demonstrates how Arabic varieties can be seen as separate, distinct and not mutually intelligible by some native speakers, instead of looking at it as one language system. This view of Arabic contradicts the 'Arabic as one' vision and some recent studies that indicate a high degree of mutual intelligibility between closely and distantly related dialects (e.g., Čéplö et al. 2016; Abu-Melhim 2014).

### 'Imagine If We Hadn't Done [the Dialect]. I Wouldn't Really Understand'

Karima explains that inserting the dialect in the course is a gate to understanding the day-to-day communication. This was clear to her when she watched Lebanese and Syrian TV series (two other dialects of the Levant region). She says,

> it's quite useful because that's how people speak in their everyday life, and I think I realize this when I started watching those TV series in Arabic and all the phrases and the words that I recognized were in dialect and I thought, OK, imagine if we hadn't done it. I wouldn't really understand.
> 
> . . . when someone enters a place and they say كيفك [how are you – Levantine dialect] or sometimes they pronounce it a little bit different and I suppose cause it's two different dialects in in the TV . . . things like question words that I recognize somewhere, small phrases like انا كمان me too [dialect]. (post-interview)

Karima's view of the dialect aligns with Shiri's (2013) findings that teaching at least one variety opens a door to understanding local dialects and cultures.

## *Bridging Languages, Bridging Cultures*

The previous two sections dealt with how learners reflect on the multilingual/multidialectal realities around them and how they move between languages for several functions. This point illustrates one more function in detail, to linguaculture, that is, to use one's whole linguistic repertoires to reflect on, discuss and understand one's and each other's culture. From this perspective, language education goals are reconceptualized from focusing on learners' progress compared to a native speaker's level to developing 'linguacultural mobility' (Leung and Scarino 2016: 91) and 'expanding the meaning-making repertoires of individuals' (ibid. 2016: 88). As Ushioda (2017: 477) elaborated, 'this holistic constitutive view of language learning places value on a person's capacity to operate effectively between languages and cultures as informed and educated speakers and mediators'. The following two excerpts show how translanguaging is used to operate within and build bridges to understand different cultural practices as well as connect at a deeper level. The first excerpt, English as a lingua franca is used to discuss different perceptions of the learner and teacher/researcher while the second excerpt, Arabic varieties (MSA and dialect) and English were used to show gratitude and maintain connections at the end of the course.

### Excerpt 1

Almost at the end of the course, Emy attended a birthday party for her non-Arab Muslim neighbours. She was curious how things are in the Arab world, and how close the culture is in terms of costumes, food, dance . . . and so on. She was also wondering about the reason behind offering many dishes at parties, which is, to her, different compared with European culture, but which could be similar to her country, Argentina. She asked if this could be an act of 'showing off' or showing social status. Having similar traditions, the teacher/researcher tried to explain her own perspective. The following dialogue uncovers our perspectives on one simple cultural occasion.

> **Emy:** There is also something well, maybe in it's different in different countries, but there is something like also showing off right? A little bit?
> **Teacher/Researcher:** For whom it depends, showing off?
> **Emy:** Like the bigger, the more food, the more. It's like higher social status or like people like to show. Like you know I mean more.
> **Teacher/Researcher:** I don't think it's– No, we never thought about it in this way. It's maybe more of the more, it's like when you have different types of food. That's like how love this family have or like it's just like

it's showing love. That's the idea, that's like showing love to the people that are coming. Something like that. It's like hospitality and love more than showing off.
**Emy:** Yeah, yeah, it's like it is and you care.
**Emy:** But it's nice. It's nice. Yeah, alright yeah, now you know we will have that more for Christmas and New Year. Yeah, a lot of but that's everywhere right? But that's the moment that, well, I feel a bit different like it with Europe in the sense that when I go to my parents in law. We maybe they will ask. They will have more like three dishes, but like instead like making soup and then in main dish and then some you know desert, maybe it will be a couple of things and then desert and salad or something. Yeah, I imagine Argentina would have so many dishes. Much more food will be like eating for a week.

This excerpt shows our attempts to make meaning of a single social act through our own intersubjectivities. The teacher/researcher tries to reflect on her traditions at parties and festivals as it is quite similar to those of Emy's neighbours. To her, the diversity of dishes provided was always a symbol of love, joy, hospitality and generosity for the invited people. Emy compared back to both European and Argentinian cultures to further understand the similarities/differences. Discussing the differences in our cultures was a first step to reflect back on our behaviours and our assumptions of the self and other – to develop understanding and to build bridges towards understanding the other. Zhu (2015) mentions that translanguaging challenges the focus on cultural difference to avoid miscommunication. Instead, differences can be critically utilized to express multiple perspectives of each learner's community and culture (ibid.). This act shifts from the focus on the linguaculture of the target language to dynamically interact with the linguaculture of each of the participants/learners.

## Excerpt 2

In the final post-course interview, the ending dialogue with Hanin and her expression of gratitude show the soft boundaries and fluid transition between languages, dialects, and a small hint to cultural hospitality.

**Hanin:** Thank you so much جزاك الله خير [may God reward you with goodness, Islamic expression of gratitude]
**Teacher/Researcher:** شكرا كتير [thank you so much, Levantine dialect]
**Hanin:** You keep my number; you don't know along the years. Maybe something would come up. I'll come into London, and we can have some tea or coming to Istanbul, and we could meet inshaa Allah [god's willing (literally), Islamic and cultural expression that means hopefully (metaphorical/implied meaning)].

**Teacher/Researcher:** شاي بالنعنع!؟ (laugh) [mint tea!?[2]]
**Hanin:** أو مرمية [or sage] because it is what I haven't tried.
**Teacher/Researcher:** Oh yeah. thenاذا مرمية [then sage it is]
**Hanin:** نعم [yes]
**Teacher/Researcher:** (laugh) ان شاء الله اكيد ان شاء الله [God's willing, sure insha allah].

This quote emphasizes the interrelations and flexible use of languages and dialects (Arabic, English), (*Fusha, Ammiyyah*) and (cultural, Islamic expressions). The quote shows that dealing with these languages and varieties does not seem to be dichotomous or distinct; they are, rather, part of one communicative system/interaction. It shows how languages, dialects and cultures are enveloped together in one simple conversation. In this way, translanguaging practices create transformative spaces that transcend the nature of learner/teacher relationship that could be restricted by monolingual regulations, keeping the connections beyond the language barriers. Translanguaging allows learners to expand on their linguistic repertoire and their relations without feeling the shame of failing to be a monolingual in the target language. Instead, translanguaging practices are used to expand their linguistic and cultural systems and their relations (Trentman 2021).

## Conclusion

This research moves from and challenges the still existing AFL orthodoxies/monolingual/monocultural hierarchies by encouraging learners to flexibly draw on their rich range of semiotic resources. This chapter looked at AFL learners' reflections on their multilingual and multidialectal environments as well as their linguacultural dynamics inside and outside the classroom. In this study, translanguaging worked as a reflective bridging tool between different languages, worlds and cultures. The chapter illustrated translanguaging potentials in providing those learners with a powerful safe space to negotiate meanings, maximize understanding of language barriers, add a joyful element to their conversations, build bridges to understand each other's cultures and connect at a deeper level. The wider implication of this research extends beyond the AFL context to other languages as the translanguaging pedagogical approach could contribute to making the classroom a space for building social justice/reducing inequalities by shifting the language learning goals from focusing on the target language ideal native speaker to give space to home languages, minority languages and dialects as well as all linguistic and cultural repertoires that learners develop through their lifetime.

## Notes

1 I use the term 'native speakers' here indicating the wide literature discussing the sociolinguistic phenomenon of Arabic, mulitglossia. From a translanguaging perspective, however, the term 'native speakers' in the language learning context might be problematic. The critique of the appropriateness of this term is discussed later in this chapter.

2 Fresh mint or wild sage tea is a daily beverage for many Palestinians and is offered to guests as part of their hospitality.

## References

Abourehab, Y., and M. Azaz. (2020), 'Pedagogical Translanguaging in Community/Heritage Arabic Language Learning', *Journal of Multilingual and Multicultural Development*, 41: 1–14.

Abu-Melhim, A. (2014), 'Intra-Lingual Code Alternation in Arabic: The Conversational Impact of Diglossia', *Theory and Practice in Language Studies*, 4 (5): 891–902.

Al Masaeed, K. (2020), 'Translanguaging Practices in L2 Arabic Study Abroad: Beyond Monolingual Ideologies in Institutional Talk', *The Modern Language Journal*, 104 (1): 250–66.

Al-Batal, M. (2018), 'Dialect Integration in the Arabic Foreign Language Curriculum: Vision, Rationale, and Models', in M. Al-Batal (ed.), *Arabic as One Language: Integrating Dialect in the Arabic Language Curriculum*, 3–22, Washington, DC: Georgetown University Press.

Al-Batal, M., and C. Glakas. (2018), 'Dialect Integration: Students' Perspectives Within an Integrated Program', in M. Al-Batal (ed.), *Arabic as One Language: Integrating Dialect in the Arabic Language Curriculum*, 260–78, Washington, DC: Georgetown University Press.

Azaz, M., and Y. Abourehab. (2021), 'Should Standard Arabic Have 'The Lion's Share'? Teacher Monolingual Ideologies in L2 Arabic Through the Lens of Pedagogical Translanguaging', *Intercultural Communication Education*, 4 (1): 90–105.

Badawı, M. (1973), *Mustawayāt al-ʿarabiyya al-muʿāṣira fī Miṣr*, Cairo: Dār al-Maʿārif.

Bassiouney, R. (2009), *Arabic Sociolinguistics: Topics in Diglossia, Gender, Identity, and Politics*, Washington, DC: Georgetown University Press.

Blanc, H. (1960), 'Stylistic Variations in Spoken Arabic: A Sample Inter-Dialectical Educated Conversation', in C. Ferguson (ed.), *Contributions to Arabic Linguistics*, 79–161, Cambridge, MA: Harvard University Press.

Blommaert, J. (2010), *The Sociolinguistics of Globalization*, Cambridge: Cambridge University Press.

Canagarajah, S., and I. Liyanage. (2012), 'Lessons from Pre-Colonial Multilingualism', in M. Martin-Jones, A. Blackledge and A. Creese (eds.), *The Routledge Handbook of Multilingualism*, 49–65, London: Routledge.

Cenoz, J. (2017), 'Translanguaging in school contexts: International perspectives', *Journal of Language, Identity and Education*, 16 (4): 193e198.
Cenoz, J. (2019), 'Translanguaging Pedagogies and English as a Lingua Franca', *Language Teaching*, 52 (1): 71–85.
Cenoz, J., and D. Gorter. (2014), 'Focus on Multilingualism as an Approach in Educational Contexts', in A. Creese and A. Blackledge (eds.), *Heteroglossia as Practice and Pedagogy*, 239–54, Berlin: Springer.
Cenoz, J., and D. Gorter. (2019), 'Multilingualism, Translanguaging, and Minority Languages in SLA', *The Modern Language Journal*, 103: 130–5.
Čéplö, S., J. Bátora, A. Benkato, J. Milička, C. Pereira and P. Zemánek. (2016), 'Mutual Intelligibility of Spoken Maltese, Libyan Arabic, and Tunisian Arabic Functionally Tested: A Pilot Study', *Folia Linguistica*, 50 (2): 583–628.
Egaña, E. A., J. Cenoz and D. Gorter. (2015), 'Teachers' Beliefs in Multilingual Education in the Basque Country and in Friesland', *Journal of Immersion and Content-Based Language Education*, 3 (2): 169–93.
Ferguson, C. (1959), 'Diglossia', *Word*, 15: 325–40.
Galante, A. (2020), 'Pedagogical Translanguaging in a Multilingual English Program in Canada: Student and Teacher Perspectives of Challenges', *System*, 92: 1–10.
García, O. (2009), *Bilingual Education in the 21st Century*, Oxford: Blackwell.
Holes, C. (2004), *Modern Arabic: Structures, Functions, and Varieties*, Washington, DC: Georgetown University Press.
Leung, C., and A. Scarino. (2016), 'Reconceptualizing the Nature of Goals and Outcomes in Language/s Education', *Modern Language Journal*, 100 (Supplement 2016): 81–95.
Makalela, L. (2015), 'Moving Out of Linguistic Boxes: The Effects of Translanguaging Strategies for Multilingual Classrooms', *Language and Education*, 29: 200–17.
Makoni, S., and A. Pennycook, eds. (2007), *Disinventing and Reconstituting Languages*, Bristol: Multilingual Matters.
May, S., ed. (2014), *The Multilingual Turn: Implications for SLA, TESOL and Bilingual Education*, New York: Routledge/Taylor and Francis.
Nassif, L., and K. Al Masaeed. (2020), 'Supporting the Sociolinguistic Repertoire of Emergent Diglossic Speakers: Multidialectal Practices of L2 Arabic Learners', *Journal of Multilingual and Multicultural Development*. https://doi.org/10.1080/01434632.2020.1774595.
Ortega, L. (2019), 'SLA and the Study of Equitable Multilingualism', *Modern Language Journal*, 103 (Supplement 2019): 23–38.
Otheguy, R., O. García and W. Reid. (2015), 'Clarifying Translanguaging and Deconstructing Named Languages: A Perspective from Linguistics', *Applied Linguistics Review*, 6: 281–307.
Parkinson, D. (1985), 'Proficiency to Do What? Developing Proficiency in Students of Modern Standard Arabic', *Al-Arabiyya*, 18: 11–44.
Ryding, K. C. (2006), 'Teaching Arabic in the United States', in K. M. Wahba, Z. A. Taha and L. England (eds.), *Handbook for Arabic Language Teaching Professionals in the 21st Century*, 13–20, New York: Routledge.
Scarino, A. (2014), 'Situating the Challenges in Current Languages Education Policy in Australia Unlearning Monolingualism', *International Journal of Multilingualism*, 11: 289–306.

Shiri, S. (2013), 'Learners' Attitudes Toward Regional Dialects and Destination Preferences in Study Abroad', *Foreign Language Annals*, 46 (4): 565–87.
Trentman, E. (2021), 'Reframing Monolingual Ideologies in the Language Classroom: Evidence from Arabic Study Abroad and Telecollaboration', in B. Dupuy and K. Michelson (eds.), *Pathways to Paradigm Change: Critical Examinations of Prevailing Discourses and Ideologies in Second Language Education*, 108–32, Boston, MA: Cengage Learning.
Ushioda, E. (2017), 'The Impact of Global English on Motivation to Learn Other Languages: Toward an Ideal Multilingual Self', *The Modern Language Journal*, 101: 469–82.
Wei, L. (2018), 'Translanguaging as a Practical Theory of Language', *Applied Linguistics*, 39: 9–30.
Williams, C. (1994), *Arfarniad o ddulliau dysgu ac addysgu yng nghyd-destun addysg uwchradd ddwyieithog*, Unpublished PhD thesis. Bangor: University of Wales Bangor.
Williams, C. (1996), 'Secondary education: teaching in the bilingual situation', in C. Williams, G. Lewis and C. Baker (eds.), *The language policy: taking stock*, 193–211, Llangefni, UK: CAI.
Younes, M. (1990), 'An Integrated Approach to Teaching Arabic as a Foreign Language', *Al-Arabiyya*, 23 (1/2): 105–22.
Younes, M. (2006), 'Integrating the Colloquial with Fuṣḥā in the Arabic as a Foreign Language Classroom', in K. Wahba, Z. Taha and L. England (eds.), *Handbook for Arabic Language Teaching Professionals in the 21st Century*, 157–66, Mahwah, NJ: Lawrence Erlbaum.
Younes, M. (2015), *The Integrated Approach to Arabic Instruction*, London: Routledge.

# Part III
# Beyond Stereotypes and Discrimination

# CHAPTER 6

# Modern Language Pedagogy beyond *Sombreros* and *Toreros*

## *Candace Skibba*

As a primer for this chapter, I propose the following question: From our own learning as professors to the ways in which we facilitate learning in our students, to the ways in which we carry out our own lines of inquiry, how are we intentionally prioritizing inclusivity and anti-racism?

Please take a moment to consider this question prior to reading the chapter. The intention here is to open a dialogue between and among the readers of this volume so that the shared experiences and opinions can be regenerative as well as co-created. In so doing, I acclaim the work of those with whom I am dialoguing and those with whom I have had the pleasure of sharing a teaching and learning space while I simultaneously disclaim myself as expert.

The teaching of modern languages is not neutral. Language itself is not neutral. Culture is not neutral. And yet, there is a sense that if one teaches modern languages, by proxy, one is engaging in ways of teaching that are inherently culturally informed and therefore anti-racist, inclusive and radical. Being versed in the cultural and linguistic heritage of a certain part of the world, while interesting and valuable, does not automatically prompt cultural humility. Rather, it is through a radical pedagogy that goes beyond the content matter and is situated in the ways in which we, as instructors, structure the hierarchy and authority of our classrooms that work to negate neutrality.

There have been many methodologies of language teaching that have come and gone in popularity, from the grammar-translation method to more communicative approaches. And while the purpose of this chapter is not to review the history of modern language teaching methodology, it is compelling to recognize the dichotomies that have existed in methodology as well as pedagogy. Among the many conversations that I have been exposed to in over twenty years of language instruction, one of the most ubiquitous 'arguments' has been language versus content, to which I will add context. Should we introduce grammatical concepts with basic content so as to avoid cognitive overload? Should students parse out structures of the language they are learning through deductive reasoning while engaging in content analysis? Similarly, when discussing language acquisition, shall we focus on the teaching or learning of the language? Consequently, are we focused more heavily on the instructor (curriculum, materials, methods, assessments) or the student (grades, growth, knowledge)? I will leave this discussion for those more engaged in this discourse. However, it is important to my argument here in that it demonstrates the propensity to bifurcate, which I find problematic. How can we engage in grammatical and structural elements of language without incorporating content and context? How are we evaluating the teaching and learning processes when we don't recognize that they are dependent upon one another? And, finally, how are we to decolonize language learning without focusing not solely on the instructor or the student, but also on the spaces (literal and figurative) among and between them? In this erasure of division, we find radical pedagogy.

In order to engage in radical pedagogy, it is necessary to investigate the ways in which educators are engaging with students *as well as* the ways in which educators are educating themselves and their institutions. That, in and of itself, is a radical act in that it supposes that educators are learners themselves. Although this may seem obvious, the discourses surrounding learning and acquisition of knowledge tend to focus on expertise, specialization and depth. While these are all admirable qualities in the pursuit of knowledge and intellectualism, they do not leave much room for further inquiry and analysis. The impetus on educators in higher education being the 'experts' in their fields presupposes that there is a finite amount of information to gather and process. Once that level has been reached and the professors profess, they are at the pinnacle of their career.

In this chapter I aim to discuss pedagogy from a non-neutral standpoint beginning with a brief overview of pedagogical and cultural theory that informs my analysis. The majority of the chapter will focus on the ways in which we have been shaped and formed into language educators, while the remainder of the chapter will provide a few opportunities for rethinking this formation.

## In Dialogue With –

When beginning this research in the Fall of 2018, I had no idea how much it would inform my own teaching, scholarship and worldview. The search for pedagogical understanding was initially prompted by a teaching experience that left me feeling empty and misguided. Fortunately, I found solace in the creation of the Radical Pedagogy Reading Group. We began with Paolo Freire's *Pedagogy of the Oppressed* and continued reading from bell hooks, Jacques Rancière's *The Ignorant Schoolmaster*, Berg and Seeber's *The Slow Professor*, *My Freshman Year: What a Professor Learned by Becoming a Student* by anthropologist Cathy Small and Rebekah Nathan, and even looked to performance pedagogy in Guillermo Gómez-Peña's *Exercises for Rebel Artists: Radical Performance Pedagogy*. The outcomes of these conversations were many and rich and included topics such as (i) dismantling expectations of what the students think the rules should be, (ii) enabling students to feel comfortable with uncomfortability, (iii) balancing teaching the historical/canon without imposing the thoughts/values/ways of thinking of such, (iv) bringing emotionality into the classroom, (v) demonstrating that there are spaces for ambiguity, and even (vi) what it means to 'know' things? What came of this group was an understanding that despite our different levels of 'expertise' in our various fields, we were all connected (and, in a sense, equalized) by our interest in pedagogy. I had rarely had the privilege of sharing such rich conversations that, for me, made my chosen career path much more meaningful. It was in that space that I began to realize that to truly challenge the premises of neoliberal education, it is necessary to focus not only on what we are teaching, but also *how* we are teaching it. As my interest has grown, I have come to depend upon those voices with whom we entered into dialogue in that group.

## The Focus on Expertise – Hiding Behind Content and Staying in Your Lane

There is little doubt that the academy prioritizes expertise and accumulation of knowledge. Much of what constitutes success in higher education is proving this fact. Therefore, many of us spend our time reading and writing in an attempt to become the foremost thinkers in our fields. We are trained to prove our theories by dialoguing with those infamous scholars included in the reading lists of our doctoral programmes. We are tasked with reading all that has been written about our topic of analysis such that what we say and how we say it is as original as possible. Where is the room for further inquiry? Where is the room for re-analysis? Cultural analysis, context and understanding in 2022 is quite different from that of twenty years ago. Can one be an expert if one hasn't updated one's knowledge along with the times?

It is interesting to highlight the more recent focus on interdisciplinarity and how this might fit into further analysis of the question of hiding behind content. Some of us have always considered ourselves interdisciplinary in the sense that our chosen content may shift, but our theoretical grounding and interlocutors are fairly constant. Example – I look at film *and* literature as my primary texts. Although they are different mediums and require different forms of examination and interpretation, the lens through which I view these texts is related. Whether I am focusing on the most recent novel by Juan José Millás or the latest film by Pedro Almodóvar, my approach is informed by and in conversation with feminist theory, disability studies and queer theory – which is not to say that I avoid other possible lenses through which to engage. In my work, these lenses are also those through which I view pedagogy. The knowledge gained through an understanding of theory informs my understanding of the primary texts. And yet, that knowledge does not necessarily indicate a more or less apt, rich or intellectual analysis. In fact, there are many times that, in discussion with students and/or colleagues whose fields of knowledge are not related, my perspective and understanding grow immensely. In my opinion, this is the beauty of learning – it is a co-creation in which growth happens at all levels and is not necessarily directly related to expertise.

In higher education, the understanding is that an educator has the credentials to teach based upon what they know about the subject. However, having knowledge and sharing that knowledge are not the same thing. It is not what you teach – but how you teach it. What most people who are not in higher education do not realize is that most professors were never taught to teach. If they were lucky, they were thrown into the classroom as teaching assistants and made to figure it out. In my case, my first venture into the college classroom came when I was twenty-two years old, had a bachelor's degree and absolutely no training in education. Since then (some twenty years ago), I have had one semester of training in methodology that pertains specifically to my discipline, but nothing about pedagogy as a concept.

Suffice it to say, I follow the premise that knowledge is co-created and in constant flux. As educators, we have been given the privilege to engage with our students, embracing a reciprocal process by which we are able to further our inquiry. However, there are many who suggest that in order for the students' analyses to be 'at our level', they must reach a certain metric or degree. Ironically, most of the students that I have the pleasure to surround myself with are most likely infinitely more intelligent than I am. That might suggest my own inadequacies but I don't see it that way. Instead, I see it as an invitation for further inquiry *together* – with respect for all that each member brings to the table.

What might a model of teaching look like that encourages this understanding of learning? Perhaps it might be sharing the knowledge that the instructor has with their students while scaffolding discourse so as to empower all participants to engage in the co-creation of further knowledge. Example – after many years of incorporating the now cult classic film *Mujeres al borde de un ataque de nervios (Women on the Verge of a Nervous Breakdown)* – Pedro Almodóvar 1988) – into various levels of my teaching of the Spanish language and Hispanic cultures, publishing a chapter in which I analyse this film (among others) as a representation of psychiatric disability that challenges Western constructs of normalcy, and presenting on this and other Almodóvar films at numerous conferences and guest lectures, there is so much yet to be gained from listening to the perspective of my students. That is one of the many reasons that I am in this field, as the interpretation and analyses of language, film and literature are infinite.

## The Focus on Expertise – Language, Identity and Bias

In some ways being a non-native speaker of the language has always come with challenges in that there is a constant sense of imposter syndrome – a topic that has become the focus of a growing amount of research within higher education.[1] From an institutional perspective I have felt othered by my discipline due to being in a school of humanities on a campus that is highly STEM oriented. This is further othered by the fact that I teach and research in another language. There is an inherent colonial preference for the study of English or American literature – if one is to study literature. I am also a woman – which provokes another type of othering. When beginning my teaching journey, a young person of a mere twenty-two years, I was teaching in my own language – English lessons to young children in a small language school in Salamanca, Spain. This time, I was the native speaker of the language being taught. However, my students – aged five to ten – didn't have the slightest regard for that fact. They could tell that I was uneasy in my lack of experience. They had no real interest in learning English any more than they did in learning anything. As children, they wanted to play and let off some steam. Had I been further along in my experience, I might have come up with a play-based learning curriculum. Perhaps I would have taken them outside to learn from the environment. I might have even shown them cartoons in English. But I had no idea what I was doing. It is amazing that by the sheer fact that I am a native speaker, I was hired. I wonder now if someone with my exact credentials were to present themselves as a non-native speaker of English or as a BIPOC native speaker of English, would they have been hired?

    Fast forward some twenty-five years later. I am tasked with facilitating the Senior Seminar for modern languages majors. The topic is cultural humility. As this is a new course for me, I am awkwardly putting together readings, speakers and conversation prompts to provoke discussion around what they have learned over the course of the past three plus years. In so doing, there is an inadvertent questioning of the learning that they have carried out. One of the class conversations defaults not to the languages that these students have learned, but, rather, English. Part of our exercise in cultural humility is to reflect on the hegemony of English, as a commodity *and* as a way in which to view the world. Though it is difficult to parse out, we work together to consider the meaning/connotation/definition of certain words and how they shape our understanding of our environments. We then look at words and structures in the languages that they have learned (Spanish, French, Chinese and Japanese) to investigate certain concepts in those languages that have no translation. The goal is to work towards a shared understanding while paying special attention to shifts in worldview as well as linguistic hegemony.

The beauty of this type of course is that I am unable to position myself as expert. I am learning about cultural humility right along with them. I do not speak or read the languages that more than half of the students in my class have studied. Our shared and co-created knowledge is – for me, at least – somewhat addictive. In many cases, the questions that we are considering regarding language and power, cultural hegemony, have not been brought up in their language learning. Why have these topics been left out of the textbooks and curriculum?

There are those, such as Uju Anya, who posit that the lacuna in language education is due, in part, to the fact that 'racism is deeply woven into all our educational institutions, practices, and interactions' (2021: 1055). Anya carries out research that intends to view language education through the lenses of critical race theory (CRT) and critical race pedagogy (CRP). Her work suggests that those lenses, while being implemented in analyses of some topical areas, are largely missing in world language (WL) teaching in the United States. Hence, her work provides 'recommendations for conducting more WL research guided by CRT and propose[s] a CRPWLT to promote more effective and inclusive practice' (2021: 1058). This radical pedagogy consists of three steps:

1) Step one in CRPWLT is to conduct inquiry and self-assessment of language programme policies, stakeholders, practices and materials through the lens of CRT to determine if and to what extent they promote Black students' meaningful, equitable participation and success in WL.

2) The second step in CRPWLT calls for a careful examination of power and inequity in language teaching. This requires educators' awareness of their racial identities and positionality in racial hierarchies, which influence their perception of materials, how they teach and their attitude towards and treatment of their students.

3) The final, most important step in CRPWLT is translating understandings from inquiry and self-reflexivity into a liberatory practice for anti-racism and social justice. (2021: 1065–6)

While Anya's work focuses on language learning, bell hooks' work implicates the entire institution of higher education. 'If we examine critically the traditional role of the university in the pursuit of truth and the sharing of knowledge and information, it is painfully clear that biases that uphold and maintain white supremacy, imperialism, sexism, and racism have distorted education so that it is no longer about the practice of freedom' (1994).

While this chapter focuses on language learning and teaching, it is worth noting that change is needed at all levels of education.

With that in mind, it is notable to consider how few educators were provided the opportunity to engage in this type of thinking in their own growth as pedagogues. In the very little training that I've had, the majority has been based upon how to create assessments, how to write syllabi, how to engage students in class, and so forth. How to think critically in a language classroom was not part of the discourse. And yet, why not? Some may have been trained or are originally from parts of the world in which critical thinking is not only avoided but also frowned upon. Others worry about the possible loss of control when they carry out discussions of this nature. Also, some are likely to fear their authority risked by veering from the course objectives that they created. The first suggestion, therefore, is for language educators to consider their own learning, background and propensity to engage in difficult and critical conversations both in and outside of the classroom.

Another phase would be to begin to think critically about the cultures of the languages that we are teaching. No language is devoid of discrimination. There are no cultures of innocence with regard to overt power plays, aggression, othering. This is simply the age in which we live. So – why not use that as the basis for a curriculum that challenges established norms within the languages themselves and the cultural hierarchies, as well as the methodologies of the classroom?

What might this look like? In a brief encounter with a colleague as we are passing through the entrance to the building where our offices are housed, I give him a shout-out for his participation in a conversation about the Russian invasion of Ukraine. This colleague teaches Russian. His powerful statement was, 'It is difficult to teach Russian on a day like today'. His response was to create an exercise for his early learners in which they read about the attacks in Russian from a Russian news source – not in an effort to corroborate the violence and unprovoked aggression – but to face the difficult topic with a critical lens. There is the potential for this type of exercise to be messy and go off the rails. Imagine that there is a student in the class who is pro-Russia, perhaps from a family of Russian oligarchs who are funding this effort. There might also be a student whose heritage is Ukrainian and who has distant relatives that have been displaced. Should the conversation then be avoided so as to maintain control and composure? That is the default for many of us. For a multitude of reasons – fear of job security, fear of retribution, fear of being called out for progressive or radical thinking – we might feel disempowered to engage in these ways. How do we make that shift? There is no clear answer. Fortunately, in my case, my colleagues and the leaders of my department are supportive and receptive to these interventions.

## Teachers as Students: The Anti-Racist Pedagogy Syllabus

It is necessary and relevant to mention that I come from a Modern Languages Department that houses eight languages and over forty faculty members. Beginning in the summer of 2020, our department began working on a combination of initiatives to incorporate anti-racist, inclusive and radical pedagogies. We have also created programming that highlights Black intellectuals/artists from around the world. Another avenue of discourse has been inviting speakers who analyse how racist behaviour manifests in the target culture – be it Spain, China or Egypt. And yet, we have so much to learn from one another and from our students. To that end, our work has formed around the following learning objectives:

**PART ONE:**

Personal reflection on our socialization and worldview by:

1. interrogating our position in the department, college, university, city, country – in sum, in our multiple communities – and how race and culture influence our views
2. examining past and present examples of anti-blackness in the regions we study
3. understanding the impact of white supremacy in our own disciplines with attention to gaining more familiarity with marginalized discourses.

The BIG QUESTION:
*How do we talk about DEI within a department that is ethnically diverse and therefore might have different perceptions of racism, inclusivity and equity?*

**PART TWO:**

Reflection and action in our syllabi, course content and overall pedagogy.

1. questioning the content we include and prioritize;
2. recognizing multiple approaches to different learning styles;
3. identifying the biases in the materials and assessment tools we use;

4. questioning assumptions about expectations we have of our students;
5. workshopping our syllabi to employ anti-racist pedagogy;
6. exploring anti-racist content to incorporate across our curriculum;
7. developing strategies to address [racial] conflicts and tension.

These objectives have informed our learning over the past two years. Currently, we are in the process of evaluating our goals so as to develop a plan for 2022–3.

## Lost Opportunities – On Analysing the Ways in Which the Materials Are Racist

One of the proposed initiatives moving forward is evaluation of the texts that we use in our curriculum through the lenses of critical race theory and critical race pedagogy. In many of the elementary and intermediate texts, there is a scaffolded approach. Vocabulary is introduced at the beginning of the chapter. Then, there are a series of exercises that follow in which the students are meant to first identify the correct word or words, then use the words in sentences and then interact with peers generally either creating questions based on a certain bank of vocabulary or creation of a dialogue incorporating the vocabulary. The idea is that there is a gradual growth – identify, use in simple context, use in complex context, create within context, create and exchange within context. The context itself is determined by the text. And then the same iteration takes place with the structural elements of language as they are scattered throughout the chapter. If this isn't a colonial creation, I don't know what is. There is very little critical analysis in this absorption of language: very little self-reflection on what the words and structures mean to the students in their own current contexts, in the cultural situations that are reflected in the texts, and, most importantly, in those cultural contexts that are left out of the text.

An example might be found in the explanation of prepositions in the Spanish language. First, it must be recognized that prepositions are one of the more difficult constructions when learning English. Therefore, it is necessary to acknowledge my own privilege of having learned English as my primary and native language. This simple L1 contextualization is something that is rarely discussed. Even among native speakers of English who have learned anything other than Standard English (which means most of us), there are varying linguistic practices of prepositions. In a video lesson from the *Leaders Project* (2014) at Teacher's College of Columbia University, the instructor explains that in African American English, there can be omission of prepositions:

Example – 'Get out my room' – omission of the preposition 'of' that would be used in Standard English.

This is but one example of the ways in which dominant linguistic understanding of the L1, the language in which the text is used, is exclusionary. It is quite possible that a student of Spanish in their erstwhile learning process might feel alienated due to a lack of identification with the grammatical explanation in their own language. Of course, there are limitations to the amount of variation that the textbooks can include. However, depending upon not only the L1 of the students, but also their demographics, an understanding of this type of situation would be more inclusive.

What happens when discussing daily life if daily life isn't what is represented in the images provided? How alienating must some of these manufactured situations feel to students who have no point of reference from which to enter into these discourses? What can we as instructors do to guide/empower students to use critical thinking to push back against these norms?

One such exercise that I have carried out with my students in the intermediate levels is a project-based assignment in which they (i) take a critical look at the so-called 'culture' sections of the text, (ii) determine whether each cultural section is engaged in critical analysis, (iii) zoom out to look at the entirety of the culture sections to analyse representation, expected normalcy and potential bias and (iv) with that knowledge, the students create their own culture section. They produce a PowerPoint presentation (that oftentimes emulates the structure of the text) and narrate their thought process – the intended audience being textbook editors and publishers.

One of the most illustrative examples of the power of this exercise was in my intermediate Spanish II course during the Spring semester of 2021. The student shared with me that she had had a hard time in her previous language courses – in particular one in which upon proposing a report on her Philippine heritage, the instructor told her that this topic wasn't relevant enough. Relevant enough? In one fell swoop of racist and colonial thinking, this instructor invalidated the existence of the colonized space (the Philippines) as well as its people (my student).

## Conclusion

While this work continues, we must ask ourselves what our role is moving forward. While some may suggest that our work as analysts and investigators of language and culture is inherently anti-racist, others may not agree. Is the process of co-creation and co-learning for us as instructors a form of anti-racist pedagogy? Are we engaged in pedagogy that is truly radical and that understands the limitations of our own knowledge and power? What are needed are frank conversations regarding these issues so as to demonstrate the potential for language learning to align with anti-racist methods, and prioritization of BIPOC and LGBTQ+ voices. We have the potential to be the leaders in shifting teaching strategies to be more inclusive.

## Note

1 For further contextualization, see *The Chronicle of Higher Education*, as well as *Faculty Focus*.

## References

Anya, U. (2021), 'Critical Race Pedagogy for More Effective and Inclusive World Language Teaching', *Applied Linguistics*, 42 (6): 1055–69.

hooks, b. (1994), *Teaching to Transgress*, New York: Routledge.

Leaders Project. (2014), *Adjectives, Adverbs, Prepositions and Contractions (Grammar Fundamentals: Module 04)*, 29 August. Available online: https://www.leadersproject.org/2014/08/29/grammar-fundamentals-for-a-pluralistic-society-module-4-adjectives-adverbs/.

# CHAPTER 7

# Third-Person Pronouns, Gender and the Han Gaze in the Chinese Modern Languages Classroom

*Derek Hird*

## Introduction

Critical gender and race theories are not generally associated with language learning in the Chinese modern languages classroom.[1] This chapter argues they should be, taking as its case study third-person pronouns, a key area of discussion in contemporary gender identity and expression debates.

To set the scene, this chapter begins with a brief account of how third-person pronouns are taught in two highly popular Chinese-language textbooks in UK higher education Chinese-language programmes: *New Practical Chinese Reader* (NPCR) and *Integrated Chinese* (IC) – NPCR introduces 他 tā (he) in Lesson Two and 她 tā (she) in Lesson Three. In a Lesson Three dialogue titled '她是哪国人' (what's her nationality), NPCR notes: 'There are two Chinese characters for the third-person singular "tā": one is "他", used for a male; the other "她", refers to a female' (Liu 2002: 26). *IC* introduces 他 and 她 in a dialogue about a family photo in Lesson Two, but without any further explanation in the 'Language Notes' column (Liu et al. 2010: 42–3). In both textbooks, third-person pronouns are presented as if they are inevitably binary and ahistorical. However, as we shall discover in what follows, such assumptions are incorrect: gendered binary third-person pronouns in Chinese are a twentieth-century invention that privileges the masculine; inclusive ways of expressing third-person pronouns are available. Chinese-language educators have a choice: they can choose to reinforce the patriarchal structures in which binary third-person pronouns are embedded or they can challenge them. This chapter lays out the latter path.

With its focus on gendered asymmetries in Chinese, this chapter addresses the volume's core question: How can modern languages be taught so that they challenge rather than reinforce social inequalities? The chapter questions the role of modern language teaching in reproducing normative language policy and practice, specifically in relation to gender. It unmasks ideologies and hegemonies that lie behind linguistic discourses (Duchêne and Heller 2011; Heller and McElhinney 2017) and advocates culturally sustaining inclusive linguistic and cultural pluralism as a means to transform the learning environment (Alim and Paris 2017). It holds that students and teachers must work together in democratic dialogue to challenge and transform educational and social practices (Freire 2005; hooks 2003).

This chapter sketches out relevant 'metadiscursive regimes' (Makoni and Pennycook 2005) of modernity that have shaped discourses of gender and race in modern China. As a case study, it analyses Chinese third-person pronouns, informed by critical feminist discourse analysis and transgender linguistics. Finally, inspired by critical anti-racist pedagogy in ELT, it sets out a critical pedagogy toolkit for the modern languages classroom and applies it to teaching Chinese third-person pronouns.

# Contexts and Concepts

## *Metadiscursive Regimes*

Charles L. Briggs defined metadiscourses as 'discourses that seek to shape, constrain, or appropriate other discourses' (1993: 389). The binary division of two sexes, male and female, is a metadiscourse of modernity that became prominent in Europe from the eighteenth century (Laqueur 1990). Another example is John Locke's (1632–1704) notion of language as an abstract vehicle for decontextualized truth, separate from nature and society, which positioned Western European languages as the universal tongues of modern cosmopolitan subjects (Bauman and Briggs 2003). One of the most powerful and insidious European metadiscourses of modernity defined racial difference by attributing immutable characteristics to different 'races', arranged into a hierarchy dominated by the 'white man' (Pennycook 1998: 95–101). These metadiscourses are among those that have deeply shaped capitalist modernity and coloniality, which, as two sides of the same coin, have acted together to stifle alternative epistemologies (Mignolo 2007: 450–51).

European metadiscourses did not spread by magic to the rest of the world: they circulated through colonial discursive regimes and were taken up by local elites in their quest to become modern subjects (Leezenberg 2009). Many early-twentieth-century young Chinese intellectuals, who revered Western literature and largely reviled 'traditional' Chinese culture, enthusiastically advocated the creation of male and female third-person pronouns in the style of European languages, although not without contestation (Huang 2009). The incoming colonial discourses often intersected with locally embedded historical discourses, reinforcing rather than challenging existing gendered and racial inequalities (Dikötter 1996; Kubota 2020).

## *The Han Gaze*

Hegemonic European notions of race were taken up by local Chinese elites in the late nineteenth century. By the early twentieth century, when Chinese nation-building discourses were already circulating widely, the idea of a Han race had been institutionalized as the millennia-old 'nation race' (*minzu* 民族) identity of the vast majority of people in China, the descendants of the Yellow Emperor (Dikötter 1996: 596; Joniak-Lüthi 2015: 7). In 1954, the Communist state initiated an ethnic classification project that, through a process of variously merging and discarding local identities, eventually created a taxonomy of fifty-five 'minority nationalities' (*shaoshu minzu* 少数民族), each mapped to a language (Mullaney 2004). There is a widespread consensus in Han society to this day that the Han are smarter and harder-working than minority ethnicities, who are deemed less developed than the Han and associated with physiological and cultural characteristics that demarcate them as conspicuously different from the Han (Joniak-Lüthi 2015: 45–54). The dominant Han 'race' have taken it upon themselves to define other ethnic identities and to place them lower than the Han in a racial hierarchy; they have also allowed Han-ness to operate as an unmarked category in much the same way that whiteness and maleness are often rendered invisible in discussions about race and gender (Joniak-Lüthi 2015: 50–1: Mullaney 2012: 3).

In addition to a collective Han identity, many Chinese intellectuals, writers and officials drew on European nation-building discourses to argue for a common national language to help foster national sentiment and cohesion. During a process of several decades, a national language was forged: Modern Standard Chinese. It was based predominantly on the Mandarin spoken in Beijing and was defined officially in 1956 as Putonghua 普通话 ('common tongue') under the Communist government (Chen 2004). Modern Standard Chinese mainly took the phonology, lexis and syntax of well-educated Beijing residents as its norms. Due to its status as the official standard, Modern Standard Chinese is associated with 'good education, intelligence, social sophistication, authority, and formality' (Chen 2004: 56). Regional varieties of Putonghua have conventionally been dismissed as corrupted non-standard forms and the official position since the 1950s has been to reduce the use of non-Mandarin languages (Chen 2004: 45, 57–8). Beijing-based Mandarin and Han ethnicity have become key twin markers of Chinese national identity, with Mandarin increasingly displacing and even replacing minority languages (Irgengioro 2018: 332; Joniak-Lüthi 2015: 53). China's many hundreds of languages offer rich and plural ways of expression, but all except Mandarin have been increasingly marginalized since the Republican era. Current language policy continues to assert the linguistic hegemony of Mandarin (Han and Wu 2020).

The acclaimed US novelist Toni Morrison has eloquently identified the pernicious effects of the dominant 'White gaze', which enforces 'patriarchal, cisheteronormative, English-monolingual, ableist, classist, xenophobic, Judeo-Christian gazes' (Alim and Paris 2017: 2–3). While it would be unwise to draw wholesale comparisons, there are parallels between the White gaze and the Han gaze (Mullaney 2012, 2). While the White gaze privileges the White Anglo-Saxon Protestant linguistic-cultural norms of north-eastern US Ivy-League elites, the Han gaze elevates Han Confucianism and educated-class cultural and linguistic Beijing-centrism as its standards, to the detriment of people without the requisite social, cultural, racial and linguistic capital.

Alim and Paris ask: 'What if the goal of learning and teaching with youth of color was not ultimately to see how closely students could perform White middle-class norms, but rather was to explore, honor, extend, and, at times, problematize their cultural practices and investments?' (2017: 3). In China, the Han gaze utilizes Mandarin, among other tools, to shape and limit discourses and to discriminate against less empowered minorities of all backgrounds (Joniak-Lüthi 2015: 45–54). How, then, does one challenge the Han gaze and Mandarin linguistic hegemony to give China and the Sinophone world's rich multilingualism and multiple social strata a central role in Chinese-language pedagogies in the Chinese modern language classroom? More specific to the focus of this chapter, in what ways can third-person pronouns be taught that challenge, rather than reinforce, the Han gaze? Given that racial and gendered discourses are often deeply intersecting and mutually supportive, any effective response to the Han gaze must also consider patriarchal social and linguistic structures.

## *Patriarchy and Linguistic Sexism*

Across the globe, still today, the intersectionality of local patriarchies and hegemonic Euro-American knowledge systems continues to reinforce male dominance and the marginalization of women (Kubota 2020). Discourses of race and gender have worked together to produce subjects with unequal status. Western colonial and patriarchal constructions of race and gender were not simply imposed upon colonized societies; local elites, themselves reliant on racialized and gendered ideologies and practices for their status and power, took up these elements of Western discourses to build modern nation states and to cultivate nationalism among ordinary people. During the development of China as a nation-state, historically embedded local patriarchies have interacted with Western patriarchies to perpetuate male privilege in China, despite women's activism and some government efforts to address gender inequalities. During this process, China's elites – who remain overwhelmingly Han, male and concentrated in mega-metropolises such as Beijing and Shanghai – have continued to utilize patriarchal Han chauvinism when it serves their interests, including in language policies and practices.

Linguistic analyses demonstrate that historically embedded patriarchal morphology, lexis and syntax – both overt and covert – perpetuate and legitimize men's dominance over women through language norms (e.g., Li 2020; Moser 1997; Tso 2015). Despite the Chinese language ostensibly appearing genderless through its not having masculine or feminine forms, Tso argues that 'linguistic sexism' arising from 'masculine hegemony' can be found in 'the morphology of Han characters; Chinese vocabulary (occupational terms and forms of address); the Chinese pronoun system; Chinese word order; Chinese four-character idioms; and Chinese proverbs' (2015: 1).

Characters containing the *nǚ* 女 radical include those used to identify female roles in the family; a further set of characters including 女 signify characteristics associated with femininity, such as *jiāo* 嬌 (pampered, spoiled), *nèn* 嫩 (delicate), *wǎn* 婉 (gentle, restrained) and *zhuāng* 妝 (to adorn oneself, dress up) (Tso 2015: 2). Media and anthropological research show that dominant discourses circulating in the Chinese media and everyday conversations persistently reproduce notions of gender difference that naturalize women's aptitude for domestic and caring responsibilities (e.g., Evans 2021; Zhang and Jamil 2015). Even more insidiously, many characters bearing negative associations include 女, such as *jí* 嫉 (jealousy), *dù* 妒 (envy), *lán* 婪 (greedy), *wàng* 妄 (presumptuous), *xián* 嫌 (dislike, resentment), *jiān* 奸 (wicked, evil, treacherous), *jiān* 姦 (adultery, rape), *yāo* 妖 (demon, evil, bewitching) and *nú* 奴 (slave) (Tso 2015: 2). In a corpus study of 287 million characters, Li Lan found that out of thirty-six verbs containing the 女 radical, fourteen were pejorative; and that thirteen out of fifty-two characters describing women's appearance were negative (Li 2020: 112). Equivalent sets of characters that include the male character *nán* 男, denoting male family roles, masculine attributes, and negative associations, do not exist. Indeed, 男 is not used as a radical at all: two previous instances, *shēng* 甥 (nephew) and *jiù* 舅 (uncle), having been reclassified due to their scarcity (Hodge and Louie 1998: 60).

When male and female roles are paired, the normative sequence places the male first. Examples include *nánnǚ* 男女 (male and female, man and woman), *fùmǔ* 父母 (father and mother), *bàmā* 爸妈 (dad and mum), *fūfù* 夫妇 and fūqī 夫妻, *zǐnǔ* 子女 and *érnǔ* 儿女 (son and daughter), and *xiōngdì-jiěmèi* 兄弟姐妹 (brothers and sisters). The male signifier is thus placed in the same position as the signifier for good in good/bad pairings, examples of which include *shìfēi* 是非 (right and wrong), *duìcuò* 对错 (correct and incorrect) and *róngrǔ* 荣辱 (honour and disgrace) (Moser 1997: 3–5; Tso 2015: 6).

Occupational roles are another area in which linguistic sexism is pervasive. Prestigious occupations are assumed to be undertaken by men; the prefix 女 is used if the position is held by a woman: for example, *nǚ fǎguān* 女法官 (female judge), *nǚ* yīshēng 女医生 (female doctor) and *nǚ jiàoshòu* 女教授 (female professor). Correspondingly, some feminized low-status jobs require a 男 prefix if held by men: for example, *nán hùshi* 男护士 for a male nurse (Moser 1997: 15; Tso 2015: 3).

A list of sexist *chéngyǔ* 成语 (four-character sayings) and proverbs in Chinese would be too long to include here. Many examples can be found in Tso (2015: 6–8), such as *fàngdàng-yínjiàn* 放荡淫贱 (debauched, loose and lewd), which describes a woman with many lovers; conversely, a man with many lovers is described as *fēngliú-tìtǎng* 风流倜傥 (elegant and unrestrained).

From these examples, it is evident that third-person pronouns form just one part of an urgently needed broader project to research, challenge and overcome the masculine bias in Chinese and its role in maintaining social patriarchy.

## Analytical Frameworks

The core twin aims of this chapter, to critique the asymmetry inherent in the Chinese third-person pronoun framework and to propose inclusive pedagogical practices as a means to transform it, require conceptual frameworks that help identify unequal power relations and show ways to undo them. The following conceptual approaches are useful for that purpose: Michele Lazar's feminist critical discourse analysis (FCDA), Kirby Conrod's application of linguistic performativity to pronouns and Ryuko Kubota's critical anti-racist pedagogy.

Developed from critical discourse analysis, FCDA holds that social practices both reflect and constitute discourse, but further recognizes that while many social practices are gendered, they are often taken as normal, natural and based on common sense, which obscures power differentials and limits ways of acting as gendered beings (Lazar 2014). FCDA therefore seeks to 'show up the complex, subtle and sometimes not so subtle, ways in which frequently taken-for-granted gendered assumptions and hegemonic power relations are discursively produced, sustained, negotiated, and challenged in different contexts and communities' (Lazar 2007: 142). FCDA inspires this chapter's critical approach to the interrelationship between gender and language and attention to power relations in Chinese third-person pronouns.

Conrod's linguistic performativity lens on third-person pronouns is a useful way of approaching the ways third-person pronouns in many languages limit gendered subjectivities to just male and female, excluding and misgendering people with transgender identities. Conrod deploys Judith Butler's theory of performativity to argue that pronoun use is 'part of the way that a collective society decides and creates the social gender of an individual referent' (2020: 8). When pronoun use does not align with someone's sense of identity, that is, when misgendering occurs, it causes feelings of 'discontinuity, fragmentation, or conflict' (2020: 8). Misgendering, whether accidental or intentional, inflicts a type of symbolic violence, through its oppression of people who are already marginalized in terms of their gender identity. (2020: 38). Conrod's linguistic performativity approach shows the urgent need for Chinese modern language teachers to transform third-person pronoun pedagogies, and, indeed, all linguistic sexism, or be complicit in perpetuating oppressive and patriarchal inequalities embedded in the Han gaze.

As discussed earlier, patriarchal oppression does not operate in isolation: it intersects with other hegemonic regimes producing complex inequalities that affect individuals differently depending on their identity markers and social practices. Linguistic inequalities reflect these multiple forms of oppression, including linguistic discrimination on the basis of gender, sexuality, race, ethnicity, age, ability, religion and nationality (Kubota 2020). Ryuko Kubota's (2021) concept of 'epistemological racism' provides a useful means of analysing how the Han gaze intersects with oppressive linguistic gender structures such as binary third-person pronouns. According to Kubota, epistemological racism pervades discourse and knowledge in distinction to individual racist acts and institutional racism, although epistemological racism informs the latter two phenomena. Epistemological racism acts as a lens through which social and cultural practices are viewed. For example, mainstream festivals in the United States celebrate the heritage and culture of White people above other groups (Kubota 2021: 240). In China, a comparison can be drawn with the dominance of Han culture and Confucianism, which shapes the meaning of Chineseness and national norms of behaviour. The language associated with the Han elite, Beijing Mandarin, has come to dominate Chinese linguistic policy through the government's increasing imposition of Putonghua as the principal national language; the use of other languages in the public sphere has correspondingly reduced (Zhu 2014). The imposition of Putonghua in education and the media not only marginalizes and disempowers minority languages and cultures, but it also sidelines non-Beijing-based regional variants of Mandarin. Kubota (2021: 240) points out the complicity of people of colour in supporting White supremacy in the United States. Han supremacy and the superiority of Putonghua are the central tenets of an ideological racism in China that educators worldwide are complicit in supporting if they uncritically teach 'standard Chinese' and 'Chinese culture' to their students.

## Third-Person Pronouns

The Chinese language employed the character 他 – which contains the ungendered 'person' radical 亻 – as a genderless third-person pronoun until the early twentieth century, when progressive intellectuals familiar with European literature sought to create a feminine pronoun to help liberate women. In 1917, poet and linguist Liu Bannong 刘半农 (1891–1934) proposed 她 as a feminine pronoun in which the female radical 女 replaced the person radical (Dan 2021; Huang 2009: 17; Jortay 2021: 123–4). Other attempts to create feminine pronouns had mixed success: essayist and translator Zhou Zuoren's 周作人 (1885–1967) proposal for a post-subscript 女 after 他 did not catch on, whereas the originally genderless Shanghainese/Hokkien pronoun for he/she, *yī* 伊, enjoyed popularity with some writers and feminists as an alternative to 她 in the 1920s and 1930s (Huang 2009: 19, 64–75). A new masculine third-person pronoun using the male radical 男 was created to form a balanced pair with 她, which the poet Liu Dabai 刘大白 (1880–1932) attempted but failed to popularize (Ling 1989; Cheng 2016: 103; Moser 1997: 11).

Some writers and intellectuals welcomed the new pronoun 她 as a means of making female gender visible. Others, however, were concerned about the emergence of a hierarchy of pronouns: men's privileged status shown by the universal person radical, then women marked by their gender and finally animals and non-animate objects represented by a third tā: 它. Opponents of differentiation argued that as first- and second-person pronouns were not gendered, there was no need to gender third-person pronouns (Huang 2009). On public posters, female students crossed out the person radical in 他, replacing it with the male character 男 to protest the subordination of women in the newly gendered personal pronoun system; and the writer Cheng Zhanlu 程瞻庐 (1879–1943) complained that 她 forced a gender upon people, such as eunuchs, who did not fit into a binary gender framework (Jortay 2021: 125). By the 1930s, however, 她 had become firmly established, defeating its non-Mandarin rival 伊, most likely because of its closeness in character formation and identical pronunciation with 他 in Mandarin; the historically embedded habit of not differentiating third-person pronouns in everyday speech was hard to shift (Huang 2009: 148–9). Under this framework, adding the suffix *mén* 们 to any of the third-person pronouns creates the plural form. However, when referring to a mixed group of people the masculine form, 他们, is used, even if just one of the group is male: this adds a further layer of discrimination against women.

Scholarly investigations of 她 may also perpetuate patriarchal assumptions. In 1989, Chinese-language scholar Ling Yuanzheng 凌远征 wrote:

> Since the third-person pronoun in Chinese was originally genderless, there was an objective need to create feminine and neutral characters 她 and 它 for the third-person singular. Thus, there was no need to denote masculinity; and since there was no need for such a character, to create one naturally would have been superfluous. (Ling 1989, translated by Moser 1997: 11)

As Moser (1997: 11) points out, Ling's reasoning endorses an asymmetrical arrangement that relegates women to their own 'special class'. Through equating universal personhood with masculinity and justifying feminine differentiation, this kind of view operates at the intersection of local and Western patriarchies and reinforces men's linguistic hegemony.

More recently, the rise of transgender activism and identities has built fresh momentum behind finding alternatives to this outdated, reductive and discriminatory gender binary. Proposals include replacing 亻 and 女 with X or 无, which would denote unknown gender or no gender, respectively (Bergundy 2021; Lai 2020). Growing numbers of people and organizations are simply dispensing with characters and using the pinyin form 'ta' as a genderless third-person pronoun (Dan 2021). There are even calls to dispense with 她 altogether and return to using 他 in its initial function as a gender-inclusive pronoun (Cheng 2016). Nevertheless, progressive efforts to pluralize or de-gender third-person pronouns have not yet entered mainstream language use, let alone been recognized by official bodies. This lack of progress is due in part to the embeddedness of gender-binary third-person pronouns in Modern Standard Chinese; yet it is also a consequence of the persistence of patriarchal attitudes, evidenced, for example, by the social backlash faced by liberal gender activists in China in the last decade (Wu and Dong 2019).

Reading the history of 她 through a conceptual synthesis of FCDA, linguistic performativity and epistemological racism brings attention to the intersections of gendered and racial linguistic regimes and their productive power. The creation and adoption of the explicitly feminine-marked 她 and the masculine coding of the previously genderless 他 by the male-dominated intellectual elite in the early Republican era rendered women more visible in Modern Standard Chinese but not on equal terms with men. If the Shanghainese/Hokkien 伊 had been adopted, the result would still have been a third-person pronoun framework based on a gender binary, but at least both genders would have been represented in identical visual form through the person radical 亻. Unfortunately, the dominance of educated Beijing Mandarin – a marker of cultural capital that deeply informs the Han gaze – prevented 伊 from gaining sufficient traction, despite support for it from leading authors and feminist publications.

That the gender binary found in colonial European languages was the model on which reforms were premised highlights the elevation of European norms above other possibilities. This situation arose because many of the intellectual elite in China (as elsewhere) subscribed to the hierarchy of national development propagated through the epistemologically racist metadiscursive regimes of colonial modernity. According to this logic underpinning these regimes, Western European women's supposed higher social status was linked in part to the presence of a feminine third-person pronoun; however, this association is not factually borne out, as gendered third-person pronouns are found in numerous languages throughout the world in very varied societies (Siewierska 2013).

Meanwhile, people who identify as non-binary do not have the means to express fully their identity in mainstream discourse and will continue to be misgendered as long as no inclusive third-person pronoun option exists. Chinese-language teachers have a choice: they can either reinforce this symbolic violence by teaching gender-binary pronouns, or they can call out this discriminatory framework and work with learners to create gender-inclusive practices for use in the classroom and society.

The gendered inequality and limitations in Chinese third-person pronouns, the linguistic sexism that permeates the morphology, lexis and syntax of Chinese and the marginalization of minority ethnicity and non-Mandarin 'Han' languages other than the official Putonghua, all clearly demand a progressive response.

## Critical Gender Pedagogy in the Modern Languages Classroom

From a critical pedagogy perspective, teachers of languages should discuss linguistic oppressions and work collaboratively with students to identify linguistic oppressions and to develop non-oppressive ways of teaching and learning languages. In the context of English Language Teaching, Ryuko Kubota (2021) sets out five principles of critical anti-racist pedagogy. Working on the premise that these principles can be adapted into critical pedagogic approaches to multiple oppressive structures and practices, this section sets out a critical pedagogy toolkit for the modern languages classroom and applies it to the issue of gender-binary third-person pronouns in Chinese.

Kubota's first principle is 'de-essentialising racism', which recognizes that injustice is caused by multiple oppressions and calls for an intersectional approach to help understand how they interact. The first tool in the toolkit is therefore *intersectionality*. Kubota's second principle is 'de-simplifying racism', acknowledging that racism is multilayered: it is structural and epistemological as well as the result of individual behaviour. Thus the second tool is *multilayerism*. The third principle Kubota puts forward is 'de-silencing anti-racism', meaning that racism must be openly discussed in the language classroom. The third tool, then, is *open discussion*. Kubota's fourth principle is 'decolonizing antiracism', which encourages teachers and students to gauge their positionality in colonial hierarchies; and her fifth principle is 'exercising critical reflexivity', which enables teachers and students to recognize their complicity in oppressive regimes and the privileges they attain through their identity markers. The toolkit's fourth tool combines these two principles into *critical decolonization and reflexivity*. Kubota recommends using her principles to increase critical awareness and engage in dialogic approaches. With those aims in mind, the four tools this section has derived from Kubota's principles – *intersectionality*, *multilayerism*, *open discussion*, and *critical decolonization and reflexivity* – can be used to shape pedagogical methods that include dialogic communication with students to enhance their critical awareness of linguistic and social oppressions.

Applying these tools to teaching Chinese third-person pronouns could involve the teacher initiating *open discussions* with students that examine the *intersectionality* (gender, race, nation-building, etc.) and *multilayerism* (epistemological, structural and individual dimensions of gendered and racial discrimination) inherent to the inequalities and exclusions perpetuated by the gender- binary model of 他 and 她. The discussion could cover the gender hierarchies, linguistic sexism, silencing of transgender identities, the Han gaze and educated Beijing Mandarin-centrism that have contributed to the imposition of an asymmetric third-person pronoun system. Students could investigate the use of pronouns by individuals (e.g., in Chinese-language social media posts), structurally (e.g., in the textbooks stipulated in the course syllabus), and epistemologically (e.g., in mainstream media discourses on gender). Putting the spotlight on their own use of this pronoun system, students and teachers could engage in *critical decolonization and reflexivity*, including critically reflecting on their own complicity, through colonial hierarchies and other identity privileges, in oppressive gender frameworks. A further, crucial step would be for students and teachers to discuss inclusive classroom protocols for the use of third-person pronouns in Chinese, such as encouraging students to state their own pronouns in Chinese and deciding upon suitably gender-inclusive Chinese third-person pronouns when discussing people whose gender identity and pronouns are unknown. Outside the classroom, activities could include talks, round-table discussions, inclusive curriculum development, continuing professional development, and attention to hiring practices (Kubota 2021: 243–4).

# Conclusion

Language curricula, textbooks and pedagogies still generally persist in framing language learning as a neutral process of technical skills development. The politics of language teaching and learning is thus often startlingly absent from the modern languages classroom. Consequently, many language teachers, whether unwittingly or not, reinforce oppressive and discriminatory linguistic regimes and structures. Worse still, it is not as if this critique is new: critical analysis of language and power has been taking place in critical sociolinguistics, linguistic anthropology and cultural studies for decades. Modern language teaching needs to catch up.

Drawing from feminist critical discourse analysis, performative linguistics and critical anti-racist pedagogy, this chapter has highlighted how the metadiscursive regimes of colonialism/modernity taken up by Chinese intellectuals in the early twentieth century, and their intersection with locally embedded patriarchal, racial and linguistic hierarchies, resulted in a third-person pronoun framework that associated men with universal personhood, discriminated against women, reduced gender options to a strict binary, reinforced normative Beijing Mandarin pronunciation and dismissed inclusive non-Mandarin alternatives. Deemed a progressive move by its proponents, the adoption of 她 as the third-person feminine pronoun has in reality had far-reaching harmful consequences. Yet, many Chinese-language teachers continue to reinforce the gendered, linguistic and racial hierarchies embodied in this one character by failing to take a critical approach to language teaching.

Drawing from Kubota's critical anti-racist pedagogy for the ELT classroom, this chapter has outlined a critical pedagogy for the modern language classroom that emphasizes the need for students and teachers to engage in *open discussion* of the *intersectionality* of discursive regimes and the *multilayerism* of oppressive acts and structures, and *critical decolonization and reflexivity* regarding their identity privileges and complicity in reinforcing social and linguistic hierarchies. Through critical reflexivity and dialogic engagement, teachers must work with students to find inclusive linguistic solutions that do not produce linguistic and social inequalities. Transforming the language classroom into a site of critical language learning revitalizes modern language learning by connecting language with the fundamental social justice challenges of our time.

## Note

1 The term 'modern languages' is retained here because it is a widespread terminology across various contexts. Nevertheless, it cannot be exempted from decolonizing critiques as it is embedded in the matrix of coloniality/modernity: see footnote 2 in the Introduction.

## References

Alim, H. S., and D. Paris. (2017), 'What is Culturally Sustaining Pedagogy and Why Does it Matter?', in D. Paris and H. S. Alim (eds.), *Culturally Sustaining*

*Pedagogies: Teaching and Learning for Justice in a Changing World*, 1–24, New York: Teachers College Press.

Bauman, R., and C. L. Briggs. (2003), *Voices of Modernity: Language Ideologies and the Politics of Inequality* (Studies in the Social and Cultural Foundations of Language; no. 21), Cambridge and New York: Cambridge University Press.

Bergundy, R. (2021), 'Debate Over New Gender Neutral "They/Them" Chinese Character', *That's Shanghai*, July 27. Available online: https://www.thatsmags.com/shanghai/post/33131/debate-over-new-gender-neutral-they-them-chinese-character (accessed 7 June 2022).

Briggs, C. (1993), 'Metadiscursive Practices and Scholarly Authority in Folkloristics', *The Journal of American Folklore*, 106 (422): 387–434.

Chen, P. (2004), *Modern Chinese: History and Sociolinguistics*, Cambridge: Cambridge University Press.

Cheng, V. T. (2016), 'Radical Equity: A Case Study of the Use of Chinese Third-Person Pronouns in Taiwan's Third Grade Social Studies Textbooks', *Intercultural Communication Studies*, XXV (3): 99–111.

Conrod, K. (2020), 'Pronouns and Gender in Language', in K. Hall and R. Barrett (eds.), *The Oxford Handbook of Language and Sexuality*, 1–45, Oxford: Oxford University Press. https://doi.org/10.1093/oxfordhb/9780190212926.013.63.

Dan, W. (2021), 'The Search for Non-Binary Pronouns in Chinese', *multilingual.com*, 26 July. Available online: https://multilingual.com/the-search-for-non-binary-pronouns-in-chinese (accessed 7 June 2022).

Dikötter, F. (1996), 'Culture, "Race" and Nation: The Formation of National Identity in Twentieth Century China', *Journal of International Affairs*, 49 (2): 590–605.

Duchêne, A., and M. Heller. (2011), *Language in Late Capitalism: Pride and Profit*, London: Routledge.

Evans, H. (2021), 'Patchy Patriarchy and the Shifting Fortunes of the CCP's Promise of Gender Equality Since 1921', *The China Quarterly*, 248 (1): 95–115.

Freire, P. (2005), *Pedagogy of the Oppressed: 30th Anniversary Edition*, New York: Continuum.

Han, Y., and X. Wu. (2020), 'Language Policy, Linguistic Landscape and Residents' Perception in Guangzhou, China: Dissents and Conflicts', *Current Issues in Language Planning*, 21 (3): 229–53.

Heller, M., and B. McElhinny. (2017), *Language, Capitalism, Colonialism: Toward a Critical History*, Toronto: University of Toronto Press.

Hodge, B., and K. Louie. (1998), *The Politics of Chinese Language and Culture: The Art of Reading Dragons*, London and New York: Routledge.

hooks, b. (2003), *Teaching Community: A Pedagogy of Hope*, New York: Routledge.

Huang, X. 黄兴涛. (2009), *Ta zi de wenhua shi – Nüxing xin daici de faming yu rentong yanjiu* 她字的文化史—女性新代词的发明与认同研究 [*A Cultural History of the Chinese Character Ta (She) – On the Invention and Identification of a New Female Pronoun*], Fuzhou: Fujian jiaoyu chubanshe.

Irgengioro, J. (2018), 'China's National Identity and the Root Causes of China's Ethnic Tensions', *East Asia*, 35 (4): 317–46.

Joniak-Lüthi, A. (2015), *The Han: China's Diverse Majority*, Seattle, WA: University of Washington Press.

Jortay, C. (2021), 'War of Words and Gender: Pronominal Feuds of the Republican Period and the Early PRC', in S. Kehoe and G. Wielander (eds.), *Cultural China 2020: The Contemporary China Centre Review*, 122–8, London: University of Westminster Press.

Kubota, R. (2020), 'Confronting Epistemological Racism, Decolonizing Scholarly Knowledge: Race and Gender in Applied Linguistics', *Applied Linguistics*, 41 (5): 712–32.

Kubota, R. (2021), 'Critical Antiracist Pedagogy in ELT', *ELT Journal*, 75 (3): 237–46.

Lai, C. (2020), '"X也" and "Ta": The Gradual Rise of Gender-neutral Pronouns in Chinese', *Ariana*, July 10. Available online: https://www.arianalife.com/topics/gender-equality/x%E4%B9%9Fand-ta-the-gradual-rise-of-gender-neutral-pronouns-in-chinese/ (accessed 7June 2022).

Laqueur, T. (1990), *Making Sex: Body and Gender from the Greeks to Freud*, Cambridge, MA: Harvard University Press.

Lazar, M. M. (2007), 'Feminist Critical Discourse Analysis: Articulating a Feminist Discourse Praxis', *Critical Discourse Studies*, 4 (2): 141–64.

Lazar, M. M. (2014), 'Feminist Critical Discourse Analysis: Relevance for Current Gender and Language Research', in S. Ehrlich, M. Meyerhoff, and J. Holmes (eds.), *The Handbook of Language, Gender and Sexuality*, 180–99, Chichester: Wiley-Blackwell.

Leezenberg, M. (2009), 'Review of R. Bauman and C. L. Briggs, eds. (2003), *Voices of Modernity: Language Ideologies and the Politics of Inequality*, Cambridge: Cambridge University Press', *Journal of Pragmatics*, 41 (1): 173–9.

Li, L. (2020), 'Gender Representation in Chinese Language', in W. Wang (ed.), *Analysing Chinese Language and Discourse Across Layers and Genres*, Amsterdam and Philadelphia, PA: John Benjamins.

Ling, Y. 凌远征. (1989), '"Ta' zi de chuangzao lishi" "她"字的创造历史 (The Creation of the Character "Ta")', *Yuyan jiaoxue yu yanjiu* 语言教学与研究 (*Language Teaching and Research*), 4: 139–51.

Liu, X. 刘珣. (2002), *Xin Shiyong Hanyu Keben 1* 新实用汉语课本 1 (*New Practical Chinese Reader 1*), Beijing: Beijing Yuyan Daxue chubanshe.

Liu, Y., T. Yao, N. Bi, L. Ge, and Y. Shi. (2010), *Integrated Chinese* (3rd ed.), Boston, MA: Cheng and Tsui Company.

Makoni, S., and A. Pennycook. (2005), 'Disinventing and (Re)Constituting Languages', *Critical Inquiry in Language Studies: An International Journal*, 2 (3): 137–56.

Mignolo, W. D. (2007), 'Delinking: The Rhetoric of Modernity, the Logic of Coloniality and the Grammar of De-Coloniality', *Cultural Studies*, 21 (2–3): 449–514.

Moser, D. (1997), 'Covert Sexism in Mandarin Chinese', *Sino-Platonic Papers* 74. Available online: http://sino-platonic.org/complete/spp074_chinese_sexism.pdf (accessed 7 June 2022).

Mullaney, T. (2004), 'Ethnic Classification Writ Large: The 1954 Yunnan Province Ethnic Classification Project and its Foundation in Republican-Era Taxonomic Thought', *China Information*, 18: 207–41.

Mullaney, T. (2012), 'Critical Han Studies: Introduction and Prolegomenon', in T. Mullaney, J. Leibold, S. Gros, and E. Vanden Bussche (eds.), *Critical Han*

*Studies: The History, Representation, and Identity of China's Majority*, 1–22, Berkeley, CA and Los Angeles, CA: University of California Press.

Pennycook, A. (1998), *English and the Discourses of Colonialism*, London and New York: Routledge.

Siewierska, A. (2013), 'Gender Distinctions in Independent Personal Pronouns', in M. S. Dryer and M. Haspelmath (eds.), *The World Atlas of Language Structures Online*, Leipzig: Max Planck Institute for Evolutionary Anthropology. Available online: http://wals.info/chapter/44 (accessed 7 June 2022).

Tso, W. (2015), 'Masculine Hegemony and Resistance in Chinese Language', *Writing from Below*, 2 (1). Available online: https://writingfrombelow.org/death-and-the-maiden/masculine-hegemony-and-resistance-in-chinese-language/ (accessed 7 June 2022).

Wu, A., and Y. Dong. (2019), 'What is Made-in-China Feminism(s)? Gender Discontent and Class Friction in Post-Socialist China', *Critical Asian Studies*, 51 (4): 471–92.

Zhang, L., and M. Babar Jamil. (2015), 'Gender Inequality in Chinese News Discourse: A Critical Discourse Perspective', *International Journal of English Linguistics*, 5 (2): 36–46.

Zhu, G. (2014), 'The Right to Minority Language Instruction in Schools: Negotiating Competing Claims in Multinational China', *Human Rights Quarterly*, 36 (4): 691–721.

# CHAPTER 8

# On Facing Racism in ELT

# Black Teachers and Racially Relevant Pedagogies in Discussion[1]

*Gabriel Nascimento*

English language teaching (ELT) has driven many concerns among scholars, educators and stakeholders in educational systems about the interplay of racism and language education (Kubota and Lin 2006; Anya 2016; Flores and Rosa 2015).

In Brazil it is not particularly a novelty in language studies since Ferreira (2002, 2007, 2015, 2019) has published extensively on language, racism and critical race literacies for nearly two decades until now. Conversely, she was one of the few scholars to question language education within our racial inequalities in Brazil.

I myself attempt to put it into two ways: (i) I engage in discussing autobiographical narratives of black teachers who constitute a minority among English language teachers in Brazil; (ii) and I bring into question colonial fashions to understand what I term 'linguistic racism', which obscures the situation of our raciolinguistic policies (Flores and Rosa 2015), and also our sociolinguistic approaches on language education (Flores and Rosa 2015) in pursuit of linguistic practices that support racism and racist practices which frame monoglossic languaging (García 2009).

In this chapter I seek to go beyond my own work and recent scholarship on race and language studies that enquires about autobiographical narratives to locate how racism is set. I intend to understand which linguistic practices can serve as support for the anti-racist agenda.

Ladson-Billings (1994) highlighted the value in positive students' narratives about teachers who were very important to black children in the post-apartheid era in the United States. She contrasts assimilationist pedagogies to culturally relevant pedagogies where African American teachers are drawn as familiar to students in black neighbourhoods, influential for how students look at themselves as readers and how post-apartheid education could help students survive systemic racism (Bonilla-Silva 2021).

This paper derives from research on language education in Southern Bahia where teachers are preparing to offer a degree in anti-racist practices in language teaching. This paper will discuss the premises of racially relevant pedagogies, as inspired by culturally relevant pedagogies (Ladson-Billings 1994) that inform my current research. In order to do so, I will explore collected narratives of my black teachers in Southern Bahia to analyse how they contributed as a racially relevant pedagogy to my life story and career.

## Language and Racism in Brazil

In Brazil, racism has been mostly neglected in sociological studies in the light of economic theorizations that inherit from both Marxist and liberal theoretical frameworks the vision that only social class matters in Brazil.

Race does not appear in the foreground in a country where most people originate from slavery and the slave trade, as reportedly more than 52 per cent identify as black or brown in Brazil. As Telles (2014) argues, census agents and policies on census in Brazil fostered the racial nowhere in Brazil because informants' self-identification came to be taken into consideration by governments only recently.

Self-identification thus led to educational policies where black people, most of the population, could be read significantly as most of the imprisoned, illiterate[2] and unemployed, and victims at gunpoint of a genocide perpetrated by police brutality and paramilitary squads.

Among policies that encourage anti-racist practices are the quota reservations for public universities since 2003 and laws that shape constitutional envisioning on fighting racism, such as (i) racial equity legislation, where racism is fought through providing more rights for black people; and (ii) the Afro-Brazilian and African culture and history law, where policymakers ensure the teaching of black history and African history and culture in public schools.

Slavery has been resisted for long in Brazilian history. For more than 388 years, Brazilian identity was shaped under the arguments of Brazil as a racial paradise, following the abolition of slavery in 1888, the most longstanding enslavement in the Americas.

As Ferreira and Camargo (2014) claim, the idea of Brazil as a racial paradise has decisively influenced language education in Brazil. A brief explication of how this ideology is constructed was given by black scholar Henry Louis Gates when he embarked on a journey to Brazil, where he visited black communities to contend that colour-blind ideologies undermine the hypothesis of racial inequalities in Brazil.[3]

Remarkably, racial inequality seems to be deniable since both openly conservative theorists (Freyre 1986) and leftist ones (Hollanda 2012) lead us to conclude that leftist or conservative positions do not differ considerably when we look at racism in Brazil (Windle 2019).

Language has long served for framing racist ideologies (in which black people are considered languageless, not even able to speak creolized Brazilian Portuguese) and also to be used under racist bias, by which covert and overt racism organize. In colonial times Bantu languages coming from Africa paved internal aspects that corroborate the hypothesis on Pretoguese, the black way to speak Portuguese, although it is not taught at school. This is to say that even under colonial and racist bias, African peoples influenced Brazilian languages towards many directions, including creolizing Portuguese (see Lucchesi 2019, for more on creolization in Brazil), but not performing ways of how to bring black bodies back in language (De Souza 2019).

De Souza (2019) sheds light on how to react as language users, in a response to southern epistemologies and decolonial theories, where bringing bodies back involves re-engaging embodiments lost in colonialism and in current coloniality. Decolonial pedagogies then should face colonial lenses by returning to primary views on modernity that pre-modern peoples used to read modernity. In that way, we are rereading ourselves and rereading modernity in ourselves.

Inevitably, I am attempting to theorize educational contexts where it is believed that one should not see colour as an exclusionary factor, but whereby black people remain underrepresented (Flores and Rosa 2015; Anya 2016). Anya (2016) explores bilingual education among black learners in an international case study where their personhood and speakerism is driven in accordance to their ancestral views on Brazilian Portuguese and blackness in urban scenarios. In doing so, she clarifies that even in the US African American communities, people have not been adequately included in bilingual education policies.

In our case, indigenous communities were targeted by bilingual education after the Portuguese invasion, and Africans were limited to enslaved positions with no schooling opportunities. Contrastively, Bantu languages have been retained in Brazilian Portuguese as an implicit aftermath of how language education ignored Africans in their European acculturation and domestication, at the same time when Africans were a pivotal influence on how Brazilians speak nowadays. Words like Samba, pemba, caçula, bunda and so forth, double-negation sentences like those also existing in African American Vernacular English ('I am not going nowhere') and vowel-centred pronunciation of words that in Portugal are not pronounced with vowels between consonants (e.g., a.di.vogado that in Portugal does not have /i/ after d) are clear examples that Brazilian Portuguese has gained from the huge contributions of Africans who were ignored in language education.

I am not suggesting that we should not develop language teaching for black communities, but that these policies come from the same context where indigenous peoples were educated towards domestication.

Flores and Rosa (2015) offer a great deal on how additive and subtractive approaches contribute to encouraging minoritized communities to replace their language communities if they intend to gain more opportunities. Sociolinguistic approaches that substitute error analysis for appropriateness are also a shared aspect in sociolinguistic studies in Brazil along with what is said to be a pedagogy of variation. Severo and Gorski (2017) remark that sociolinguistic studies (and also the pedagogy of variation) often lack insights brought by studies in the sociology of language. They also lack aspects from fields like anthropological linguistics (Irvine and Gal 2000; Kroskrity 2005) that do not ignore interaction and perception in language formations. Heller (2007) among other scholars provides different methods for how we could connect bilingualism to sociolinguistic approaches more socially.

Irvine and Gal (2000) draw on Michael Silverstein to consider how speakers perceive of languages and how languages are formed into linguistic differentiations and not through structural aspects. Language ideologies (Kroskrity 2005) serve to understand anthropological aspects that link language to their interactional uses and semiotic processes on how we index things around us.

Such accounts highlight how varying factors obscure language ideologies in what I term 'linguistic racism', that is, linguistic and non-linguistic practices and ideologies that make languages exist as a factor for racial inequalities. Furthermore, it also tells us that we cannot go on without questioning southern epistemologies that read the South as unique, homogeneous and fixed.

# Rereading Southern Epistemologies in Black Lived Experiences: The South of the South

Lived experiences (Fanon 2008; Alcoff 2006) are clear examples of how we can read resistance to the modern/colonial/Eurocentric/patriarchal world. Fanon (2008) recuperates colonial experiences of then Antilleans (now Martinicans) to oppose humanism. As globally set, humanism gathers the views on how Europeanness is framed internationally, where the concept of human comes from Europe as the zero-point hubris (Castro-Gómez 2007, 2021). Humanism is not a universal construct, but a local aspect entailed in European experiences that compels every single person in the planet as if he/she would conceive of the same ethnocentric sense of Europeanness based upon liberalism, capitalism and alleged free market. In a sense, it is ignored that early ways to face modernity also continue in some ancestral territories in Africa and in the Americas.

Fanon (2008) points out lived experiences as sociogeny emerging from black peoples in contrast with psychogenesis of white humanism. Humanism sets out a zone of nonbeing:

> There is a zone of nonbeing, an extraordinarily sterile and arid region, an utterly naked declivity where an authentic upheaval can be born. In most cases, the black man lacks the advantage of being able to accomplish this descent into a real hell. (Fanon, 2008: 2)

Worth noting that the opposite of nonbeing, where black people are limited to, is the zone of being, that Grosfoguel (2016) captures thus:

> The people below the line of the human are considered subhuman or non-human; that is, their humanity is questioned and, as such, negated (Fanon, 2008). In the latter case, the extension of rights, material resources and the recognition of their subjectivities, identities, spiritualities and epistemologies are denied. (Grosfoguel 2016: 10)

Lived experiences point to ontologies versus epistemologies, which we depart from or by which we are read, concerning real experiences imposed on us by colonialism. On the other hand, there are scholars who attempt to 'southernize' epistemologies that according to Sousa Santos (2014) shall be explicated through the concept of global lines of abyssal thinking versus ecologies of knowledges:

> Modern western thinking is an abyssal thinking. It consists of a system of visible and invisible distinctions, the invisible ones being the foundation of the visible ones. The invisible distinctions are established through radical lines that divide social reality into two realms, the realm of 'this side of the line' and the realm of 'the other side of the line'. The division is such that 'the other side of the line' vanishes as reality, becomes nonexistent, and is indeed produced as nonexistent. Nonexistent means not existing in any relevant or comprehensible way of being. Whatever is produced as nonexistent is radically excluded because it lies beyond the realm of what the accepted conception of inclusion considers to be its other. What most fundamentally characterizes abyssal thinking is thus the impossibility of the copresence of the two sides of the line. (Sousa Santos, 2014: 189)

Abyssal thinking that divides the world, and regulates the very possibility for emancipatory dimensions, performs global lines that can work only towards downplaying the other in its borders or lines.

In the light of abyssal thinking, epistemicide poses significant lines that prevent consideration of the other as capable of languaging. In our case, we are speaking of others who are blackened[4] and racialized as stemming from centuries of enslavement, and who are multilingual in origin, even though not regarded that way (Makoni and Mashiri 2007; Canagarajah and Liyanage 2012; Makoni and Pennycook 2012). Postabyssal thinking thus is an alternative, but,

> if not actively resisted, abyssal thinking will go on reproducing itself, no matter how exclusionary and destructive the practices to which it gives rise. As I have shown in the previous chapters, political resistance thus needs to be premised upon an epistemological break: there is no global social justice without global cognitive justice. This means that the critical task ahead cannot be limited to generating alternatives. Indeed, it requires an alternative thinking of alternatives. A new postabyssal thinking is thus called for. Is it possible? Are there any conditions that, if adequately valued, might give it a chance? This inquiry explains why I pay special attention to the countermovement I mentioned above as resulting from the shake-up of the abyssal global lines since the 1970s and 1980s. Postabyssal thinking starts from the recognition that social exclusion in its broadest sense takes very different forms according to whether it is determined by an abyssal or a nonabyssal line, as well as that, as long as abyssally defined exclusion persists, no really progressive postcapitalist alternative is possible. (Sousa Santos 2014: 189)

The very problem with the conceptualization of epistemologies of the Global South is that it gives rise to an alternative South that comes true in many Souths indeed. There is no room for such an alternative that does not read critically how white people from the South are not the South before black people.

Epistemologies of the Global South go on focusing primarily on epistemologies, rather than gathering local histories that can situate the global dimensions (Mignolo 2000; De Souza 2011) to re-situate both the South of the Global South and diversities in the southern epistemologies.

Opposing homogeneous views on epistemologies of the Global South do not ignore how we can read abyssal thinking towards fighting epistemicide. Furthermore, abyssal thinking can be reclaimed in terms of the theorizations on the nonbeing zone that Fanon (2008) argues. More broadly, if we connect southern epistemologies to lived experiences we are better able to understand racism, gendered positions and so forth.

I speak from the South of the South where we are stuck in racial dimensions from where we cannot depart because race is not a matter of choice or a position that is organized by chance.

Black lived experiences resist epistemologies that do not ensure that black ontologies matter. As departing from both lived experiences and the South of southern epistemologies, I will now explore culturally relevant pedagogies to push for racially relevant pedagogies.

## Culturally Relevant Pedagogies and Racially Relevant Pedagogies: Why 'Racial'?

Teaching education research in general has handled identity negatively where failure is expected to be present in the autobiographical narratives of black teachers, who generally experience high rates of racial inequality.

As I have been protesting since the beginning of this chapter, we should overcome the idea that racial inequalities allow only homogeneous narratives from where teachers are supposed to narrate themselves. Accordingly, slaves or ex-slaves designed their own identities in multimodal ways, like the rebellions where manifestos were written in both Brazilian Portuguese and Arabic languages that enslaved Africans brought, and artistic and cultural manifestations on which resistance relied and relies. As Guerreiro Ramos (1954) addressed, critical stances in academia have neglected the real lives of black people and have given preference to third-person narratives where black people's lives are told through the eyes of white scholars. In turn, Gates Jr. (1988) returns to how enslaved Africans edited the sense of vernacular language and their bound representations into new ones, where indexed representations may vary from the way the standard language portrays black people and the way it is interpreted by black people as rhetorical figures that unveil the invention around race and language (see Gates Jr., 1988 for more).

It helps me a lot on my way to rethinking anti-racist teaching education. Ladson-Billings (1994) follows the opposite performance of searching for failure in black teachers' professional stories. Since the wake of civil rights in the United States, the post-apartheid contexts urged a divide between culturally relevant teachers and assimilationist teachers, as follows:

Among other factors, Ladson-Billings (1994) makes use of her personal narratives and those from students in black communities where teachers share the same neighbourhood spaces as students and parents, like the church, unlike white teachers who come from outside and do not seem to join the community cultural sites. As she puts it about black teachers:

> I learned that the teachers held conceptions of knowledge that were different from many of their colleagues. For these teachers knowledge was flexible and contestable. Just because something appeared in a textbook they did not feel obligated to accept it. They were careful to search for the warrants that supported curriculum assertions, and they regularly vetted materials by looking for other ways to substantiate claims. (Ladson-Billings, 1994: 10)

TABLE 8.1 Conception of Self and Others by Culturally Relevant Teachers and Assimilationist Teachers. Retrieved and Adapted from Ladson-Billings (1994)

| Culturally Relevant | Assimilationist |
|---|---|
| Teacher sees herself as an artist, teaching as an art. | Teacher sees herself as a technician, teaching as a technical task. |
| Teacher sees herself as part of the community and teaching as giving something back to the community, encourages students to do the same. | Teacher sees herself as an individual who may or may not be a part of the community; she encourages achievement as a means to escape community. |
| Teacher believes all students can succeed. | Teacher believes failure is inevitable for some. |
| Teacher helps students make connections between their community, national and global identities. | Teacher homogenizes students into one 'American' identity. |

White teachers infrequently offer students the possibility to read beyond scholarly reading classes, which she finds as the contrary of new opportunities:

> In second grade my classmates and I all read from the same Dick and Jane basal reader. I was chastised more than once for reading ahead. But during that year I was also chosen to attend a special reading class. Unlike today's remedial reading classes, that class was reserved for accelerated readers. We were a select group of about five or six students and we went to reading class each day for about thirty to forty minutes. There we read 'real' books, not basal textbooks, about faraway places and interesting people. Our teacher was Mrs. Gray, a tall, elegant African American woman who seemed to love children and the idea that she could expose them to new experiences. One Saturday just before Christmas break Mrs. Gray took the class downtown on the subway train to see the dancing fountains and the Christmas display at John Wanamaker's, Philadelphia's landmark department store. I had been in Wanamaker's many times to shop with my mother, but this was the first time I could remember being taken for the express purpose of being entertained. 'Now remember,' admonished Mrs. Gray, 'when we get downtown people will be looking at us. If you misbehave they're not going to say, look at those bad children. They're going to say look at those bad colored children!' She did not have to tell us twice. We knew that we were held to a higher standard than other

people. We knew that people would stare at us and that the stares would come because of our skin color. Despite the 'burden of blackness,' it was a magical visit. I felt special. I felt important. I felt smart! (Ladson-Billings 1994: 34)

Her narratives and her informants' narratives prompt significant reflection in teaching education about how we are dealing with successful African American Education (or Ant-racist education) when we talk to real people, chiefly in black communities. These stories we have in common she terms culturally relevant pedagogies, which analyse how African American educators are dream keepers at the level of protecting black children's dreams.

Others have proposed culturally responsive pedagogies (Gay 2000) and culturally sustaining/revitalizing pedagogies (Paris and Alim 2017; McCarty and Lee 2014) as alternative directions to further culturally relevant pedagogies. Drawing on Django Paris, McCarty and Lee (2014) present that culturally relevant pedagogy

> goes beyond being responsive or relevant to the cultural experiences of minoritized youth in that it 'seeks to perpetuate and foster – to sustain – linguistic, literate, and cultural pluralism as part of the democratic project of schooling'. (McCarty and Lee 2014: 102)

Such accounts prompt me to propose that teaching education should engage in participatory action research (Kemmis 2006), where solutions are not found by chance but co-constructed with teachers' own participation.

Ladson-Billings has shown insistently that we are focused on cataloguing failure instead of successful practices that could teach us even more. As Guerreiro Ramos (1954) observes for how real black stories resist, successful education exists in mostly black communities, including our Brazilian ones.

I am from a small village where most teachers are black, and from whom I have learned so much in terms of primary literacies that taught me about Brazilian history, slavery and colonization, as shown in Figure 8.1.

As targeted in my PhD dissertation, where I collected narratives to understand my life story towards my career as English language professor, teacher educator and applied linguist, I grew up in a poor community where most black students (black people account for most of the total population, as it is in the whole country) get involved in crime due to lack of opportunities. Many of my friends could not enter university via affirmative actions because they died, became pregnant or are either unemployed or employed in poorly paid occupations. Education was thus very important to my life, as its relative absence was to theirs. The fact that I could enter university and they could not shows how racism creates obstacles for most of us, depending on how dark we are.

FIGURE 8.1 *School parade in Banco Central, rural area of Ilhéus-BA. Retrieved from and donated by teacher Vivaci Ferreira's personal archive. Reproduced with the permission of Vivaci Ferreira.*

Schooling practices of black teachers worked to help me perceive of education as a chance to leave the non-human conditions (Fanon 2008) chasing after me back then. School parades (*gincanas,* theatre performances and so on) arising from games all the community dwellers could participate in influenced the journey I took to write and think of myself as an intellectual. My first poems symbolize how these moments were very particular to the way I came to pursue a career in teaching education and as a writer.

Returning to my autoethnographical narratives, I heard primarily black teachers speaking about my experiences as a black student from that community, which have significantly helped my life story towards my career.

One of the participants, Cintia (pseudonym), was the first and only black principal I had in life that moved to Banco Central, unlike several teachers who do not recognize that community as their own. Ladson-Billings (1994) assumes these familiar connections with territory occur in general among black teachers and can be catalogued as culturally relevant pedagogies.

In my notes on Cintia's narratives in conversation, I point out that

> Cintia's sensitiveness, Gabriel reflects while Cintia speaks, made him and more children eat a more robust merenda (snacks distributed by governments at schools) at a time when we underwent hunger. (Adapted from Nascimento, 2020)

On a day when I proposed an internal newspaper when I was around six years old, she took the chance – even under predictable impossibilities that precariousness compelled for our lives – to say yes and open the secretary's room for me to write using the typing machine.

Culturally relevant pedagogies led me to propose racially relevant pedagogies to rethink both the interplay of language education, language and racism, and culturally relevant pedagogies, especially in Brazil from where I speak. I decided to replace 'culturally' with 'racially' because 'culturally' has been used in literature to give less importance to racism in Brazil. Whereas racism has cultural origins that have been used to discriminate, 'cultural' is also used as a way to accommodate the understanding that racism is in culture and therefore we must tolerate it or get adapted to it.

Racially relevant pedagogies do not differ consistently from culturally relevant pedagogies, but they attribute value to 'racially' to confront racist ideologies and racist formations in Brazil as inspired by what I myself did with linguistic racism, which differs from the context of the Global North where language ideologies seem to speak globally, whereas I am always analysing locally.

## Conclusion

In sum, I see emerging connections between language education, language and racism, southern epistemologies and racially relevant pedagogies in my work: First, as a teacher educator whose work derives from epistemologies arising from my own ontology as a black teacher of black students.

Second, as I do not see the Global South homogeneously, the data I collected show it to be possible that teachers might at the same time ignore or act before humanism, modernity and the abyssal lines by which they are divided. If contrasted with the zone of nonbeing that black people live in, black teachers urge potential pedagogies from their bodies that are not regarded as pedagogies by the academic curriculum.

My own experiences work to provide my analysis with how my teachers embodied culturally relevant pedagogies and were very influential for the way I followed opportunities in life.

The core values of racially relevant pedagogies attempt to recuperate the body stolen by coloniality (De Souza 2019), but also to go ahead by marking the unmarked in language, like whiteness, racism and suchlike.

Future developments will then be responsible for demonstrating how black teachers in language education in Brazil also have attitudes towards racism in Brazil that, whether catalogued or not, have groundbreaking lessons for us.

## Notes

1. This chapter is supported by The National Council for Scientific and Technological Development (CNPq) and developed in the Language and Racism Network, Federal University of Southern Bahia, Brazil.
2. We shall criticize concepts on literacies that embrace literacy from the scholarly positions in educational contexts. Blommaert (2008) offers a great deal to this question by using the ethnography of texts to urge grassroots literacies.
3. Henry Louis Gates' visit to Brazilian black communities is shown in Episode 2 of his "Black in Latin America", a four-part series on the influence of African descent on Latin America that premiered on PBS in 2011. For more information see https://www.pbs.org/wnet/black-in-latin-america/.
4. As I am putting forward, I do not consider black people are black in origin. Blackened, in accordance with Fanon (2008), means that blackening is a process in which Black people are tied by racism.

## References

Alcoff, L. M. (2006), *Visible Identities: Race, Gender, and the Self*, New York: Oxford University Press.
Anya, U. (2016), *Racialized Identities in Second Language Learning: Speaking Blackness in Brazil*, New York: Routledge.
Blommaert, J. (2008), *Grassroots Literacy: Writing, Identity and Voice in Central Africa*, London: Routledge.
Bonilla-Silva, E. (2021), 'What Makes Systemic Racism Systemic?', *Sociological Inquiry*, 91: 513–33.
Canagarajah, S., and I. Liyanage. (2012), 'Lessons from Pre-Colonial Multilingualism', in A. Blackledge and A. Creese (eds.), *The Routledge Handbook of Multilingualism*, 49–65, London: Routledge.
Castro-Gómez, S. (2007), 'Descolonizar la universidad: La hybris del punto cero y el dialogo de saberes', in S. Castro-Gómez and R. Grosfoguel (eds.), *El giro decolonial: Reflexiones para una diversidad epistémica más allá del capitalismo global*, 79–91, Bogotá: Siglo del Hombre Editores.
Castro-Gómez, S. (2021), *Zero-Point Hubris: Science, Race, and Enlightenment in Eighteenth-Century Latin America* (*Reinventing Critical Theory*), Lanham, MD: Rowman & Littlefield Publishers.
De Souza, L. M. T. M. (2011), 'Engaging the Global by Re-Situating the Local: (Dis)locating the Literate Global Subject and His View from Nowhere', in V. de Oliveira Andreotti and L. M. T. M. De Souza (eds.), *Postcolonial Perspectives on Global Citizenship Education*, 68–86, London: Routledge.
De Souza, L. T. M. (2019), 'Introduction and Decolonial Pedagogies, Multilingualism and Literacies', *Multilingual Margins*, 6: 1–15.
Fanon, F. (2008), *Black Skin, White Masks*, London: PlutoPress.
Ferreira, A. J. (2002), 'In-Service Teacher Educators and the Developing of Critical Teaching: Cultural Plurality – "Race" and Ethnicity in ELT Education in

Brazil', *Educate – The London Journal of Doctoral Research in Education*, 1: 1–86.
Ferreira, A. J. (2007), 'What Has Race/Ethnicity Got to Do With EFL Teaching?', *Linguagem & Ensino*, 10: 211–33.
Ferreira, A. J. (2015), 'Autobiographical Narratives of Race and Racism in Brazil: Critical Race Theory and Language Education', *Muitas Vozes*, 4: 79–100.
Ferreira, A. J. (2019), 'Social Identities of Black Females in English Language Textbooks Used in Brazil and Cameroon: Intersectionalities of Race, Gender, Social Class and Critical Racial Literacy', *REVISTA*, X (4): 20–40.
Ferreira, A. J., and M. Camargo. (2014), 'Racismo Cordial no Livro de Língua Inglesa Aprovado pelo PNLD', *Revista da Associação Brasileira de Pesquisadores(as) Negros(as) – ABPN*, 6: 177–202.
Flores, N., and J. Rosa. (2015), 'Undoing Appropriateness: Raciolinguistic Ideologies and Language Diversity in Education', *Harvard Educational Review*, 85 (2): 149–71.
Freyre, G. (1986), *The Masters and the Slaves: A Study in the Development of Brazilian Civilization*, Berkeley, CA: University of California Press.
García, O. (2009), *Bilingual Education in the 21st Century: A Global Perspective*, Oxford: Wiley-Blackwell.
Gates Jr., H. L. (1988), *The Signifying Monkey: A Theory of African-American Literary Criticism*, Oxford: Oxford University Press.
Gay, G. (2000), *Culturally Responsive Teaching: Theory Research and Practice*, New York: Teachers College Press.
Grosfoguel, R. (2016), 'What is Racism?', *Journal of World-System Research*, 22 (1): 9–15.
Guerreiro Ramos, A. (1954), 'O problema do negro na sociologia brasileira', *Cadernos do Nosso Tempo*, 2 (2): 189–220.
Heller, M. (2007), *Bilingualism: A Social Approach*, Basingstoke: Palgrave Macmillan.
Hollanda, S. B. (2012), *Roots of Brazil*. Notre Dame, IN: University of Notre Dame Press.
Irvine, J. T., and S. Gal. (2000), 'Language Ideology and Linguistic Differentiation', in P.V. Kroskrity (ed.), *Regimes of Language: Ideologies, Polities, and Identities*, 35–84, Santa Fe, NM: School of American Research Press.
Kemmis, S. (2006), 'Participatory Action Research and the Public Sphere', *Educational Action Research*, 14 (4): 459–76.
Kroskrity, P. V. (2005), 'Language Ideologies', in A. Duranti (ed.), *A Companion to Linguistic Anthropology*, 496–517. Malden, MA: Blackwell Publishing.
Kubota, R., and A. Lin. (2006), 'Race and TESOL: Introduction to Concepts and Theories', *TESOL Quarterly*, 40 (3): 471–93.
Ladson-Billings, G. (1994), *The Dreamkeepers: Successful Teachers of African American Children* (2nd ed.), San Francisco, CA: Jossey Bass.
Lucchesi, D. (2019), 'Language Contact in Brazil and the Genesis of Creole Languages', *Journal of Ibero-Romance Creoles*, 9 (1): 334–57.
Makoni, S., and P. Mashiri. (2007) 'Critical Historiography: Does Language Planning in Africa Need a Construct of Language as Part of Its Theoretical Apparatus?', in S. Makoni and A. Pennycook (eds.), *Disinventing and Reconstituting Languages*, 62–89, Clevedon: Multilingual Matters.
Makoni, S., and A. Pennycook. (2012), 'Disinventing Multilingualism: From Monological Multilingualism to Multilingua Francas', in A. Blackledge and A.

Creese (eds.), *The Routledge Handbook of Multilingualism*, 439–53, London: Routledge.

McCarty, T. L., and T. S. Lee. (2014), 'Critical Culturally Sustaining/Revitalizing Pedagogy and Indigenous Education Sovereignty', *Harvard Educational Review*, 84 (1): 101–24.

Mignolo, W. (2000), *Local Histories/Global Designs*. Chichester: Princeton University Press.

Paris, D., and H. S. Alim. (2017), 'What is Culturally Sustaining Pedagogy and Why Does it Matter?', in D. Paris and H. S. Alim (eds.), *Culturally Sustaining Pedagogies: Teaching and Learning for Justice in a Changing World*, 1–24, New York: Teachers College Press.

Severo, C. G., and E. Gorski. (2017), 'On the Relation between the Sociology of Language and Sociolinguistics: Fishman's Legacy in Brazil', *International Journal of the Sociology of Language*, 243: 119–32.

Sousa Santos, B. de. (2014), *Epistemologies of the South: Justice against Epistemicide*, Boulder, CO: Paradigm Publishers.

Telles, E. (2014), *Pigmentocracies: Ethnicity, Race, and Color in Latin America*, Chapel Hill, NC: The University of North Carolina Press.

Windle, J. (2019), 'Neoliberalism, Imperialism and Conservatism: Tangled Logics of Educational Inequality in the Global South', *Discourse-Studies in the Cultural Politics of Education*, 40 (2): 1–12.

# Part IV
# Textbook Discourses

# CHAPTER 9

# The First Encounter

# Representations of Gender and LGBTQ+ in Textbooks for Learners of Dutch and Swedish as a Foreign Language

*Josef Wikström and Juul Wolters*

## Introduction

The question of representation of historically oppressed or marginalized groups in textbooks in foreign languages has received increased attention during recent years. Scholars have investigated topics such as minorities in Russian textbooks (Azimova and Johnston 2012), diversity in university reading lists (Schucan Bird and Pitman 2019), gender roles in Japanese EFL textbooks (Lee 2014) and representations of historically marginalized groups in textbooks in the United States of America (Brandle 2020). What is common for all of these studies is the idea, brought forward by discourse analysts such as Fairclough (1992), that what we say about the world, and how we describe it, is essential for how we give meaning to the very same world later on (Winter Jörgensen and Philips 2000: 11). The way the world is described might have an even higher importance when it comes to textbooks in foreign languages. As Azimova and Johnston (2012: 337) point out, in some cases this is the only contact with the language's culture the students have.

The objects of this study are the representations of gender and sexual orientations in textbooks in two relatively minor Germanic languages, Dutch and Swedish. The Dutch language has approximately twenty-four million speakers and is the official language in six countries (the Netherlands, Belgium, Suriname, Aruba, Curaçao and Sint-Maarten). Around 414,000 learners around the globe are learning Dutch as a foreign language (Feiten and cijfers - Taalunie 2020). Swedish is taught at around 225 universities and studied by approximately 18,000 students outside of Sweden (Svenska institutet 2017) and spoken by approximately ten million people (Institutet för språk och folkminnen 2020). The countries in which the majority of the speakers live (the Netherlands, Belgium, Sweden and Finland) are considered some of the most equal and progressive when it comes to gender and LGBTQ+[1] rights (United Nations Development Programme 2020). We choose to use the term LGBTQ+ to keep uniformity in the article.

The questions to be investigated are therefore how the quantitative and qualitative representations of gender and LGBTQ+ appear in the analysed textbooks in Dutch and Swedish as a foreign language, how the textbooks position themselves in accordance with what is currently discussed about gender and LGBTQ+ in the countries in which the languages are spoken and how we can understand the textbooks when comparing them to the different strategies for working against oppression. In the discussion we will suggest a few ways of how to incorporate a more LGBTQ+ friendly approach in relation to what our study has shown.

## Theoretical Framework

The theoretical basis for this investigation is the idea brought forward by critical discourse analysis, that how the world is portrayed will also help constitute the meaning of the world itself. What we consider to be meaningful is a result of social practices, not an absolute truth existing outside of the symbols created by us (Winter Jörgensen and Philips 2000: 11f). Central to our study are also the ideas brought forward by Paulo Freire (2000) in his *Pedagogy of the Oppressed*, first published in 1968, of the importance of questioning the current norms in order to change the world towards being more open, equal and inclusive.

In our study we have chosen to use Kevin Kumashiro's (2002) theory of anti-oppressive education as presented in *Troubling Education: Queer Activism and Anti-oppressive Pedagogy*. In his book Kumashiro presents four different approaches to working with oppression in society, each of them dealing with two questions: How are the dynamics of oppression understood and how does this affect how we work against it? Kumashiro identifies four different ways of understanding, and subsequently working against, oppression in education currently in use. These will be presented briefly in what follows.

*Education for the Other* understands oppression as something bad and harmful that happens to the Other, and in order to work against oppression the school needs to provide places and resources which can be helpful in case something happens. The general idea is that not all students are equal, and that the school should acknowledge this instead of pretending every student is the same. Kumashiro identifies several problems with this approach, one being that oppression is not only about the oppressed, but also about the privileged. By focusing on the Other, the Other is portrayed as the problem. 'By focusing on the negative experiences of the Other, this approach implies that the Other is the problem: without the Other, schools would not be oppressing anyone' (Kumashiro 2002: 37). Furthermore, in order to address the Other, the Other needs to be defined, something which is not an easy task since several different groups are oppressed in society. The question raised is how educators can ensure everyone is included.

*Education about the Other* understands oppression as oppressive knowledge. This means that the student only gets to know about what society defines as normative, or that the information about the Other is misleading and shown via stereotypes or myths. The way schools work against this type of oppression is by adding specific units or chapters in textbooks about the Other. Even though this is an improvement if we consider that all students are addressed via this approach, the Other is still only seen as an expert on being the Other, something added to the 'real' story, and Kumashiro writes that this approach runs the risk of reinforcing the social, cultural and intellectual space and division between the Other and the norm.

*Education critical of privileging and othering* is characterized by an understanding that it is equally important to understand why certain groups are privileged, as it is to understand why certain groups are Othered. Hence, this approach focuses on the structures in place in society which allow a division between groups to happen in the first place, and how these structures are legitimized and maintained. The idea is that oppression in society will be changed if the students don't just have knowledge about Othered groups, but are also in possession of critical thinking skills to understand why these divisions appear in the first place. The students will be empowered to challenge oppression. The critique brought forward by Kumashiro is that by referring to the structure, it is implied that oppression has the same effect on everybody. This is not necessarily the case.

*Education that changes students and society* is meant to address that need to look, not only for structures in general, but also in each discourse. Kumashiro says that it is necessary to understand that in certain discourses the power balance between groups can change, and that oppression therefore must be understood according to the context in which it occurs.

## Representation in Language Teaching Textbooks

As this investigation sets out to investigate gender and LGBTQ+ representations in textbooks in Dutch and Swedish as a foreign language, we find ourselves working with two topics often used within discourse theory in practice: how the image of a nation and a specific gender is constructed. Although textbooks of foreign languages primarily deal with the language in question itself, it is impossible to think of a textbook of a foreign language leaving out descriptions of the culture and values belonging to the nation(s) in which the language is spoken. Anthony D. Smith in his *National Identity* (1991: 11) writes that the Western or 'civic' model of a nation includes a common culture and a 'civic' ideology. A textbook of a foreign language is normally full with references to such a common culture. It can be seen in a more formal way in specific chapters about important historical events in the country's history, but it can also be 'hidden'. Jackie F. K. Lee (2014) in his investigation of gender representation in Japanese EFL textbooks writes that 'the difference between the formal curriculum and the hidden curriculum is that while the former specifies openly what students are intended to learn, the latter involves that which is not openly intended but which students learn regardless' (Lee 2014: 40). Furthermore, the hidden curriculum can be divided into two subcategories, the intended and the unintended (Lee 2014: 40). In short, a text is always a manifestation of its origin, intended or unintended. The question of different representations of gender and sexual orientations has received increased attention during the last few years, as has been mentioned above. However, when it comes to Dutch and Swedish as foreign languages, there's still a gap to fill. For Dutch, Koster and Litosseliti (2021) have contributed greatly to a better knowledge of representations of gender and professions and gender and LGBTQ+ constellations in chapters about families in Dutch as a foreign language. However, with a focus on representations of LGBTQ+ only in the chapters explicitly dealing with family constellations comes a risk of what we, using Kumashiro's theory, could call education about the Other. Although representations of LGBTQ+ might be present in chapters about families, they might be invisible in other representations of society (political, scientific, historical, etc.). As for Sweden, Bromseth and Darj (2010) in their book *Normkritisk pedagogik: Makt, lärande och strategier för förändring* explain different strategies on how to work with critical education, and several scholars such as Evertsson et al. (2009); Bron-Wojciechowska (1995); de Boise (2017) have focused on gender and higher education in Sweden. However, we have yet to come across texts with a focus on the actual material used for classes in Swedish as a foreign language. Other scholars have written about the importance of creating a safe learning environment, not only to generate positive effects in the general well-being of the students, but also to achieve better academic results (Batchelor et al. 2018; Page 2017). Snapp et al. (2015) show that students themselves have highlighted the positive effects when including representations of LGBTQ+ in the curriculum. Thus, the educators are important since they can ensure that such representations are included and prioritize the creation of a safe learning environment.

## Gender and LGBTQ+ in the Netherlands and Belgium[2]

In 2001, the Netherlands became the first country in the world in which same-sex marriage was allowed. Same-sex partnership has been legal since 1998 (Ministerie van Onderwijs, Cultuur en Wetenschap 2021a). In 2003, Belgium became the second country in the world to allow same-sex marriages (Senate, n.d.). Current focus areas are women and LGBTQ+ persons both in the Netherlands (Ministerie van Onderwijs, Cultuur en Wetenschap 2021b) and in Flanders (Gelijke Kansen in Vlaanderen (Equal Opportunities in Flanders 2010)). According to the Human Development Report from 2020, Belgium and the Netherlands were ranked in the fourth place when it comes to gender equality (United Nations Development Programme 2020). Thus, it is safe to say that equality and LGBTQ+ rights are prioritized questions for both the Flemish and the Dutch governments. Although LGBTQ+ persons still face difficulties, Kuyper (2018) writes that the general attitude towards gays and bisexuals has improved since 1960 (Sociaal en Cultureel planbureau) (2018: 8–23). Kuyper also writes that the positive attitude has increased in all layers of society (2018: 15–18). The article shows that in 2016, the countries with the most positive general attitudes towards homosexuality were Iceland followed by the Netherlands, Sweden, Norway and Belgium (Kuyper 2018: 25–6).

## Conflictive Grounds – The Gender-Neutral Hen and a Third Non-Binary Gender

In the last few years, the use of the gender-neutral pronoun *hen* has increased, as an alternative to the female *zij* (she) and the male *hij* (he). After an online survey organized by the Transgender Network in the Netherlands in 2016, the gender-neutral pronoun *hen*, and its corresponding possessive pronoun *hun*, were chosen as the gender-neutral pronouns with most support among the public (Transgender Netwerk Nederland 2016). These pronouns work the same way as the English pronouns 'they' and 'them', also sometimes used as a gender-neutral version of he/she or him/her. Doubts have been raised about the possibility of *hen* to be normalized in everyday language, mostly on the basis of how difficult it is to introduce a new pronoun. The Dutch linguist Marc van Oostendorp compared the introduction of the gender-neutral *hen* in Dutch to the process in Sweden (explained later), arguing that *hen* is too different from *zij* and *hij*, while in Sweden the use of *hen* is facilitated by the similarity in pronunciation to the already existing gendered pronouns *han* and *hon* (Becker 2020). Although voices have been raised in favour of *hen* as a gender-neutral pronoun (Expreszo 2021), others have suggested *die* as another option, or simply an increased use of proper names as another way to avoid gendered pronouns (Becker 2020).

### *Third Non-binary Gender*

Since 1985 it's been possible for persons to change their birth certificate only once from male to female or vice versa according to the transgender law of 1985. In 2014 a new transgender law was accepted which allowed the possibility to report the conviction of belonging to the opposite sex to the registrar of civil status based on the submission of an expert's statement. This means that the registrar can add an addition to the original birth certificate showing the change of legal sex once the conditions have been met (Rijksoverheid 2020). In Belgium it has been possible to change sex and first name since 1 January 2018 (Ministerie van Justitie en Veiligheid 2021). Under existing legislation, it is necessary to go to court in order to change an intersex or non-binary person's sex into a neutral one (X).

## Gender and LGBTQ+ in Sweden[3]

Sweden has a good reputation when it comes to gender equality and LGBTQ+ rights. In the UN's Human Development Report 2020, Sweden found itself in the seventh position overall when comparing factors such as gender development and gender inequality (United Nations Development Programme 2020). Sweden's previous government, before the elections in 2022, declared itself as a feminist government (Socialdepartementet 2016) with a special focus on gender equality. As for LGBTQ+ rights, there's an action plan from 2021 (Regeringskansliet 2021), which explains the areas of focus in the forthcoming years. Same-sex partnership has been legal since 1995, in 2003 same-sex partners were allowed as adoptive parents and in 2009 the laws concerning marriage were made gender-neutral (Arbetsmarknadsdepartementet 2018). This, of course, does not mean that everything is ideal. Socialdepartementet (2016: 65) says there are still inequalities between the genders, both horizontally and vertically. The inequalities can be seen both in the fact that women and men work and are active in separate areas in society and in that when both men and women work in the same sector, men occupy the higher positions (Socialdepartementet 2016). During the last couple of years several discussions have arisen in Sweden regarding both gender equality and attitudes towards people with a different sexual orientation than the norm.

We will briefly mention two – the gender-neutral pronoun *hen* and the political discussion regarding legal recognition of non-binary gender.

## *The Gender-Neutral Hen*

The gender-neutral pronoun *hen* was introduced in 2012 and received many negative reactions. It was introduced as a gender-neutral alternative to the already existing *han* ('he' in English) and *hon* ('she' in English). It can be used either as a generic pronoun when the subject is unknown or irrelevant, or as a transgender pronoun, for persons who do not identify themselves as either man or woman. Gustafsson Sendén et al. (2015) investigated the attitudes towards the new pronoun between 2012 and 2014, and found that the negative attitudes expressed by the majority in 2012, had in 2014 significantly shifted to a more positive attitude. Since 2015, *hen* has been recognized and added to SAOL, the Swedish Academy Glossary (Gustafsson Sendén et al. 2015).

## *A Third Non-binary Gender*

In 2020 the Swedish Federation for Lesbian, Gay, Bisexual, Transgender, Queer and Intersex Rights (RFSL) published a debate article in the Swedish newspaper Svenska Dagbladet in which they argued that the Swedish government should introduce a legal third sex (Svenska Dagbladet 2020). A state inquiry from 2017 about the transgender people's situation in Sweden suggested that this proposal should be investigated (*Regeringskansliet* 2017). However, the prevailing idea up until today seems to be the one expressed in *Makt, mål och myndighet: feministisk politik för en jämställd framtid* from 2016, saying that although the Swedish government understands the problem with binary sexes, the division is needed in order to understand the differences in society in order to make society more equal (Socialdepartemenetet 2016: 66).

Bromseth (2010: 30–32) writes that equality between sexes can now be seen as standard in Sweden. Traditional gender roles stating that women should take care of children and men should focus on their careers are no longer prevailing attitudes in Sweden. When it comes to sexual orientation, however, Bromseth writes that even if sexual morality and pathologization are no longer common in the schools in Sweden, heterosexuality still constitutes the norm in that it is seen as the 'natural' and the 'best' sexual orientation.

# Material and Method

The investigated textbooks in Swedish are *Rivstart A1 + A2*,[4] *Rivstart B1 + B2*[5] and *Språkporten 123*.[6] All three of the investigated textbooks are popular both among teachers working in Sweden teaching foreign students, and at foreign universities and language schools teaching Swedish. Språkporten 123 is also used in Swedish upper secondary schools for the nationwide courses in Swedish as a secondary language, and for students with another mother tongue than Swedish. The investigated textbooks are all of the second edition, with Språkporten 123 being the older one, from 2012. Rivstart A1 + A2 was published in 2014 and Rivstart B1 + B2 in 2015. Complementary material such as workbooks and teacher manuals was not included in the study. As for Dutch, the textbook series *Methode Nederlands voor hoogopgeleiden anderstaligen* was chosen. The series focuses on highly educated foreigners and is used both in courses of Dutch as a second language in the Netherlands and in courses of Dutch as a foreign language abroad. The series consists of four textbooks, from absolute beginners to level C1 according to the Common European Framework of Reference for Languages (CEFR).

The titles of the books are *Nederlands in gang* (A1 until A2),[7] published in 2010, *Nederlands in actie* (From A2 until B1)[8] from 2015, *Nederlands op niveau* (from B1 until B2)[9] from 2015 and *Nederlands naar perfectie* (from B2 until C1)[10] from 2015.

The study consists of two parts – one quantitative and one qualitative. We began by counting each reference to any male, female or gender-neutral representation. For male and female representations, we looked for words in the following categories: (i) personal pronouns (such as 'she', 'her' or 'his'); (ii) names of family members (such as 'father', 'mother'); (iii) proper names (such as 'Benjamin' or 'Alicia') and (iv) representations in images. As for gender-neutral representations, we looked for (i) gender-neutral pronouns (*hen* in Swedish and Dutch) and (ii) gender-neutral proper names (such as 'Kim' and 'Robin'). We also counted each representation of any romantic or sexual relationship, and noted whether this relationship was heterosexual, queer or ambiguous. An example of an ambiguous relationship could be when someone refers to his or her husband, but we don't know the gender of the speaker itself.

After the initial counting was done, we analysed how these representations could be understood by using discourse analysis. Which are the underlying images we get from the different representations of men, women, non-binary, heterosexual relationships and queer relationships, and how do they relate to the current state of affairs in the languages' countries? Do these representations help us to 'read against common sense' (Kumashiro 2002: 62) or do they consolidate the current norms?

# Findings and Analysis

## *Dutch Textbooks*

### Women, Men and Non-binary

As seen in Table 9.1, there are more occurrences of male representation in the analysed textbooks. The higher the level of the language, the bigger the

**TABLE 9.1** Representation in the Dutch Textbooks

| Title | Women | Men | Non-binary | LGBTQ+ | Hetero | Neutral and/or ambiguous |
|---|---|---|---|---|---|---|
| Nederlands in gang – from A1 until A2 | 493 | 524 | 3 | 0 | 17 | 7 |
| Nederlands in actie – from A2 until B1 | 514 | 587 | 0 | 1 | 22 | 32 |
| Nederlands op niveau – from B1 until B2 | 435 | 750 | 5 | 7 | 10 | 8 |
| Nederlands naar perfectie – from B2 until C1 | 392 | 712 | 3 | 2 | 10 | 8 |
| **Total** | **1834** | **2573** | **11** | **10** | **59** | **55** |

difference between the amount of representations of women and men. The content in the textbooks goes from practical and concrete, for example, speaking about your family, going to the market, visiting the doctor and so forth, to more abstract content in the textbooks aimed at students at a higher language level. From having been almost even when it comes to male and female representations, starting from B1 there is a remarkable predominance of male representations. One of the chapters in the B1–B2 textbook, titled 'Progressive' describes the division of domestic tasks, stereotypes and role models between women and men in a family. With this chapter comes a set of topics to discuss in the classroom, all dealing with gender stereotypes. Of the historical persons mentioned in the textbooks the majority are men. Although the number of occurrences of male and female representations differ, the analysed textbooks avoid stereotypical representations of men and women, such as men as the working gender and women as more often being associated with good looks and suchlike. The analysed textbooks show almost a total absence of representations of non-binary. There is no mention of the gender-neutral pronouns *hen* and *hun*. The occurrences of non-binary representations are limited to names which can be used both for men and women, such as 'Luca', 'Robin' and 'Dominique'. There is some ambiguous mentioning with references such as *partner* (partner) and *iemand* and *niemand* (somebody and nobody).

## *LGBTQ+ and Heterosexual Relationships*

The way the Dutch and Belgian societies are ranked and how they present themselves as progressive and supportive in terms of gender and LGBTQ+

equality and emancipation is not transferred to the analysed textbooks. When comparing the textbooks with Kumashiro's theory of different approaches to understand and work against oppression, the books can be said to place themselves somewhere between 'Education for the Other' and 'Education about the Other', in that they contain very few examples of any sexual orientation different from the norm, and when any example is mentioned, it lacks any acknowledgement of the structures in society upholding the norms. In the quiz question about Gay Pride we can see that students have to guess what Gay Pride is. This is the first mention about Gay Pride in all the books, so the students need to have gained this information elsewhere. The example is problematic also because the 'correct' answer to the quiz question is that gay men, on this day, can be themselves without discrimination. This implies that they can't be themselves on other days, and furthermore fails to include lesbian women, bisexuals, transgendered and other LGBTQ+ persons. There is hardly any information about the relationship structures in the Dutch society and about how to think critically about how a sexual norm is upheld and maintained. The only approach that comes close to 'Education about the Other' is the writing exercise in which one of the alternatives for topics to write about is a male homosexual couple's right to become parents through adoption. It is still an interesting exercise given that the students have to think about gender and LGBTQ+ rights and learn that gay marriage is accepted in the Netherlands, but some critical questions can be raised. First of all, it forms part of an exercise in which the students can choose between four different topics. This means that the topic may not be used at all. In the case that the teacher doesn't want to give the topic any attention, it could disappear as a potential subject for discussion. Furthermore, there is no mention of lesbian couples or other LGBTQ+-couples. In this way the book excludes the question of lesbian couples adopting, which is also accepted and has been legal since 2001, just like gay marriages. The only lesbian representation itself is Maartje Wortel, who falls in love with a girl. This is an example of normalizing same-sex relationships, but does little to clarify the laws regarding LGBTQ+ rights in Dutch society.

## *Swedish Textbooks*

### Men, Women and Non-binary

In all of the three analysed textbooks, the occurrences of male representations are more than the female representations, although it is quite even, especially in the Rivstart series. Common for all the textbooks in this study is that they all understand gender as being either a man or a woman. Any other representation is not explicitly expressed in the books. This is true but for one exception – a chapter about the criminal Lars 'Lasse-Maja' Molin, in which he is described with the gender-neutral *hen*. In this chapter, the gender-neutral pronoun *hen* is also used when referring to people in general. This can be seen also when the textbooks present statistics about the Swedish way of life. The statistics are often divided between what men and women answered and any third category is not an option. By doing so the textbooks follow the current state of affairs in Sweden, as they recognize the problem of a binary gender division, while at the same time they continue to use it. In this aspect the textbooks can be said to continue the questioning of the 'Other', in that it is seen as something additional to the existing norm. When referring to people in general the books use the Swedish word *man*, which could be replaced by *en* in order to avoid taking the male gender as the general gender. Having said this, it is notable how, in the Rivstart series, men and women are constantly given non-stereotypical roles when it comes to professions and family roles. Women are given stereotypical male professions, such as working as a chef, a doctor, a web designer, a lawyer or an engineer, while men are given more or less stereotypical female professions, such as a hairdresser, a flight attendant or a waiter. We read about a female microbiologist who works too much to be able to cook food at home and pick up her kids from the kindergarten, something her husband, who works as a translator, does. Språkporten 123 is the textbook with the highest inequality between the genders, and it is also the book that does less to question the stereotypical male and female roles. The student can read about Princess Diana, the Mona Lisa and the 'Swedish woman', and although the expressed objective seems to be to question the 'myth' surrounding these topics, the texts discuss the different theories and ideas which are part of the myth, more than they question how they came to be a myth in the first place. The reader of the text 'the Swedish woman', for example, doesn't get to hear from Swedish women and how they feel about the myth, but, rather, from a male author explaining why the myth isn't true, and how it is not a sexual invitation when a Swedish woman looks a stranger in the eye. The problem doesn't seem to be that there's a myth about 'the Swedish woman', but that what is said within the notion of the myth is incorrect.

## *LGBTQ+ and Heterosexual Relationships*

When it comes to the amount of explicit representations of heterosexual relationships versus explicit representations of gay relationships, all three of the Swedish textbooks had in common that heterosexual relationships were predominant. Out of all explicit relationships, the LGBTQ+ relationships occupied 6 per cent, 10 per cent and 11 per cent in the textbooks. Out of the total of twenty-six representations of gay relationships, nineteen of these occurrences were found in chapters explicitly talking about typical versus atypical families in Sweden. However, it is worth mentioning that especially in

TABLE 9.2 Representation in the Swedish Textbooks

| Title | Women | Men | Non-binary | LGBTQ+ | Hetero | Neutral ambiguous |
|---|---|---|---|---|---|---|
| Rivstart A1 + A2 | 847 | 872 | 3 | 3 | 33 | 18 |
| Rivstart B1 + B2 | 920 | 1017 | 65 | 9 | 50 | 28 |
| Språkporten 123 | 1483 | 1993 | 0 | 14 | 61 | 57 |
| Total | 3250 | 3882 | 68 | 26 | 144 | 103 |

Rivstart A1 + A2, the few existing representations are often uncommented. In the first chapter the textbook deals with how to present yourself, and among other topics such as name, profession and origin, we also learn how to describe our relationship status. The specific words for presenting oneself as single, in a relationship, married and so on are accompanied by a section informing the learner that same-sex marriages have been allowed in Sweden since 2009. In the same chapter we learn that Agnes has a girlfriend who's currently living in the United States of America. In the following chapter, when dealing with different pronouns in Swedish, we learn that Bengt and Kenneth are married, and in chapter 8 when talking about the grammatical construction of the present perfect tense we learn that a woman once tried parachuting since her girlfriend gave her the adventure as a birthday gift. In general, LGBTQ+ representations are portrayed as something very uncomplicated, but there are, as previously mentioned, only three occurrences.

Rivstart B1–B2 has a more historical approach, and the reader learns about Swedish history and historical persons, such as the homosexual painter Eugène Jansson and the Swedish criminal Lars Molin from the nineteenth century, famous for dressing up in women's clothes. The chapter is also the only one in which the gender-neutral pronoun *hen* is used. The other occurrences of LGBTQ+ representations are found in a chapter about typical Friday evenings in Sweden, in which a lesbian couple talk about their habits together with their kids, and a section about different types of families, including the so-called *regnbågsfamiljen* (LGBTQ+ parenting). Worth mentioning is the chapter about the history of Sweden, in which both the fight for gender equality and the gay movement are mentioned, not as a separate section of the chapter, but together with other events divided by the decade in which they happened. This makes the feminist and gay movement an integrated part of the history of Sweden, although the role of the privileged heterosexual community is left uncommented.

Språkporten is the textbook with the most opportunity to discuss themes such as oppression and privileges in that it is aimed at language learners at the C1–C2 level. The chapters are a mix of texts written specifically for this textbook and excerpts from texts written in other media, such as newspaper articles and novels. In Språkporten, however, there's only one single occurrence of a non-heterosexual relationship to be found outside of the specific chapter about families in Sweden – a short remark on how Leonardo da Vinci's possible homosexuality has been debated. The other occurrences are all found in the chapter about the Swedish family, in which the student is informed about the gender-neutral marriage law and homosexual families. The chapter mentions that it used to be a criminal offence to be openly gay in Sweden, and that children in families with same-sex parents according to studies do not differ in terms of development when compared to children in heterosexual families.

## Discussion

Although some attempts can be found in the textbooks, it is not possible to say that the textbooks actively question the structures allowing the 'othering' to happen. They never manage to question (heterosexual) male privileges, although they to some degree manage to incorporate gender equality, and to a lower degree, LGBTQ+ as an integrated part of Swedish and Dutch societies. The ambiguous/neutral relationships in the textbooks could serve as an entrance to discussions and critical thinking about relationships and the meaning of LGBTQ+ in these countries, although it is left to the educator to incorporate this in the classroom. Besides textbooks, which have the potential to give a more inclusive representation of the society they try to portray, the educator has a big responsibility in creating a more inclusive learning environment. By creating a safe environment, the educator can, in the position of designing the course (Blackburn and Miller 2017), increase the overall well-being and health among students, as well as awareness regarding LGBTQ+ (Batchelor et al. 2018; Page 2017; Snapp et al. 2015). Several scholars have pointed out the need to first analyse the existing curriculum in order to see where there is a gap to fill in the existing curriculum (Blackburn and Buckley 2005; Page 2017; Snapp et al. 2015). In the analysed textbooks we could say that the introduction of the personal pronouns represents such a gap. The educator can inform about the possibility to use the gender-neutral *hen* and how the pronoun originated. Another gap could be found in some of the chapters about families. If not present in the book, the various forms of families in the society can be presented and explained. The ambiguous and neutral gender occurrences could be used to avoid stigmatizing non-normative relationships. Snapp et al. (2017: 255) write that students feel LGBTQ+ should be included in history classes and classes about relationships. As presented earlier, Rivstart B1–B2 does include both the women's rights movement and LGBTQ+ in its history chapter, but the history chapters in the examined Dutch textbooks don't.

## Conclusions and Implications

There is a difference between how the societies in the Netherlands and Sweden are presented in the textbooks, compared with what we know about gender equality and the situation for LGBTQ+ in the mentioned countries. The examined textbooks are male-biased in numbers, although the representations themselves are not stereotyped. The third non-binary gender is, however, barely mentioned, nor explained except in one occurrence in one of the Swedish textbooks. The books are very heterosexual-oriented and the Dutch books even more so than the Swedish ones. There are some neutral and ambiguous examples which could be used to normalize non-normative relationships. When it comes down to LGBTQ+ and gender representations, the educator should play an active role in showing such representations, since the examined textbooks hardly do it, and the educator has to have a critical and active role in order to make the students aware of how the Swedish and Dutch societies are structured. With that said, our investigation shows a need for authors and publishers of textbooks in foreign languages to address the gaps between what is practised in the countries, and what is shown in content and approach in the textbooks. A student interested in learning Dutch or Swedish may very well do so because of the reputation these countries have in terms of gender equality and LGBTQ+ rights. It would be appropriate if the textbooks also reflected these parts of the Dutch and Swedish societies.

Future research could be done with more didactic L2 material for a more complete representation of each language and culture and also be carried out for languages and cultures other than Dutch and Swedish. Another topic for future research could be to investigate what effect the different methods have on the students.

## Notes

1 Other terms used in other research and media are LHB, LHBI, LGBTQ, LGBTQIA (L for lesbian, H for homosexual, B for bisexual, T for transgender, Q for queer and questioning together, I for intersex and A for asexual). We are aware that it is a sensitive subject and we aim to be as inclusive as possible. We decided to use LGBTQ+ (lesbian, gay, bisexual, transgender, queer or questioning) and the '+' as it stands for every other representation of sexual and romantic (non-)preference, (non-)gender or (non-)biological sex such as intersex, pansexual and non-binary.

2 In this research the main focus is on the Netherlands since the textbooks used for this chapter focus on the Netherlands. Occasionally Belgium is used to show the common grounds in, for example, politics and to give an extra comparison.

3  In this research the main focus is on Sweden since that is the focus of the textbooks used for this chapter, although Swedish is one of Finland's official languages as well.
4  Levy Scherrer, P. and Lindemalm, K. (2014). *Rivstart A1 + A2 Textbok* (2nd edn.). Stockholm: Natur & kultur
5  Levy Scherrer, P. and Lindemalm, K. (2015). *Rivstart B1 + B2 Textbok* (2nd edn.). Stockholm: Natur & kultur.
6  Åström, M. (2012). *Språkporten: [svenska som andraspråk 1, 2, 3]*. (2nd edn.). Lund: Studentlitteratur.
7  de Boer, B., van der Kamp, M. and Lijmbach, B. (2010). *Nederlands in gang*. Bussum: Coutinho.
8  de Boer, B., van der Kamp, M. and Lijmbach, B. (2012). *Nederlands in actie* (3rd edn.). Bussum: Coutinho.
9  de Boer, B. and Ohlsen, R. (2015). *Nederlands op niveau* (2nd edn.). Bussum: Coutinho.
10 Palmer, E. and van 't Wout M. (2015). *Nederlands naar perfectie* (1st edn.). Bussum: Coutinho.

# References

Arbetsmarknadsdepartementet. (2018), 'Historik om utvecklingen av hbtq-personers rättigheter i Sverige'. Available online: https://www.regeringen.se/artiklar/2018/06/historik-om-utvecklingen-av-hbtq-personers-rattigheter-i-sverige/ (accessed 14 October 2021).

Azimova, N., and B. Johnston. (2012), 'Invisibility and Ownership of Language: Problems of Representation in Russian Language Textbooks', *The Modern Language Journal*, 96 (3): 337–49. https://doi.org/10.1111/j.1540-4781.2012.01356.x.

Batchelor, K. E., M. Ramos, and S. Neiswander. (2018), Opening Doors: Teaching LGBTQ-themed Young Adult Literature for an Inclusive Curriculum, The Clearing House: A Journal of Educational Strategies, Issues and Ideas, 91 (1): 29–36. https://doi.org/10.1080/00098655.2017.1366183.

Becker, S. (2020), 'Is het Nederlands klaar voor het genderneutrale "Hen loopt"?', *Trouw*, 8 October. Available online: https://www.trouw.nl/cultuur-media/is-het-nederlands-klaar-voor-het-genderneutrale-hen-loopt~b5fb2e1b/?utm_source=link&utm_medium=social&utm_campaign=shared_earned (accessed 31October 2021).

Blackburn, M., and M. C. Miller. (2017), *Equity by Design: Teaching LGBTQ-Themed Literature in English Language Arts Classrooms*. https://files.eric.ed.gov/fulltext/ED580428.pdf.

Blackburn, M. V., and J. Buckley. (2005), 'Teaching Queer-Inclusive English Language Arts', *Journal of Adolescent & Adult Literacy*, 49 (3): 202–12. https://doi.org/10.1598/jaal.49.3.4.

de Boer, B., and R. Ohlsen. (2015), *Nederlands op niveau* (2nd ed.), Bussum: Coutinho.

de Boer, B., M. van der Kamp, and B. Lijmbach. (2010), *Nederlands in Gang*, Bussum: Coutinho.
de Boer, B., M. van der Kamp, and B. Lijmbach. (2012), *Nederlands in actie* (3rd ed.), Bussum: Coutinho.
Brandle, S. M. (2020), '"It's (Not) in the Reading: American Government Textbooks" Limited Representation of Historically Marginalized Groups', *PS: Political Science & Politics*, 53 (4): 734–40. https://doi.org/10.1017/s1049096520000797.
Bromseth, J. (2010), 'Förändringsstrategier och problemförståelser: Från utbildning om den Andra till queer pedagogik', in J. Bromseth and F. Darj (ed.), *Normkritisk pedagogik: Makt, lärande och strategier för förändring*, 27–54, Uppsala: Centrum för genusvetenskap, Uppsala universitet.
Bromseth, J., and F. Darj. (2010), *Normkritisk pedagogik: Makt, lärande och strategier för förändring*, Uppsala: Centrum för genusvetenskap, Uppsala universitet.
Bron-Wojciechowska, A. (1995), 'Education and Gender in Sweden', *Women's Studies International Forum*, 18 (1): 51–60. https://doi.org/10.1016/0277-5395(94)00097-2.
de Boise, S. (2017), 'Gender Inequalities and Higher Music Education: Comparing the UK and Sweden', *British Journal of Music Education*, 35 (1): 23–41. https://doi.org/10.1017/s0265051717000134.
Evertsson, M., P. England, I. Mooi-Reci, J. Hermsen, J. de Bruijn, and D. Cotter. (2009), 'Is Gender Inequality Greater at Lower or Higher Educational Levels? Common Patterns in the Netherlands, Sweden, and the United States', *Social Politics: International Studies in Gender, State & Society*, 16 (2): 210–41. https://doi.org/10.1093/sp/jxp008.
Expreszo. (2021), *Wat stel ik voorop: Mijn eigen ongemak of die van iemand die anders aangesproken wil worden*. Available online: https://expreszo.nl/wat-stel-ik-voorop-mijn-eigen-ongemak-of-die-van-iemand-die-anders-aangesproken-wil-worden/ (accessed 31 October 2021).
Fairclough, N. (1992), *Discourse and Social Change*, Cambridge: Polity.
*Feiten & Cijfers - Taalunie*. (2020), 'Feiten & cijfers'. Available online: https://taalunie.org/informatie/24/feiten-cijfers (accessed 31 October 2021).
Freire, P. (2000), *Pedagogy of the Oppressed* (30th anniversary ed.), New York: Continuum.
Gelijke Kansen in Vlaanderen (Equal Opportunities in Flanders) (2010), 'LGBT Policy in Flanders – A Brief Introduction – (D/2010/3241/375)'. Available online: https://publicaties.vlaanderen.be/view-file/7938 (accessed 30 October 2021).
Gustafsson Sendén, M., E. A. Bäck, and A. Lindqvist (2015), 'Introducing a Gender-Neutral Pronoun in a Natural Gender Language: The Influence of Time on Attitudes and Behavior', *Frontiers in Psychology*, 6. https://doi.org/10.3389/fpsyg.2015.00893.
Institutet för språk och folkminnen. (2020), 'Om svenska språket'. Available online: https://www.isof.se/lar-dig-mer/kunskapsbanker/lar-dig-mer-om-svenska-spraket/om-svenska-spraket (accessed 15 November 2021).
Koster, D., and L. Litosseliti. (2021), 'Multidimensional Perspectives on Gender in Dutch Language Education: Textbooks and Teacher Talk', *Linguistics and Education*, 64: 100953. https://doi.org/10.1016/j.linged.2021.100953.

Kumashiro, K. (2002), *Troubling Education: Queer Activism and Anti-Oppressive Education*, New York and London: Routledge.
Kuyper, L. (2018), 'Opvattingen over seksuele en genderdiversiteit in Nederland en Europa'. Available online: https://www.scp.nl/publicaties/publicaties/2018/05/17/opvattingen-over-seksuele-en-genderdiversiteit-in-nederland-en-europa (accessed 2 November 2021).
Lee, J. F. (2014), 'A Hidden Curriculum in Japanese EFL Textbooks: Gender Representation', *Linguistics and Education*, 27: 39–53. https://doi.org/10.1016/j.linged.2014.07.002.
Ministerie van Justitie en Veiligheid. (2021), 'Nieuwe regeling voor transgenders – Federale overheidsdienst Justitie, Federale Overheidsdienst Justitie'. Available online: https://justitie.belgium.be/nl/themas_en_dossiers/personen_en_gezinnen/transgenders (accessed 31 October 2021).
Ministerie van Onderwijs, Cultuur en Wetenschap. (2021a), 'Gelijke rechten LHBTI's'. Available online: https://www.rijksoverheid.nl/onderwerpen/lhbti-emancipatie/gelijke-rechten-lhbtis (accessed 30 October 2021).
Ministerie van Onderwijs, Cultuur en Wetenschap. (2021b), 'Emancipatie. Sectoren | OCW in cijfers'. Available online: https://www.ocwincijfers.nl/sectoren/emancipatie (accessed 31 October 2021).
Page, M. L. (2017), 'From Awareness to Action: Teacher Attitude and Implementation of LGBT-Inclusive Curriculum in the English Language Arts Classroom', *SAGE Open*, 7 (4): 215824401773994. https://doi.org/10.1177/2158244017739949.
Palmer, E., and M. van 't Wout. (2015), *Nederlands naar perfectie* (1st ed.), Bussum: Coutinho.
Regeringskansliet. (2017) 'Transpersoner i Sverige – Förslag för stärkt ställning och bättre levnadsvillkor'. Available online: https://www.regeringen.se/rattsliga-dokument/statens-offentliga-utredningar/2017/11/sou-201792/ (accessed 15 November 2021).
Regeringskansliet. (2021), 'Handlingsplan för hbtqi-personers lika rättigheter och möjligheter'. Available online: https://www.regeringen.se/informationsmaterial/2021/01/handlingsplan-for-hbtqi-personers-lika-rattigheter-och-mojligheter/ (accessed 15 October 2021).
Rijksoverheid. (2020), 'Bijlage 2 Eindrapport onderzoek geslachtsregistraties'. Available online: https://www.rijksoverheid.nl/documenten/kamerstukken/2020/07/03/bijlage-2-eindrapport-onderzoek-geslachtsregistraties (accessed 31 October 2021).
Schucan Bird, K., and L. Pitman. (2019), 'How Diverse is Your Reading List? Exploring Issues of Representation and Decolonisation in the UK', *Higher Education*, 79 (5): 903–20. https://doi.org/10.1007/s10734-019-00446-9.
Smith, A. D. (1991), *National Identity*, London: Penguin.
Snapp, S. D., H. Burdge, A. C. Licona, R. L. Moody, and S. T. Russell. (2015), '"Students" Perspectives on LGBTQ-Inclusive Curriculum', *Equity & Excellence in Education*, 48 (2): 249–265. https://doi.org/10.1080/10665684.2015.1025614.
Socialdepartementet. (2016), *Makt, mål och myndighet: Feministisk politik för en jämställd framtid*, Stockholm: Socialdepartementet.
Svenska Dagbladet. (2020), 'RFSL: Sverige bör införa ett tredje kön', *SvD.se*, 27 July. Available online: https://www.svd.se/sverige-bor-infora-ett-tredje-kon (accessed 1 November 2021).

Svenska institutet. (2017), 'Många vill lära sig svenska'. Available online: https://svenskaspraket.si.se/sa-arbetar-vi/manga-vill-lara-sig-svenska (accessed 15 November 2021).
Transgender Netwerk Nederland. (2016), 'Zo maak je na toiletten ook taal genderneutraal'. Available online: https://www.transgendernetwerk.nl/non-binair-voornaamwoord-uitslag/ (accessed 31 October 2021).
United Nations Development Programme. (2020), 'The Next Frontier: Human Development and the Anthropocene', *Human Development Report 2020: Overview*. Available online: http://hdr.undp.org/sites/default/files/hdr_2020_overview_english_0.pdf (accessed 16 October 2021).
Winther Jørgensen, M., and L. Phillips. (2000), *Diskursanalys som teori och metod*, Lund: Studentlitteratur.

# CHAPTER 10

## 'For Us Foreigners, Licking Our Fingers Clean Is a Good Habit'

## On Learning Chinese and Learning about Discourse from Chinese-Language Textbooks

*Séagh Kehoe, Paul Kendall, Gerda Wielander*

In this chapter, we introduce critical pedagogic approaches adopted at the University of Westminster in the context of a uniquely structured curriculum that combines the teaching of Chinese language and culture in the same module.[1] Building on the authors' own teaching experience, we discuss the ways in which we have used our Chinese cultural studies lectures to productively interrogate some of the problematic discourses that arise across Chinese-language textbooks. We argue this approach provides a critical language pedagogy that encourages students to identify, examine and critique ideological underpinnings of linguistic-cultural texts. Through this approach, we are able to address issues of monolingualism and monoculturalism as well as heteronormativity as expressed in the Chinese-language textbooks; this pedagogical approach also facilitates discussions on decanonization and critically reviews established teaching practices that often run along ethnic fault lines. Our approach provides a critical language pedagogy that critiques oppressive linguistic-cultural systems, in this case the PRC dominant, Han-centric (see also Hird's chapter), heteronormative system expressed in some of the most widely used Chinese-language textbooks.

Textbooks are a cornerstone of many language learning courses at all levels of education around the world. They offer students and teachers a ready-made structure and syllabus, help to standardize instruction and provide a record and measure of what has been taught, as well as a variety of learning resources. As sociocultural artefacts, however, textbooks also represent particular constructions of the social world and are the products of complex webs of political decisions, historical events, educational beliefs and policies and cultural realities (Curdt-Christiansen and Weninger 2015; Bori 2018; Block and Gray 2017). In this sense, they embody different kinds of ideologies, legitimize specific types of knowledge and contribute to the circulation of particular representations and stereotypes (Canale 2016).

In Chinese studies, much has been written about the ways in which textbooks have been used by the state and cultural elites as a way of transmitting dominant ideologies in primary and secondary education in the PRC (Liu 2005a, 2005b; Wang 2016). Yet, despite the vast expansion in the provision of Chinese-language courses outside of the PRC in recent decades, there has been relatively little attention to how China and its relationship with the world are depicted in textbooks for Chinese-language learners around the world. What kinds of ideologies are at play across these textbooks and what kinds of critical pedagogical practices might educators use to interrogate them in the classroom?

We start by providing an institutional background against which we were able to introduce our approach, and then proceed to analysing three examples of textbook discourse and our ways of challenging these through critical pedagogy. We then provide critical reflections of our own practice before setting out the main points in the conclusion.

## Interrogating the Ways We Teach Language and Culture

The opportunity to revisit the way in which language and culture are taught at the University of Westminster presented itself as part of the university's decision to change the credit model in the 2016/17 academic year. When redesigning the core modules in modern languages, we aimed to address the following prevalent issues in modern languages teaching: (i) the disconnect between language and culture teaching resulting from different staff groups (sometimes in different departments) delivering the respective classes, entrenching a division that, at least in Chinese studies, often runs along ethnic lines; (ii) the lack of intellectual stimulation as experienced and expressed by students in the student surveys; (iii) the lack of a sense of belonging to a course cohort as a result of students in the same class being enrolled on a variety of combined degree pathways; (iv) the discrepancy in intermediate learners between their level of language proficiency and their academic knowledge about relevant subject areas; (v) the lack of critical engagement with the discourses on Chinese culture as presented in the textbooks; and (vi) the high cost of addressing all these issues through separate module provision.

The prevalent mode of delivery of modern languages degrees is a distinction between language modules and the intellectually more stimulating cultural studies or history modules that provide the relevant context for the study of language. In most institutions, these types of modules are delivered by different staff groups; language classes tend to be delivered by staff in language centres who may or may not be on academic contracts and who often are native speakers of the relevant languages. In the case of Chinese, these classes are almost exclusively offered by native speakers of Chinese who are mostly also from China. Cultural classes are often delivered by research-active staff who do not consider language teaching as part of their skill set; there is also a perceived hierarchy between language teaching and other types of teaching. In the context of shrinking student numbers on many modern language degrees, this significantly contributes to the cost of delivering modern languages degrees, as it can become difficult to fill academics' timetables where such narrow specialisms are claimed. It has also contributed to the splitting off of the 'functional' language element of teaching into language centres and the 'content' elements of modern languages degrees into other disciplines like history, politics and so forth. These structural realities translate into students' experiencing 'language' and 'content' as two separate spheres of learning: one difficult but not intellectually stimulating (surely a contradiction in terms but a prevalent evaluation), the other intellectually stimulating and accessible.

The new language core modules introduced at Westminster in 2016/17 consist of six teaching hours per week made up of the following elements. A one-hour lecture in which the entire student cohort across all levels of proficiency and course combinations comes together is the first class of the week and sets the theme for the remaining classes of the week. Its theme is based on the main topic of the textbook's lesson for the week. This may be an introductory lecture to China that includes basic information on Taiwan, Hong Kong and the Chinese diaspora, usually missing in the textbooks used at UK universities which are predominantly produced in the People's Republic of China. The lecture also introduces some key terms in Chinese. All lecturers involved in the delivery of this element are also involved in Chinese-language teaching, either through oral tutorials or a seminar group. The cultural aspect of the module is therefore not only thematically connected to the language seminars, but there is also a personal connection through the identity of the lecturer. Lectures are delivered in English in the first and second years, but partly delivered in Chinese in the final year of study.

In its original conception, the lecture was followed by a one-hour tutorial in small groups which focuses on oral skills. In the tutorials, students were grouped by subject combination, and where cohorts were big enough, by level of proficiency. For example, all students of Chinese and international business were in the same tutorial group. The tutorials provided an opportunity for identity building within the same pathway and introduced additional vocabulary that may be of special interest for a business student, for example. At a higher level, the preceding lecture provided a natural talking point for tutorial discussions. In practice, we had to make adaptations as individual cohorts are not always big enough to allow for disciplinary divisions in the tutorials which, in the second year, are now mostly used to review the content of the previous week. These two learning units (lecture and tutorial) are followed (on two different days) by two two-hour seminar blocks where students were meant to come together based on their levels of proficiency (beginner and intermediate in the first year of study, for example) and, in the case of beginners, would work through the textbook whose theme was critically introduced in the weekly lecture. In practice, the language tutorials of the following week proved the more suitable vehicle to continue the criticality of the lectures.

The same pattern and rationale were adopted for all modern language core modules. These core modules are complemented by cross-cultural, thematic option modules, some, but not all of which, have seminars in the degree languages. 'Concepts of Happiness across Cultures' was one of the most popular ones with a thematic lecture in English for all students and seminar groups in which relevant sources and examples were studied in Arabic, Chinese, French or Spanish. Through this particular thematic lens it is possible to introduce philosophical, sociological, anthropological, economic and popular cultural aspects while engaging the students in something that feels personally relevant to them and hence enhances engagement.

The design and delivery of this pattern required us to interrogate and let go of a number of orthodoxies and dominant discourses around language learning. One is the assumption, directly linked to the disconnect between allegedly functional language teaching and stimulating cultural teaching, that one requires a high level of proficiency in a language in order to be able to have interesting thoughts or conversations. Most textbooks start with simple everyday conversations in order to teach basic language structures. Both lectures and tutorials are designed to complement this approach by showing that simple words and structures can be used to express knowledge or abstract ideas as well as everyday matters of life. Beyond addressing issues (i), (ii) and (v) listed previously, this approach also actively combats the false assumption widely prevalent in society that poor or basic language skills are a reflection of poor education or low levels of intelligence. By requiring students to talk about complex matters in simple terms we also create an awareness of the disconnect between the ability for complex thought and the need for complex language to express these among the students.

Secondly, adopting a thematic approach for the lectures that broadly follows themes arising from the textbook in order to create integrity and consistency between the language and culture elements of the module requires letting go of received orthodoxies of knowledge and traditional (more often than not chronological) approaches to delivering cultural content. It also requires letting go of an established canon of texts and allowing for both gaps and the inclusion of 'unorthodox' or 'lesser' themes. Agreeing on the lecture themes can in itself become a very useful staff development session in the context of decolonizing the curriculum and reflecting on one's own unconscious biases about what constitutes the most important knowledge or scholarship about China.

Thirdly, the removal of the distinction between language and culture teaching by involving relevant academics in all aspects of the module has given rise to a higher appreciation of language pedagogy among research-active colleagues, leading to new collaborations and intellectual projects like this one. It is worth noting that the editor of this volume was part of the academic team that devised the new languages curriculum at Westminster as described earlier.

Finally, combining language and culture teaching has provided a much needed opportunity to interrogate language textbook discourses. As noted earlier, language textbooks across a range of educational contexts have been variously critiqued for contributing to and perpetuating cultural stereotypes and legitimizing specific types of knowledge (Canale 2016; McConachy 2018). As Azimova and Johnston (2012: 347) point out, while 'no textbook can fully convey the richness and diversity of those groups and individuals who are users of the language, it is nevertheless important to try'. In the sections that follow, we introduce two Chinese-language textbooks, as previously and currently used at the University of Westminster. We then discuss some of the key discourses that run through them, and the strategies we have developed as part of our Chinese cultural studies lectures to interrogate these discourses.

## The Textbooks

New Practical Chinese Reader (NPCR) is a series of six levels of textbooks. First published in 1981 as Practical Chinese Reader and now moving into its third edition, the set was compiled under the sponsorship of the China National Office for Teaching Chinese as a Foreign Language (NOTCFL) and is published by Beijing Language and Culture University Press. It is targeted at beginner and intermediate adult learners of Standard Mandarin outside of China. NPCR is explicit in its intentions to combine the teaching of Chinese language and culture, claiming that 'the content of the texts is closely related to Chinese culture with an emphasis on introducing Chinese customs and Chinese behavioural culture' (2010: II). Each level is made up of between ten and thirteen lessons. Lessons begin with a dialogue or story about a cast of international students studying Chinese, first in their home countries and later in China, and their interactions with their teachers, friends and partners, most of whom are Chinese citizens. Dialogues and stories are followed by new vocabulary, grammar, exercises and finally a 'Cultural Note' in English.

Integrated Chinese (IC) is a set of four levels of textbooks. Now in its fourth edition, the set was first published in 1997 by ChengTsui, a Boston-based independent publisher of Asian language learning textbooks and education materials. Like NPCR, IC's target population is beginner and intermediate adult learners in higher education outside of China. While it is particularly widely used in the United States, it is also increasingly being taken up in UK universities. Each level is made up of ten lessons. Similar again to NPCR, the lessons begin with a dialogue or story about the lives of students learning Chinese and their friendships and relationships with native speakers of Chinese in both the United States and China. Lessons then cover new vocabulary, grammar, exercises and finally, a section on 'Cultural Literacy' in English that aims to 'promote students' awareness of cultural diversity in the world' (2016: IX).

At Westminster, NPCR (until 2019) and IC (at present) have been used in language seminars and tutorials for the first two years of study in the Chinese undergraduate degree.[2] In line with the approach described earlier, the task has therefore been to link these Chinese-language sessions to cultural studies lectures by critically mapping weekly lecture topics onto the themes of textbook lessons. However, when putting this into practice, lecturers found that somewhat different strategies were needed for the first and second years of undergraduate study. In the first year, lectures consist of general introductions to essential topics in Chinese studies (e.g., language, religion and education) while most students are complete beginners in Chinese. The critical links between lecture and textbook learning have therefore been relatively loose, with limited potential for bringing Chinese-language content into lectures, while the beginner textbooks are not as saturated by problematic discourse as at intermediate level, given the simplicity of language involved. However, by the second year, students were able to build on knowledge from the first year to tackle more specific topics. At the same time, the textbooks start to introduce students to more opinions and abstract concepts.

The following paragraphs focus on this second year. These examples show how cultural studies lectures have challenged textbook discourses through two intertwined strategies: complicating what the textbooks say; and uncovering what they do not say. They also show how lectures have fed back into language learning through the critical examination of 'authentic' Chinese-language texts. Our analysis focuses on three discourses that particularly permeate both textbooks – and also figure prominently in CCP discourse – although we note that word count does not allow us to provide detailed analysis of further shared discourses in these textbooks, such as the celebration of middle-class consumption and conceptualization of Han-minority difference. Our identification of these discourses stems from years of scrutinizing these textbooks during the process of teaching, as well as our knowledge of the wider discursive realms within which these textbooks operate as they represent the PRC, its history and its relationship with the wider world.

## Analysis

### *Discourse 1: Historical Change*

Both NPCR and IC tend to make strong contrasts between the past and the present, with NCPR in particular pushing a narrative of linear progress. A typical example of this can be seen in IC4 Lesson 12. Titled 'Changes in China', the lesson follows the characters on a trip to Nanjing. There, they reflect on how Nanjing has changed, in rather blunt and vague terms, noting that what was once a quiet city is now 'full of newly built high-rises and cars,' as well as foreign tourists and businesses. Nanjing is presented as an attractive combination of the 'traditional' and the 'modern', where heritage and development exist in harmony, where 传统建筑 (traditional architecture) stand next to 高楼大厦 (high-rise buildings). When the group travels to Yunnan in Lesson 13, however, there is no discussion of change or its impact on local cultural practices. Here, the 'architecture, clothing, and food and drink of the different ethnic groups' are unaffected by the politics of development. Representations of this kind both obscure the realities of state-led rapid development and its related tensions in Tibet, Xinjiang and other ethnic regions across the PRC, while also echoing long-standing Chinese state discourses of the country's ethnic minority populations as outside of history (Schein 1997; Gladney 1994). Elsewhere, IC is more specific in the moments of change to which it refers, for example, 'after 1950' and 'since the Reform and Opening Up'.[3] Nonetheless, the series is highly selective about what aspects of historical change it represents. Lesson 18, for instance, sees the cast visiting the National Museum of China, discussing defining historical moments and figures from the Qin dynasty (221–206 BC) to the fall of the Qing dynasty and the Republican era in the early-twentieth century, with no reference made to the Mao era (1949–76). This is true of the book more broadly. For instance, whether in the case of lessons on environment, gender relations or education, there is little to no engagement with or even acknowledgement of the legacies of the Mao era in contemporary China.

While IC texts express some occasional ambivalence about change and development in China, NPCR is more celebratory and often promotes a narrative of linear progress. Terms such as 'in the past', 'before', 'historically', in feudal times' and 'nowadays' make frequent appearances and emphasize positive change. This is especially clear in Lesson 40 (part 2) where, when describing women's status in China, the text describes how 'during China's more than two thousand years of feudal society, women had no social status . . . . Now the situation is different, women [ . . .] have an equal position with men. This is China's social progress.' Similarly in Lesson 47 (part 1), characters remark: 'before the implementation of Reform and Opening Up, the living standards of Chinese people were much lower than they are now,' while in Lesson 48 (part 1) a discussion of the One-Child Policy sees one character remarking: 'from the 1970s onwards, the one-child policy became a basic policy in China. In recent decades, China has successfully controlled population growth. Today, China's population growth rate is lower than the world average.' NPCR's representation of historical change chimes closely with Chinese state discourses, which stress a homogeneous national time with the purpose of proving the inevitability and legitimacy of Communist rule (Dirlik and Zhang 1997; Callaghan 2004; Wu 2005).

Discussions of gender in NPCR and IC Chinese somehow manage to refer to the recent past without mentioning the Mao era by name. Indeed, both textbooks seem somewhat embarrassed by the Mao era and its historical legacy, preferring instead to stress the continued presence of 'traditional' culture in contemporary China. Again, this does not align well with research in Chinese studies, which has stressed the transformative character of the Mao era (e.g., Karl 2010), as well as its continuing legacy (e.g., Li and Zhang 2016; Sorace, Franceschini and Loubere 2019).

Our response at Westminster has been to take existing textbook themes situated in the contemporary world and either re-situate these themes within the Mao era or reconsider these themes in the light of Maoist legacies. For example, our cultural studies lecture responds to the IC's positive description of Nanjing by introducing its negative representation as post-socialist dystopia in the 2016 animation *Have a Nice Day!* This film-length animation complicates IC4's representation of Nanjing in numerous ways. Firstly, its creator, Liu Jian, does not flinch from presenting the darker elements of life in urban China, with his depiction of a criminal underworld whose financial dynamism ultimately drives the city's construction. Secondly, Liu draws heavily on Maoist imagery, both in his representation of the city, with the inclusion of sites such as Nanjing Yangtze River Bridge (a celebrated Mao-era construction project) and in the incorporation of socialist realism into his own animation style. Thirdly, he presents the contemporary cityscape as either in decay or under construction; a park entrance is shown with peeling paint and missing Chinese characters, while a bus stop is depicted against a backdrop of rubble and cranes. Liu's animation is, of course, a pessimistic work of fiction rather than a neutral account of the city (if such a thing can exist). Thus, rather than introducing his animation as 'the truth' about Nanjing, the lecture treats it as a counterweight to the uncritical, touristic image of Nanjing found in IC4. *Have a Nice Day!* also feeds back into language learning: it is used to ask students to reflect in Chinese on how they would describe their hometowns and accompanying histories, and also introduces students to 'non-standard' Chinese that cannot be found in NPCR or IC.

## *Discourse 2: Women's Status*

Both NPCR and IC contain a full lesson on women's status in China. In IC4, Lesson 15 is titled 'Gender Equality' and covers improvements and setbacks from the Mao era (albeit not mentioned by name) to Reform and Opening Up to the present, including issues such as gender discrimination in education and employment. It describes how, 'historically [. . .] women's status in the family and in society was much lower than that of men' but 'after 1950, the situation changed gradually', before going on to say that some forms of gender inequality have 'resurfaced' since Reform and Opening Up (122). The lesson also praises the contemporary household as 'perhaps the place of greatest gender equality in Chinese society' (122), using the example of one 'model husband' who, as long as there is no football game on TV, is willing to help out by cooking and washing dishes. Nowhere is the structural issue of patriarchy or state repression of grassroots feminist movements acknowledged or discussed; instead, the gender pay gap is quickly dismissed in vague terms as something 'determined by the market' (124). Moreover, as many scholars have long argued, in the post-Mao era, there remain significant disparities in housework time between men and women and the household remains a site of male-domination (Luo and Chui 2019; Honig and Hershatter 1988). Much of this, rather than 'resurfacing' since the Reform and Opening Up, as the lesson suggests, is a legacy of the Mao era. As Hershatter (2019) notes, for instance, socialist discourse had little to say about the distribution or remuneration of household labour, with the expectation that women would attend to tasks in the home before, after and during their labour elsewhere.

NPRC is similar in terms of the gross simplifications and even distorted representation of women's status in modern Chinese history. Generally, however, representations of women's status are far more problematic in NPCR. Lesson 40 (part 1), for instance, in which a man interviews two women about women's status in China, the conversation proceeds from a deeply patriarchal standpoint, with comments such as 'if women stay at home, this problem [of large population] becomes relatively easier to solve' and questions such as 'You don't think there are some jobs that are more suitable for men?' In addition to the blatant sexism of Lesson 40, in Lesson 48 (part 1) two male characters discuss the benefits and drawbacks of the 'family planning policy' (计划生育), usually known in English language discourse as the 'one-child policy', without a single reference to the wide-ranging and multiple ways in which the draconian decades-long restriction impacted the lives of women (Greenhalgh 2001; Schrempf 2012; Li 1996). Consideration of the very gendered dimensions of the policy appear not even worthy of comment here, with the discussion focused primarily on the successes of the policy in allowing the PRC to achieve a population growth rate in line with the global average, a claim much contested in Chinese studies literature (Zhang 2017; Whyte, Wang and Cai 2015). Overall, NPCR's representation of women's status in China reflects much of the Chinese state's rhetoric about women's liberation and unified support for and successes of the 'family planning policy', serving to legitimize the state's claims of historical progress and downplay structural inequalities.

Chinese cultural studies research, in contrast, is far more critical and nuanced in its appraisal of gender relations during the Mao and Reform eras (e.g. Evans 2008; Hershatter 2014). Second-year lectures at the university have fed off these tensions between textbook discourse and academic literature. While the lessons in NPCR and IC present contemporary urban China as a place where patriarchy is in retreat, the accompanying cultural studies lecture responds by examining the highly patriarchal and contemporary discourse of 'leftover women' (剩女). This is a discourse which has been directed at single, well-educated urban women in their late twenties and above in recent years, admonishing them for focusing on career prospects at the purported expense of their marriage prospects (see Ji 2015; Fincher 2014). As well as attending a lecture in English on this discourse of 'leftover women', students watch two related Chinese-language videos for discussion in the following week's oral tutorials: one is an advertisement for the dating site Baihe, in which a young woman explains that she cannot be too picky in finding a husband if she wants to avoid disappointing her ailing grandmother; the other is a documentary-style piece by the cosmetics brand SK-II, in which various successful single women and their parents discuss the notion of 'leftover women'. These two videos help to complicate textbook discourse on gender in China rather than simply replacing it with another monolithic discourse: the Baihe example highlights the denigration of well-educated women who are 'picky' in choosing a husband, while the SK-II example shows that there have been robust responses to this denigration (albeit in this particular case as part of a campaign to sell cosmetics). Students at this point possess a level of Chinese whereby they can – with some assistance – understand and answer questions about the content of these advertisements. While the language textbook introduces useful vocabulary for talking about gender relations (e.g., 'equality between men and women' 男女平等; 'regarding men as superior to women' 重男轻女), the cultural studies lecture bridges the conceptual gap between the march towards gender equality described in the textbooks and the contemporary production of discourse about 'leftover women'. It also feeds back into language teaching by introducing students to 'authentic' texts that relate to this discourse of 'leftover women'.

## *Discourse 3: Cultural Practices*

Finally, while there is a sense of historical change – however problematic – in the textbook discussions of gender and Nanjing, both NPCR and IC tend to be almost completely ahistorical in their accounts of Chinese-foreign relations, with an implicit binary of unchanging, monolithic Chinese and foreign (Western) cultures. While IC does include some transnational elements and characters that are not obviously categorized as Chinese or Western, the depiction of cultural practices does not complicate the prevalent binary. Indeed, even in IC, Chinese cultural practices are often depicted in essentializing and unchanging terms. In Lesson 11, 'China's Holidays', for instance, the dialogues stick to a well-worn script about Lunar New Year, Dragon Boat Festival, Qingming Festival and Mid-Autumn Festival as traditional and timeless festivals, though a short 'Compare and Contrast' exercise later in the lesson does encourage students to reflect on how festival celebrations change over time. In Lesson 14, where the characters discuss lifestyle and health, tai chi is the main form of exercise described in the case of China. This is contrasted with 'exercises that Americans generally like', such as yoga, jogging, swimming and playing ball (96). The text does not acknowledge the wide diversity of physical exercise popular in China today nor the global flows that have long shaped sports in China and elsewhere (Shuman 2019; Fan and Lu 2012).

Indeed, Chinese culture and 'Western' culture are depicted here as closed and mutually exclusive categories of practices. We see examples of this 'Chinese culture versus not-Chinese culture motif' running throughout the IC set. In Lesson 12, for instance, the characters visit Nanjing and upon looking around at the various high-rise buildings, international brands and foreign tourists, they remark that if it were not for Chinese characters, they might have guessed they were in the United States. China has now 'melded into the world', they say, before expressing concern that this may lead to 'fewer and fewer distinctly Chinese things'. The Temple of Confucius is then held up as an example of the resilience of Chinese culture, which leads the characters to conclude that perhaps 'traditional architecture' and 'high-rises' may coexist after all. Chinese culture here and elsewhere in the book is synonymous with 'tradition', and is represented as timeless, unchanging and external to and even threatened by 'the modern' or 'Western' culture.

Similar to what we have seen of NPCR elsewhere in this chapter, discourses about cultural practice in China and 'the West' take place in very binary and even antagonistic terms. In Lesson 27, for example, when the characters discuss different eating habits, they note that when Chinese people eat they use chopsticks, whereas westerners use a knife and fork to eat. Westerners also have their own food on their own plate, they cut the food into small pieces before putting it into their mouths. If there is a bit of food on their fingers they will lick it off; Chinese people don't see this as polite.

Indeed, NPCR never misses a moment to contrast and compare China and 'the West', sometimes to comical effect. In Lesson 50 (part 2), one American character remarks, 'Every time after eating crabs, my Chinese friends and I have to say: "Americans really don't know how to eat them!" He smiled and said: "You Chinese like to eat female crabs the most, but we Americans like to eat male crabs. Today we will compare them to see which ones are delicious."' As we see here and across much of NPCR, cultural practices are represented as self-contained, mutually distinct and fixed. The series foregrounds difference, essentializing and homogenizing both China and 'the West'. This is reinforced through frequent references to the 'Chineseness' of different cultural practices, for example 'China's silk', 'China's calligraphy' and 'China's music' (Lesson 28), and assertions of a shared national origin and set of values as seen in Lesson 31's claim that 'the Yellow River is the cradle of the Chinese nation, so the Chinese people call it "Mother River"'. As scholars have noted, presenting Chinese national culture and identity as fixed is a recurring aspect of Chinese state discourse as well as orientalist discourse about China elsewhere, and is a key strategy in avoiding the renegotiation of Chinese identity by alternative voices (Lams 2017; Callahan 2012).

Our response in cultural studies lectures has been to emphasize how representations and experiences of foreignness and Chineseness in the PRC have been multiple and shifting. One lecture, for example, explores the multiple ways in which whiteness, Blackness and Chineseness (including overseas Chinese) were represented in the Mao era, with students asked to decipher various examples of visual culture, particularly propaganda posters from Westminster's China Visual Arts Project.[4] These 'authentic texts' provide depictions of a 'bad' Occident (the United States) and a 'good' Occident (Soviet Union) during the 1950s (see Landsberger 2008) in a way that complicates textbook notions of a single, static 'West'. For example, Chinese economic and architectural practices are shown as heavily influenced by the Soviet Union before it became part of the 'bad' Occident in the 1960s. They also show seemingly benevolent but ultimately hierarchical relations between China and its Third World allies (see Frazier 2017). Although propaganda during their own time, these posters can serve in the contemporary period to critique a propagandistic discourse that divides the world into China and the 'West'. Further lectures examine the diverse categories and experiences of foreigners in China from the Mao era to the present. This topic of Chinese-foreign relations has particularly appealed to students, many of whom have gone on to write related dissertations, for example, on identity among 'foreigners' who have grown up in China, on the rebranding of the Italian concession in Tianjin as a romantic, Italian-style tourist destination, and even on the representation of foreigners in the textbooks described here.

## Conclusion

Both IC and NPCR promote one-dimensional characterizations of historical change, gender relations and cultural difference, with neither providing much scope for critical reflection or questioning of the ways in which China or its relationship with the world is represented. Our cultural studies lectures, which are delivered as part of the core language module that uses these textbooks, provide a useful place to productively interrogate these discourses as socially, historically and ideologically situated products rather than a 'true' reflection of China and its relationship with the rest of the world.

This is, of course, not the only possible model for integrating language learning and cultural studies. Looking across the other languages in Westminster's modern languages programme, namely Spanish, French and Arabic, there has been considerable variation in the extent to which cultural studies lectures have been aligned with textbooks. In Spanish and French, a fairly even split between beginner and intermediate learners has made it extremely difficult to achieve this alignment, given that lectures cannot easily be simultaneously fused with two textbooks. In Arabic, there is a certain amount of alignment between lecture and textbook, but the latter displays more critical cultural awareness than NPCR and IC, so that the coming together of cultural studies research and textbook discourse has been less fractious.

Chinese has also departed from the original institutional plan in certain ways. For example, the oral tutorial has tended to review the content of the previous week's cultural studies lecture. This has facilitated a spaced repetition method of learning, so that if students learn about, for example, textbook and cultural studies discourses of gender one week, then the following week's tutorial becomes a site of consolidation. This close relationship between lecture, seminar and oral tutorial also makes it important to have a small, close-knit group of teachers, who can work across cultural studies and language teaching. In practice, our approach of linking language and cultural studies has had some very favourable results, in particular, topics to which students can bring their own personal experience can lead to very lively discussions in Chinese. For example, students have a lot to say in their tutorial about the disjuncture between the textbook depictions of gender relations and discussions of 'leftover women' in the SK-II advertisement they watch in their cultural studies lecture. Even those who otherwise tended to shy away from discussing more complex issues in Chinese were keen to participate and share their thoughts. In this case, our approach proved a very stimulating way to encourage students to identify and interrogate how and why particular discourses about gender inequality in China occur across different linguistic-cultural texts.

While the three examples in this chapter only scratch the surface of the cultural studies topics that we cover at Westminster, they demonstrate a basic underlying method of linking lecture topics to textbook lesson themes, complicating textbook discourse (and silence) by bringing in more critical voices from Chinese studies, and then feeding this critical approach back into language learning through the examination of 'authentic' Chinese-language texts. After five years of teaching this model, we feel that the biggest challenge for both teachers and students remains the time limits imposed on us. The module asks a lot of students and it is quite difficult for them to perform well in all aspects we cover. Students have reported high satisfaction with their modules; however, we have not been able to conduct in-depth reviews of both student and all-staff perceptions of Westminster's approach. However, we believe that it will nonetheless provide educators elsewhere with inspiration for a critical language pedagogy for interrogating linguistic-cultural texts in other contexts.

## Notes

1 At Westminster, we teach Standard Mandarin, or Putonghua 普通话.
2 In the final year, students move on to more 'authentic' Chinese-language texts, which allows for a relatively easy combination of cultural studies and language without the issue of textbook discourse, as described earlier.
3 The year 1950 is the date of PRC's 'New Marriage Law', which is frequently mentioned in discussions on the history of gender in China. The 'Reform and Opening Up' refers to the era of market-oriented reforms launched by Deng Xiaoping, with December 1978 celebrated as the official starting point of this era.
4 The China Visual Arts Project is a unique archival collection, comprising 843 posters dating from the 1940s to the 1980s, alongside a wealth of books, objects and ephemera. For further information about the collection, please visit: https://westminster-atom.arkivum.net/cpc

## References

Azimova, N., and B. Johnston. (2012), 'Invisibility and Ownership of Language: Problems of Representation in Russian Language Textbooks', *The Modern Language Journal*, 96 (3): 337–49.

Block, D., and J. Gray. (2017), 'French Language Textbooks as Ideologically Imbued Cultural Artefacts: Political Economy, Neoliberalism and (Self) Branding', in S. Coffey and U. Wingate (eds.), *New Directions for Research in Foreign Language Education*, 115–31, London: Routledge.

Bori, P. (2018), *Language Textbooks in the Era of Neoliberalism*, London: Routledge.

Callaghan, W. (2004), 'National Insecurities: Humiliation, Salvation, and Chinese Nationalism', *Alternatives*, 29: 199–218.

Callaghan, W. (2012), 'Sino-Speak: Chinese Exceptionalism and the Politics of History', *The Journal of Asian Studies*, 71 (1): 33–55.

Canale, G. (2016), '(Re)Searching Culture in Foreign Language Textbooks, or the Politics of Hide and Seek', *Language, Culture and Curriculum*, 29 (2): 225–43.

Curdt-Christiansen, X., and C. Weninger. (2015), 'Introduction: Ideology and the Politics of Language Textbooks', in X. Curdt-Christiansen and C. Weninger (eds.), *Language, Ideology and Education: The Politics of Textbooks in Language Education*, 1–9, London: Routledge.

Dirlik, A., and X. Zhang. (1997), 'Introduction: Postmodernism and China', *Boundary*, 24 (3): 1–18.

Evans, H. (2008), *The Subject of Gender: Daughters and Mothers in Urban China*, Lanham, MD: Rowman & Littlefield.

Fan, H., and Z. Lu. (2012), 'Representing the New China and the Sovietisation of Chinese Sport (1949–1962)', *The International Journal of the History of Sport*, 29 (1): 1–29.

Fincher, L. H. (2014), *Leftover Women: The Resurgence of Gender Inequality in China*, London: Zed Books.

Frazier, R. J. (2017), 'Making Blackness Serve China: The Image of Afro-Asia in Chinese Political Posters', in L. Raiford and H. Raphael-Hernandez (eds.), *Migrating the Black Body: The African Diaspora and Visual Culture*, 92–114, Seattle, WA: University of Washington Press.

Gladney, D. (1994), 'Representing Nationality in China: Refiguring Majority/Minority Identities', *The Journal of Asian Studies*, 53 (1): 92–123.

Greenhalgh, S. (2001), 'Fresh Winds in Beijing: Chinese Feminists Speak Out on the One-Child Policy and Women's Lives', *Signs*, 26 (3): 847–86.

Hershatter, G. (2014), *The Gender of Memory: Rural Women and China's Collective Past*, Berkeley, CA: University of California Press.

Hershatter, G. (2019), 'Women and China's Socialist Construction, 1949–78', *The Asia-Pacific Journal*, 17 (2): 1–27.

Honig, E., and G. Hershatter. (1988), *Personal Voices: Chinese Women in the 1980s*. Stanford, CA: Stanford University Press.

Ji, Y. (2015), 'Between Tradition and Modernity: 'Leftover' Women in Shanghai', *Journal of Marriage and Family*, 77 (5): 1057–73.

Karl, R. E. (2010), *Mao Zedong and China in the Twentieth-Century World: A Concise History*, Durham, NC: Duke University Press.

Lams, L. (2017), 'Othering in Chinese Official Media Narratives during Diplomatic Standoffs with the US and Japan', *Palgrave Communications*, 3 (33), https://doi.org/10.1057/s41599-017-0034-z.

Landsberger, S. R. (2008), 'Encountering the European and Western Other in Chinese Propaganda Posters', in M. J. Wintle (ed.), *Imagining Europe: Europe and European Civilisation as Seen from Its Margins and by the Rest of the World, in the Nineteenth and Twentieth Centuries*, 147–75, Brussels: Peter Lang.

Li, J., and E. H. Zhang. (2016), *Red Legacies in China: Cultural Afterlives of the Communist Revolution*, Cambridge, MA: Harvard University Press.

Li, X. (1996), 'License to Coerce: Violence against Women, State Responsibility and Legal Failures in China's Family Planning Program', *Yale Journal of Law and Feminism*, 8: 145–91.

Liu, X. (2010), *New Practical Chinese Reader* 新实用汉语课本 *Series*, Beijing: Beijing Language and Culture University Press.

Liu, Y. (2005a), 'The Construction of Cultural Values and Beliefs in Chinese Language Textbooks: A Critical Discourse Analysis', *Discourse: Studies in the Cultural Politics of Education*, 26 (1): 15–30.

Liu, Y. (2005b), 'Discourse, Cultural Knowledge and Ideology: A Critical Analysis of Chinese Language Textbooks', *Pedagogy, Culture & Society*, 13 (2): 233–64.

Liu, Yehua et al. (2016), *Integrated Chinese Series*, Boston: Cheng & Tsui.

Luo, M. S., and E. W. T. Chui. (2019), 'The Changing Picture of the Housework Gender Gap in Contemporary Chinese Adults', *Chinese Journal of Sociology*, 5 (3): 312–39.

McConachy, T. (2018), 'Critically Engaging with Cultural Representations in Foreign Language Textbooks', *Intercultural Education*, 29 (1): 77–88.

Schein, L. (1997), 'Gender and Internal Orientalism in China', *Modern China*, 23 (1): 69–98.

Schrempf, M. (2012), 'Re-Production at Stake: Experiences of Family Planning and Fertility among Amdo Tibetan Women', *Asian Medicine*, 6 (2): 321–47.

Shuman, A. (2019), 'Within or Outside International Sport? Chinese Leaders in the 1950s and 1960s', *Staps*, 125: 69–88.

Sorace, C., I. Franceschini, and N. Loubere, eds. (2019), *Afterlives of Chinese Communism: Political Concepts from Mao to Xi*, Canberra: ANU Press.

Wang, D. (2016), 'Learning or Becoming: Ideology and National Identity in Textbooks for International Learners of Chinese', *Cogent Education*, 3 (1), https://doi.org/10.1080/2331186X.2016.1140361.

Whyte, M. K., F. Wang, and Y. Cai. (2015), 'Challenging Myths about China's One-Child Policy', *The China Journal*, 74: 144–59.

Wu, H. (2005), *Remaking Beijing: Tiananmen Square and the Creation of a Political Space*, London: Reaktion Books.

Zhang, J. (2017), 'The Evolution of China's One-Child Policy and its Effects on Family Outcomes', *Journal of Economic Perspectives*, 31 (1): 141–60.

# Part V
# Teacher Education

# CHAPTER 11

# Translanguaging in Austrian Primary Teacher Education

*Theresa Guczogi*

Translanguaging has been prominently discussed as a way of supporting plurilingual children in their language and subject learning and a means to question and tackle politico-linguistic power norms.

Drawing on my own practice-led work as a lecturer in teaching English as a foreign language, I will discuss the impact of translanguaging strategies in the education of primary teacher candidates in Vienna, Austria, as a means to break discriminatory power structures both within and beyond the classroom. In this chapter, I will demonstrate how translanguaging can be used as a pedagogical approach in teacher education with the aim to equip teacher candidates to apply it in their own teaching.

Austria is a particularly rich example for the study of translanguaging strategies as 26 per cent of pupils grow up with more than one language (Bundeskanzleramt 2021). In Vienna, almost 52 per cent of pupils grow up plurilingually (Stadt Wien 2021). To contextualize language politics in Austria, I will therefore first give an overview of the role that multilingualism plays in Austrian curricula and the harmful effects that language bans have on pupils' linguistic and emotional development. I will then illustrate how translanguaging can help to open up classrooms for plurilingualism and how this challenges politico-linguistic power norms.

In order to understand how teacher education programmes can best prepare candidates for translanguaging, it is important to know which skills teachers need to successfully plan and teach translanguaging lessons. Following an overview of Orfelia García and Tatyana Kleyn's (2016) examination of skills that teachers need to apply translanguaging, I will discuss how these skills can be acquired in teacher education programmes and draw on some of my practice-led work at the KPH Wien/Krems, where I integrate translanguaging into my teaching. Teacher education studies often quoted Howard Altmann, who argues that early-career teachers teach with methods they were confronted with as learners (Altmann 1983: 24). Here, I argue that the importance of translanguaging strategies in primary education lies not only in its pedagogical power to respond to the twenty-first-century multilingual classroom, but also in its ability to challenge social linguistic hierarchies. By providing them with the experience of being in a translanguaging classroom, it is hoped that future generations of teachers will use this approach in their own teaching.

## Multilingualism in Austrian Curricula

The Council of Europe defines plurilingualism as the capacity of individuals to speak multiple languages and multilingualism as a phenomenon occurring in society (García and Otheguy 2020). In this way, plurilingualism is an asset for the individual, as well as for a globalized society. This position is also upheld by the EU through its stance that all its citizens should learn two languages in addition to their 'mother tongue' (European Parliament 2021). However, this positive view of plurilingualism is not always implemented in the systems, structures and approaches of its member states. This can be seen clearly in the position adopted vis-à-vis migrant languages of emergent plurilingual pupils in the Austrian school system. The Austrian Ministry for Education acknowledges that the Austrian school is multilingual, as 26 per cent of pupils grow up with more than one language (BMBWF 2021), and there have been initiatives like voXmi (Pädagogische Hochschule Wien 2021) to promote plurilingualism in schools. In the curricula of most schools, the use of languages other than German is not only accepted, but also promoted as a valuable resource (Fleck 2019: 98). For instance, the Austrian Primary Curriculum stipulates that statements in the pupils' home languages should be accepted and encouraged, and that any degradation of their home languages must be avoided (Lehrplan der Volksschule in Fleck 2019: 98).

The Austrian Federal Ministry of Education, Science and Research requires that *Sprachliche Bildung* (language education) focus on improving pupils' skills in the German language to facilitate their participation in instruction. Furthermore, the concept of *Sprachliche Bildung* encompasses the pupils' whole plurilingualism including their first and second language(s), home language(s) and foreign languages, as well as regional authochthonous minority languages (BMBWF 2021), which have a special status due to the *Minderheiten-Schulgesetz* (school law for minority languages).[1] Migrants' languages are mainly taught in the form of the *Muttersprachlicher Unterricht* (mother-tongue teaching). This can, in theory, take place in any language if requested by the parents for allochthonous minority languages, provided enough pupils sign up for classes in these languages and the school has the resources to facilitate them (BMBWF 2014). It, however, is mostly taught in separate groups and the other students in the class may not necessarily be confronted with their peers' languages. Only if there is a majority of pupils sharing a home language in a class is team-teaching explicitly recommended in that language (BMBWF 2014). In regular class teaching in a lot of schools, languages may be present on posters, in songs and formal exchanges like greetings and languages spoken between the children are accepted, but the focus is nonetheless on the official language of the school only (Purkarthofer 2018: 55–6) and other languages are not used during instruction. In her book *Der monolinguale Habitus der mehrsprachigen Schule*, Gogolin argues that there is a 'monolingual habitus' (2008: 30) dominating schools in Europe – that is to say, the focus on the language of instruction only. The result of this is that, because they are not able to draw on their full linguistic repertoire in their education, plurilingual pupils are systematically disadvantaged, as they are able to succeed in education in only one of the components of their linguistic repertoire. This also means that school systems do not take their pupils' linguistic resources into account and, as a result, ultimately waste their potential. Some Austrian schools have banned the use of their pupils' home languages even during breaks, which can be harmful for multiple reasons. Due to the fact that conversations during breaks are of a private nature even if they take place in public spaces like schools, a language ban during these times violates Article 29 of the United Nations Convention on the Rights of the Child (United Nations 1990). Contrary to the assumptions of some teachers, forcing pupils to speak only German during breaks does not help them to learn the language faster, as they may perceive the language of instruction as a threat to their home language(s). This can even hinder the acquisition of the new second language (Fleck 2019: 102–3). Another negative aspect of language bans is that they can create an atmosphere of mistrust between teachers and students, as well as among students (Fleck 2019: 106).

Translanguaging has the potential to tackle notions of harmful language practices by turning classrooms into more equitable spaces and has been discussed by many scholars and theorists as a means to support plurilingual children during regular classes. By allowing pupils to draw on their full linguistic repertoire during specifically determined phases of instruction, they are supported in their content and language learning which has important implications within and beyond the classroom. To establish translanguaging in the school system, it is therefore important to implement translanguaging in teacher education programmes.

# Using Pedagogical Translanguaging in Teacher Education

Utilizing pedagogical translanguaging in university lectures and seminars provides a wide range of benefits for students. Cenoz and Gorter (2017) argue that pedagogical translanguaging includes all the measures and strategies that teachers apply in order to incorporate their pupils' home languages into their instruction. Spontaneous translanguaging, however, happens during fluid discourse among pupils during or outside classes (Cenoz and Gorter in Schwarzl 2020: 35). Creating spaces for pedagogical translanguaging in teacher education programmes can facilitate students' subject learning and the understanding of content on a deeper level. Using translanguaging as a strategy in teacher education also challenges politico-linguistic norms, as translanguaging makes the students' whole linguistic spectrum visible and emphasizes the value of all languages. By providing public spaces for all languages, they are legitimized as a valuable component of learning (Kleyn 2016: 207). This in turn has the potential to effectuate political change: establishing translanguaging strategies in teacher education can play a crucial role in raising awareness of the advantages that plurilingualism can have for schools and society and to tackle the limiting and often harmful language policies in the Austrian education system, where the students' plurilingual realities are often ignored. As a result, the worth of all languages not only for individuals and their education but also for society as a whole is stressed. It is, therefore, especially important for teachers to recognize that seeing their pupils in all their facets of being also means taking notice of their whole linguistic repertoire. Kleyn argues that students 'cannot and should not be asked to leave their home language and cultural practices at the door' (2016: 203). Rather than excluding their home languages, schools must facilitate opportunities for pupils to use them as a resource for their learning. Instead of feeling ashamed of their 'deficits' in the official language of the school, they should be encouraged to feel proud of their plurilingualism. Making the effort to integrate their pupils' home languages into their instruction also has the benefit that teachers will know and understand their students better (Kleyn 2016: 203). However, in spite of the opportunities offered by multilingual learning spaces, it is known that even teacher candidates who grew up with migration languages often advocate for monolingualism in schools, as they often did not get the chance to experience their own plurilingualism as a valuable resource for instruction (Lengyel and Rosen 2012, 2015; Panagiotopoulou and Rosen 2016 in Fißmer et al., forthcoming). Some members of linguistic minorities even emphasize that during their own time at school they were ashamed of their plurilingualism and were keen to speak 'perfect' German to avoid any doubt regarding their language skills (Fißmer et al., forthcoming).

Dirim and Pokitsch therefore argue that lecturers in multilingualism must be aware of the ways in which they themselves (re-)construct language hierarchies. Since language pedagogical concepts were developed in a space that has not overcome colonial thinking, even well-intended ways of dealing with language(s) can lead to a (neo-)linguistic exclusion (Dirim and Pokitsch in Fißmer et al, forthcoming). Dirim therefore claims that teacher education programmes must take on a critical linguistic perspective and reveal how, in postcolonial times, colonial traditions are carried on by categorizing people through linguistic features (Dirim in Fißmer et al., forthcoming).

The impact of translanguaging strategies extends beyond the classroom. García et al. (2021) argue that translanguaging can tackle 'abyssal thinking' (de Sousa Santos in García et al. 2021: 1), that is, a colonial, hegemonic thinking that regards the knowledge and lived experiences of those colonized as nonexistent. In this way, they argue that colonial mindsets based on 'abyssal thinking' deeply impact the language practices in school systems and especially the way racialized bilingual pupils are viewed, who 'are continuously positioned by society and categorized in schools as deficient in language, despite the students' own understandings about their linguistic abilities' (García et al. 2021: 3). Makalela (2018) supports this argument in the context of the teaching of African languages in South Africa, which are often taught in a colonial way, that is, as separated from one another. This, however, does not mirror the plurilingual realities of their speakers, who often use three or more languages in the same conversation. He therefore advocates for an Ubuntu translanguaging pedagogy (UTP), which he has applied to teach Sepedi to speakers of other African languages in a teacher training programme in South Africa. Makalela describes the ubuntu philosophy as 'I + We = I am because you are; you are because we are' (2018: 271) and has drawn on this principle of interconnectedness between African languages to design a translanguaging course in Sepedi as an additional language. He concludes that UTP can lead to 'positive learning experiences and reaffirm[s] the student teachers' multilingual identities. In particular, the translingual principles have created a positive multilingual space and increased acquisition of the target language as well as its sister languages, without devaluating their own home languages' (2018: 277).

## Skills Teachers Need to Successfully Integrate Translanguaging

To understand how teacher education programmes can prepare future educators to approach their pupils' plurilingual realities through translanguaging, it is important to identify what skills and stances they need to integrate translanguaging into their teaching. García and Kleyn argue that teachers must shift their stance, change their lesson design and shift their interaction towards translanguaging during lessons (2016: 20).

School systems traditionally separate individual languages between spaces, hours or teachers. For example, in many Austrian primary schools, the class teacher will mainly feel in charge of developing the students' German skills, teach English during scheduled hours and leave the development of the students' home languages to the *Muttersprachlicher Unterricht* (mother-tongue) teachers. García and Kleyn argue that developing a translanguaging stance means that teachers must change their own attitudes towards what teaching languages in schools should 'look' like and where and how exchanges should happen, as this ideological shift will also change their behaviour in the classroom. This also means that teachers must build an awareness that their pupils' languages are a resource that is always available to them and their learning (2016: 20–1).

To help trainee teachers develop a supportive stance towards translanguaging, Kleyn (2016) suggests reflecting on the following questions in teacher education programmes:

- Voice: What is the role of translanguaging in providing voice to emergent bilinguals? If students are denied the use of their home language, what are the implications educationally, emotionally and politically?

- Freedom: To what extent is linguistic freedom provided to students who speak a home language that differs from the national language? Are the human and linguistic rights of these students being met? If not, what changes need to occur at the national, local and school levels?

- Access: How is access to learning content, a new language and continuing to develop a home language provided or denied to emergent bilinguals, and why? What role can translanguaging play in making learning more accessible? (2016: 218)

As well as developing a supportive stance towards translanguaging, teachers must learn to design lesson plans based on translanguaging. García, Johnson and Seltzer (2016: 21) identify three elements that are necessary for the planning of translanguaging classes. Firstly, it is essential to create collaborative and cooperative structures. As interaction plays a significant role in all content and language learning, providing multiple possibilities for collaboration is a major factor in translanguaging classes. Therefore, teachers should ensure that they plan lessons with a lot of peer-interaction. To facilitate interaction in the students' full linguistic repertoire, they are often grouped according to their home language backgrounds to prevent language barriers and support each other in their learning (García and Kleyn 2016: 22). For example, in a primary science class in Austria, the same question about what the weather is like in different seasons could be handed to all groups in German, but the pupils can discuss the topic in their home language(s) to support each other in their content learning. Secondly, by collecting varied multilingual and multimodal instructional resources such as multilingual texts, videos, films and websites, a range of perspectives can be integrated into the learning process (2016: 22). Multilingual resources can, for example, be found on the website of the *Österreichisches*

*Sprachen-Kompetenzzentrum* (Austrian language competence centre)[2] and the multilingual magazines *Trio* and *Trio Hallo Österreich* provide texts in Arabic, Bosnian/Croatian/Serbian, Dari, English, German and Turkish. Furthermore, teachers need pedagogical strategies to successfully implement translanguaging into their lesson planning, that is, knowledge of different methods, social forms and other strategies to integrate their pupils' languages into their teaching. This allows plurilingual students to publicly display their full language repertoire as 'an image of language that fits in with state and school definitions' (García and Kleyn 2016: 23). Teachers could, for example, integrate their pupils' home languages through songs and poems, encourage them to translate words or definitions or let them do research in multilingual books and on multilingual websites.

Teachers who want to work with translanguaging also have to be willing to be flexible and to spontaneously adapt to their pupils' abilities. For instance, García and Kleyn argue that 'teachers that take up translanguaging theory must also be prepared to change the course of instruction in order to respond to individual children's language repertoires' (2016: 23). As a result of this spontaneous reaction to the pupils' utterances in their multiple languages, teachers will have to react spontaneously and shift their original lesson design, for example by providing the opportunity to discuss unclarities about content in their home language groups.

## Translanguaging in Teacher Education

The majority of research about translanguaging in teacher education has been conducted as part of the City University of New York's New York State Initiative on Emergent Bilinguals (CUNY-NYSIEB).[3] As indicated in the project's name, the focus was on establishing translanguaging in English–Spanish bilingual education and on preparing student teachers for it. As part of this programme, Espinosa et al. have implemented translanguaging into teacher education at the City University of New York. The idea was to not offer translanguaging as a stand-alone course, but, instead, to integrate it throughout all bilingual, TESOL and general education programmes (Espinosa et al. 2020: 264). To help students on the teacher training course develop a translanguaging stance, in each of these courses offered, they get the chance to reflect on language profiles and journeys of themselves as well as those of other people they know. This is to help them reflect on their own way of living their plurilingualism and of how they and others view their plurilingualism. Apart from these reflections, students are confronted with translanguaging theory (Espinosa et al. 2020: 262).

Similarly, Kleyn suggests different ways of integrating translanguaging in teacher training. She argues that one important component is that trainee teachers get the opportunity to gain first experiences with the teaching of translanguaging lessons during school internships. Therefore, teacher education programmes must require teacher candidates to design lessons with translanguaging elements during school internships (Kleyn 2016: 215–16).

In all teacher education programmes, students are confronted with a range of principles and methods. These concepts are often taught only theoretically. However, to transform school systems and implement translanguaging sustainably, we must provide them with teacher education programmes in which the integration of migration languages is not taught only theoretically, but also where it can be experienced in practice (Rösch and Bachor-Pfeff 2021: 9–10; Kleyn 2016: 215–16). Using translanguaging as a pedagogical principle in teacher education can help students understand the concept on another level and hopefully motivate them to integrate it into their own teaching and, as a result, change norms of the school system as a whole.

By equipping teacher candidates with the experience of being in a translanguaging classroom, opportunities to try out translanguaging and theoretical knowledge about translanguaging, plurilingualism can be understood as the norm of the multilingual school. Kleyn also argues that translanguaging pedagogies can never be identical, as programmes and students are different and translanguaging pedagogies must therefore always be adapted to the group (2016: 215–16).

## *Strategies for Pedagogical Translanguaging in Teacher Education*

To help student teachers understand the benefits of implementing translanguaging in their future teaching, it is important to provide them with ample opportunities to experience translanguaging in their own education. Lecturers adapt a role model function regarding the way they deal with translanguaging during university seminars and lectures which, as Kleyn highlights, becomes 'critical to how candidates experience and enact it in their own classrooms' (2016: 215–16). To motivate teacher candidates to use translanguaging in their own teaching, they need to be provided with positive opportunities of experiencing translanguaging. There are various ways in which translanguaging can be applied in teacher education. Some of the strategies listed in what follows have partly been suggested explicitly for teacher education (Kleyn 2016; Espinosa et al. 2020). Others have been suggested for their use in school, but I would argue that they are also appropriate for teacher education.

Integrating multiple multilingual materials is one way of realizing translanguaging in teacher education:

- Completing course readings in multiple languages (Kleyn 2016: 215–16);

- Using multilingual dictionaries (Collins and Cioè-Pena in Kleyn 2016: 204);
- Discussing multilingual bulletin boards, signs, labels, posters, charts, books, dictionaries, iPads, maps, photographs and student work (Kleyn 2016: 204);
- Reading translations of the same texts in various languages individually, then discussing some paragraphs in small groups or the plenary (Schwarzl 2020: 62);
- Using parallel texts (Kleyn 2016: 206);
- Using electronically translated texts (Kleyn 2016: 207).

One challenge relating to finding appropriate course readings in multiple languages is that it is not always possible for lecturers who do not share their students' home language(s). However, students could be given the opportunity to conduct their own research on a topic related to the course in their home language(s), which, depending on the findings could lead to interesting discussions about language prestige in academia.

Kleyn suggests the use of parallel texts or translated texts in bilingual education to help students understand difficult words, structures and concepts, and to provide them vocabulary in both languages used (Kleyn 2016: 206). The use of parallel or translated texts in other languages could be another way to integrate the students' home languages. Electronically translated texts can help to raise the students' language awareness by making them compare and correct these texts with their source text (Kleyn 2016: 207).

Collaborative work is crucial to translanguaging, as students can support each other in their subject and language learning through peer-led learning. In teacher education, students can be grouped according to home language(s) to discuss concepts, instructions and other content at the start or during seminars and lectures. Lecturers should, however, be very sensitive regarding how they word the forming of groups based on language and should find a balance between alternating home language and mixed language groups to avoid ghettoization. Various researchers (Schwarzl 2020; Woodley and Brown 2016) have emphasized the particular challenge of class compositions where minority languages are represented only by a few speakers. In those cases, it is not always possible to collaborate in class with a home language partner. However, students who do not have home language(s) partners can be encouraged to use dictionaries and online translation programmes (Kleyn 2016: 207) and, where possible, students can draw on inter-comprehension by being paired with home language partners from similar language systems.

Multilingual oral presentations make the students' home languages visible and, as a result, emphasize the legitimization of these languages in education.

Espinosa et al. suggest that multilingual presentations in the students' home languages provide teacher candidates with a consciousness of the diversity of languages present within the classroom. As a result of giving space to multilingual presentations, 'official language practices that silence some, while privileging others' (Espinosa et al. 2020: 264) are disturbed and may be questioned, and politico-linguistic power norms are disturbed. In teacher education programmes, multilingual presentations could be designed in the following ways:

- Exposing all students to multilingual presentations or allowing them to present in language(s) not spoken by the majority of the class (Kleyn 2016: 215–16);
- Providing students with the opportunity to read aloud in their home language(s) to the group (Kleyn 2016: 207);
- Writing a paper or essay in 'home' language(s) and presenting it in class (Espinosa et al. 2020: 264);
- Reading a poem in the home language(s) (Schwarzl 2020: 62);
- Working with content bilingually, then presenting it in designated languages (Kleyn 2016: 204);
- Presenting home language practice(s) with a song or chant (Espinosa et al. 2020: 264).

Encouraging students in teacher education programmes to write essays in their home language(s) will undoubtedly benefit the individuals' learning but it will arguably present a challenge when it comes to summative assessment, since the lecturer might not have a high enough knowledge of all languages used to understand the papers. However, since teacher candidates are adult learners and it can be assumed that they will be interested in their chosen research topic, I would argue that this activity could even be used as a component of the summative assessment of a course if this piece of assessment is graded as 'completed/ not completed'.

Writing and taking notes in multiple languages is another way to put translanguaging into practice and to engage with the students' home languages and content on another level. In teacher training, the following strategies can be applied:

- Taking notes on scholarly articles and other texts in home language(s) or bilingually to construct deeper meaning (Espinosa et al. 2020: 264; Montoya in Kleyn 2016: 205);
- Writing poems in various languages (Ebe in Kleyn 2016: 204).

Plurilingual writing has the potential to help students come up with their own thoughts about an article and to better understand concepts. However, it is important to note that it might not always be possible because many students have not been alphabetized in their home language(s).

In some cases where two languages are shared by all students and the lecturer, bilingual instruction can be a way to implement translanguaging in teacher education. One example of how this can be achieved is by providing translations of the learning aims, some keywords, directions or important concepts to facilitate students with a general sense of the content at the beginning of a lesson (Kleyn 2016: 207). Another suggestion Kleyn makes is for the lecturer to explain the content in two languages and to then let the students discuss and translate the vocabulary into their home language(s) (Kleyn 2016: 204). For example, in a TEFL seminar on intercultural communication, different concepts of culture could be explained in English, as well as German, and for a deeper understanding then discussed in the students' home language(s) groups.

Applying translanguaging strategies to provide students with the experience of being in a translanguaging classroom is one key factor to integrate it into teacher education and, as a result, in a school system. It is, however, also important to provide teacher candidates with ample opportunities to reflect on this experience. Kleyn suggests discussing with the students the role that translanguaging has played for their own content and language learning. She also suggests discussing different experiences of learning through the students' home languages and the consequences of learning only through the dominant language. By doing so, larger issues like identification within a society and the role that the students' individual languages play for this sense of identity, as well as the question of how inclusive classrooms actually are regarding multilingualism, can be raised (Kleyn 2016: 205).

## Practical Suggestions for Integrating Translanguaging into Teacher Education

At the KPH Vienna/Krems, all students in primary teaching can choose their specialism in various disciplines, including English and German as a second language. Since all the courses in the *Schwerpunkt Englisch* are taught in the target language, which the majority of students have learned as a foreign language, the programme offers various possibilities to not only teach about translanguaging in theory, but also to provide teacher candidates with the experience of being in a translanguaging classroom and to apply translanguaging strategies to teach subject material in the classroom. The idea behind this is that future teachers should not only learn about different concepts in theory, but also experience them themselves during their education.

In one of the modules I teach, the curriculum includes ways of integrating multiple languages in foreign language teaching. This module is divided into two parts: a lecture on language learning and multilingualism which is taught by my colleague, and my seminar on multilingualism and intercultural communication. In the lecture, translanguaging is discussed on a theoretical level. To complement this, in my seminar on intercultural communication and multilingualism, students experience translanguaging on a practical level during multiple sessions throughout the course. I decided to use translanguaging as a pedagogical strategy throughout the course, but only to explain my rationale for doing so and to think about ways to integrate translanguaging in the students' own teaching towards the end of the course. The idea behind this was to provide the students with the experience of being in a translanguaging classroom to help them understand translanguaging on a deeper level. Another reason why I provided my students with a translanguaging experience before teaching its theory was to mitigate negative first reactions about translanguaging that might otherwise occur. Sometimes in my teaching, when I introduce students to a concept or a method, the first reaction is defensive, as they question whether it can be realized in practice. By providing them with the experience of using their whole linguistic repertoire during specific phases of my course, I wanted to prevent this immediate first reaction and to help students realize that there are, indeed, ways to integrate translanguaging into their own teaching in primary schools. In the next sections, I will outline some best practice examples of classes I have taught that include translanguaging, which can be used in other kinds of teacher education programmes as well.

### *Establishing the Students' Language Profiles*

To plan effective ways to integrate translanguaging in seminars and lectures, it is important to establish an overview of the students' language profiles at the beginning of a course. Ideally, this is connected with an activity that encourages them to reflect on their own language practices and the roles that languages play in their life. During face-to-face classes, an effective way to do this is by using the language portfolio, which was developed by Gogolin and Neumann and further developed by Krumm. In this activity, students illustrate their languages in the silhouette of a person and then explain what they have done. This gives teachers and lecturers a lot of information about the role of the students' languages in their life (Busch 2013: 36f).

Another activity for finding out about students' languages profiles designed for an online class is to create a Padlet with pictures of various items that can typically be found in a classroom, like a ruler, a blackboard, a sponge and so on, and to ask the students to label these items with all the words they know for them. After the students have labelled the photos, the group should describe what languages they recognize in the

Padlet. In a third step, each student adds a note with their name and groups words in all the languages they have knowledge in around their name before proceeding to tell the group what role each language plays in their life.

## *Contrasting Translanguaging Courses and Language Bans*

To provide the students with a first experience of translanguaging, it can be useful to provide them with the contrasting experience of being in a translanguaging classroom and being in a classroom where they are forbidden to use any language other than English, which for most of them is a foreign language. This is why in the first part of a session the lecturer advocates a language ban. The lecturer hands the students a short scholarly text in English and explains that the group will do a text jigsaw activity where small groups will read a different short section. While they are preparing a presentation with another peer about their segment, the students are not permitted to use any bilingual dictionaries or online dictionaries, to check translations into German or other languages, or to ask their peers for translations. The students are constantly reminded that they are only allowed to discuss the text in English and that they are strictly forbidden to use any other language for discussion.

In the second part of the class, the lecturer can provide the students with a translanguaging experience by asking them to annotate a text they were given to read at home with comments about each sub-section, in their strongest language(s). For this, it should be stressed that mixing languages is also possible. Then, the lecturer hands the students questions in English and tells them to discuss the questions with a partner in any language or languages they want. Where possible, multilingual students can be paired with home language partners. To give students opportunities to use their whole linguistic repertoire, students who do not share their home languages or strongest languages with anyone can be encouraged to take notes on their own. They should also be encouraged to use bilingual dictionaries at this stage. In a next step, they can discuss the questions with others in any language they want or mix languages. At the end of this stage, the text (or passages from it) can be discussed in English in the plenary and unclear sections can be read and discussed through.

After having provided the students with these two contrasting experiences regarding the inclusion and exclusion of their whole linguistic repertoire, there should be a reflection round, where the students are asked how they felt during each part of the seminar and if there was any difference regarding their understanding of the topics. A good way to do this is to use an activity in which the students have to answer questions non-verbally by locating themselves in a certain corner. Useful reflection questions can be as follows:

- How well did you understand this topic?
- How comfortable did you feel during this stage of the class?

The students then move to one of the corners, depending on whether their answer is 'I understood this very well/somewhat/not at all', 'I felt very comfortable/somewhat comfortable/very uncomfortable'.

This activity provides a good overview of how the individual group members have perceived different aspects of the seminar and it is also a good starting point for discussion. It can be a useful way to help the students reflect on their personal perceptions and feelings when a language ban is imposed onto them.

## *Language Prestige*

To start a discussion about language prestige and language power relations, students can be asked to research a topic from the seminar in their strongest language(s) as a homework exercise in preparation for a new topic. At the beginning of the seminar, students should be paired in their home language(s) groups where possible and asked to discuss the findings from their research. Again, they should be reminded that they may discuss in any language or mix languages. Each group should write down five important aspects about the topic in any language(s) they wish. These should then be written down on the board, again encouraging the students to do this in any language or languages they want to use. After this step, the students can read their terms out to the class, so all languages are presented orally as well as in written form. This can be a starting point for a discussion about whether it was difficult to find information about the topic and to guide the students towards a discussion on language prestige. Another idea behind this approach is to facilitate a better understanding of the topic for the students by encouraging them to undertake prior research in their strongest language(s) and to allow them to think about it without the boundaries of being inhibited in their subject learning by language barriers.

## Conclusion

This chapter has demonstrated that the impact of translanguaging can turn classrooms from linguistically exclusive into inclusive spaces. Allowing pupils to draw on their full linguistic repertoire in their learning can facilitate their language and content learning. On a larger scale, making all the pupils' languages visible in the classroom not only emphasize the value of all languages for the individual, but it can also lead to the questioning of politico-linguistic power norms in the school system and, as a result, society as a whole (García and Kleyn 2016: 21). Furthermore, translanguaging can serve as a means to tackle colonial norms which strictly separate the teaching of one language from all the others (Makalela 2018: 262) and categorize plurilinguals and their language practices as deficient (García et al. 2021: 8).

Teacher education programmes in multilingual societies such as Austria and especially Vienna must help raise their students' awareness that multilingualism is the norm in the world, rather than an exception (Espinosa et al. 2020: 262). It is therefore also critical that students develop a stance that their pupils' plurilingualism is not a burden, but a chance for learning, and that they learn to use this potential effectively through translanguaging. However, to sustainably implement translanguaging into a school system, students must also experience being in a translanguaging classroom in their own education. The practical examples in this chapter have demonstrated how this can be achieved in content classes for students of primary teaching held in a foreign language. However, they could also serve more broadly as an inspiration for lecturers in teacher education programmes for modern languages teachers.

## Notes

1  See https://www.bundeskanzleramt.gv.at/themen/volksgruppen.htm
2  See http://www.oesz.at/
3  See https://www.cuny-nysieb.org/

## References

Altmann, H. B. (1983), 'Training Foreign Language Teachers for Learner-Centered Instruction: Deep Structures, Surface Structures and Transformations', in J. E. Alatis, H. H. Stern, and P. Strevens (eds.), *Applied Linguistics and the Preparation of Second Language Teachers: Toward a Rationale*, 19–26, Washington, DC: Georgetown University Press.
BMBWF. 'Information zum muttersprachlichen Unterricht', 2014. Available online: https://www.bmbwf.gv.at/Themen/schule/schulrecht/rs/1997-2017/2014_12 .html (accessed 6 April 2021).
BMBWF. 'Sprachliche Bildung', 2021. Available online: https://www.bmbwf.gv.at/ Themen/schule/schulpraxis/ba/sprabi.html (accessed 1 October 2021).
BMBWF. 'Von Mehrsprachigkeit – Muttersprachlicher Unterricht – Interkulturelle Bildung', 2021. Available online: https://www.bmbwf.gv.at/Themen/schule/ schulpraxis/ba/sprabi/msmuib.html (accessed October 1, 2021).

Bundeskanzleramt. 'Schülerinnen und Schüler mit anderen Erstsprachen als Deutsch', 2021. Available online: https://www.oesterreich.gv.at/themen/bildung_und_neue_medien/schule/Seite.110005.html (accessed 13 November).

Busch, B. (2013), *Mehrsprachigkeit*, Wien: Facultas wuv.

Cenoz, J., and D. Gorter. (2017), 'Minority Languages and Sustainable Translanguaging: Threat or Opportunity?', *Journal of Multilingual and Multicultural Development*, 38(10): 901–12.

Espinosa, C. M., L. Ascenzi-Moreno, T. Kleyn, and M. T. Sánchez. (2020), 'Transforming Urban Teacher Education', in O. García (ed.), *Translanguaging and Transformative Teaching for Emergent Bilingual Students: Lessons from the CUNY-NYSIEB Project*, 257–70, New York: Routledge.

European Parliament. (2022), 'Fact Sheets on the European Union: Language Policy'. Available online: https://www.europarl.europa.eu/factsheets/en/sheet/142/language-policy (accessed 1 October 2021).

Fißmer, J., L. Rosen, and F. tom Dieck. (forthcoming), '. . . wenn hier jeder, der nicht mal richtig Deutsch werden kann – Zur (De-)Konstruktion von Sprachhierarchien in der inklusionsorientierten Lehrer*innenbildung', in A. Großhauser, A. Köpfer, and H. Siegismund (eds.), *Inklusion und Deutsch als Zweitsprache als Querschnittsaufgaben in der Lehrer*innenbildung – Konzeptuelle Entwicklungslinien und hochschuldidaktische Zugänge*, Trier: Wissenschaftlicher Verlag Trier.

Fleck, E. (2019), 'Wie viel Muttersprache ist erlaubt?', in E. Furch and M Wiedner (eds.), *Tagungsband Menschenrechtsbildung 2018. 1. Jahrestagung zur Menschenrechtsbildung an der Pädagogischen Hochschule Wien*, 95–108, Hohengehren: Schneider.

García, O., N. Flores, K. Seltzer, W. Li, R. Otheguy, and J. Rosa. (2021), 'Rejecting Abyssal Thinking in the Language and Education of Racialized Bilinguals: A Manifesto', *Critical Inquiry in Language Studies*, 18 (3): 1–26.

García, O., S. Johnson, and K. Seltzer. (2016), *The Translanguaging Classroom: Leveraging Student Bilingualism for Learning*, Philadelphia, PA: Caslon.

García, O., and T. Kleyn. (2016), 'Translanguaging Theory in Education', in O. García and T. Kleyn (eds.), *Translanguaging with Multilingual Students*, 23–47, London: Taylor and Francis.

García, O., and R. Otheguy. (2020), 'Plurilingualism and Translanguaging: Commonalities and Divergences', *International Journal of Bilingual Education and Bilingualism*, 23: 17–35.

Gogolin, I. (2008), *Der monolinguale Habitus der multilingualen Schule*, Münster: Waxmann.

Kleyn, T. (2016), 'Setting the Path: Implications for Teachers and Teacher Educators', in O. García and T. Kleyn (eds.), *Translanguaging with Multilingual Students*, 216–34, London: Taylor and Francis.

Lengyel, D., and L. Rosen. (2012). 'Vielfalt im Lehrerzimmer?!–Erste Einblicke in ein Lern-/Lehr-und Forschungsprojekt mit Lehramtsstudentinnen mit Migrationshintergrund an der Universität Köln', in *Das interkulturelle Lehrerzimmer*, 71–87, Wiesbaden: VS Verlag für Sozialwissenschaften.

Lengyel, D., and L. Rosen. (2015). 'Diversity in the Staff Room–Ethnic Minority Student Teachers' Perspectives on the Recruitment of Minority Teachers', *Tertium Comparationis*, 21(2): 161–83.

Makalela, L. (2018), 'Teaching African Languages the Ubuntu Way: The Effects of Translanguaging among Pre-Service Teachers in South Africa', in P. Van Avermaet, S. Slembrouck, K. Van Gorp, S. Sierens, and K. Maryns (eds.), *The Multilingual Edge of Education*, 261–82, London: Palgrave Macmillan.

Pädagogische Hochschule Wien. (2021), 'Was ist voXmi?'. Available online: https://phwien.ac.at/die-ph-wien/institute/institut-fuer-weiterfuehrende-qualifikationen-und-bildungskooperationen/berichte/2139-was-ist-voxmi (accessed 13 November 2021).

Purkarthofer, J. (2018), 'Sprachorganisation in Bildungsinstitutionen. Gesagtes und Ungesagtes in Kindergarten und Schule', in M. Fürstaller, N. Hover-Reisner, and B. Lehner (eds.), *Vielfalt in der Elementarpädagogik Theorie, Empirie und Professionalisierung*, 49–62, Schwalbach: Debus Pädagogik.

Rösch, H., and N. Bachor-Pfeff. (2021), 'Einleitung', in H. Rösch and N. Bachor-Pfeff (eds.), *Mehrsprachliche Bildung im Lehramtsstudium*, 7–12, Hohengehren: Schneider Verlag.

Stadt Wien. (2020), 'Exkurs: Mehrsprachigkeit von SchülerInnen'. Available online: https://www.wien.gv.at/spezial/integrationsmonitor2020/bildung/exkurs-mehrsprachigkeit-von-schuelerinnen/ (accessed 13 November 2021).

Schwarzl, L. (2020), 'Ein mehrperspektivischer Blick in das Translanguaging-Klassenzimmer-selbstbezogene Überzeugungen und Klassenklima im Fokus', PhD diss., University of Vienna.

United Nations. (1989), 'Convention on the Rights of the Child'. Available online: https://www.ohchr.org/en/professionalinterest/pages/crc.aspx (accessed 2 September 2021).

Woodley, H., and A. Brown. (2016), 'Balancing Windows and Mirrors: Translanguaging in a Multilingual Classroom', in *Making Meaning of Translanguaging: Learning from Classroom Moments*, New York: Routledge.

# CHAPTER 12

# Learning Language in All Subjects – The Key for More Equal Opportunities

## A Mixed Methods Study on the Concept of *Sprachliche Bildung* (Integrative Language Learning) in Primary Schools in Vienna and Lower Austria

*Golriz Gilak*

### Introduction and Literature Review

The understanding of content can only be as good as the understanding of language (Drumm 2017: 38). The fact that modern language teaching is necessary also, and especially, in non-language lessons is still underestimated. In Austria, the migration languages Turkish and Bosnian/Serbo-Croatian have increasingly been represented since the guest workers were employed in the 1960s. According to Statistics Austria, Romanian, Arabic, Farsi/Dari, Russian and Hungarian were also among the most widely spoken everyday languages in Austria in 2020 (Statistik Austria 2021: online). According to the Office of National Statistics in Great Britain, immigrant languages such as Polish, Punjabi, Urdu among others and minority languages such as Welsh, Scots and others belong to the common non-English languages (Office of National Statistics n.d.: online).

De Cillia (2013) describes *lebensweltliche Mehrsprachigkeit* (plurilingualism in everyday life) as a form of plurilingualism consisting of minority languages or migration languages. The majority of society does not see this form of plurilingualism as an enrichment, but, rather, as an obstacle to educational success (Dirim/Khakpour 2018: 202). Even students experience their linguistic deficits because of their plurilingualism (Michalak 2008). The monolingualism of the school which Gogolin (2008) refers to as the 'monolingual habitus of the multilingual school', leads to a neglect of minority or migration languages in the educational system. Also, strong dialectal deviations can make the acquisition of the language of instruction comparable to learning a foreign language (Leisen 2013: 39). However, linguistic diversity as an enrichment is often connected only to the competences in foreign languages, that is, languages that can be learned in the educational system (de Cillia 2013). The missing consideration of the ('everyday') languages of the students could be one of the many causes of educational disadvantages (Busse 2019: 2). After all, the constant immigration from numerous regions of the world and the globalization of work and private life lead to an irreversible change in the linguistic requirements of learners in educational institutions (Krumm/Reich 2011: 3).

However, the appreciation of all languages is not only beneficial for migrant students, but also proves to be a necessary preparation also for native children, to understand the normality of a multilingual and multicultural coexistence (Luchtenberg 2009). Every educational system should achieve equity for all students corresponding to the definition of the OECD which means that 'whatever variations there may be in education outcomes, they are not related to students' background, including socio-economic status, gender or immigrant background' (OECD 2019: online).

This research and the concept of integrative language learning are making a contribution to more equal opportunities in the educational system by following the principles of SDG 4, high-quality education:

> *The United Nations Sustainable Development Goals (SDGs) advocate for ensuring inclusive and equitable quality education and promoting lifelong learning opportunities for all (United Nations 2015). The principle that every person has a fair chance to improve his or her life, whatever his or her personal circumstances, lies at the heart of democratic political and economic institutions. Ensuring that all students have access to the best education opportunities is also a way of using resources effectively, and of improving education and social outcomes in general.* (OECD 2019: online)

The concept of integrative language learning is aimed at all students. Jim Cummins (2008) distinguishes between two registers of language: BICS (Basic Interpersonal Communications Skills) and CALP (Cognitive Academic Language Proficiency). While BICS is more tolerant of mistakes when using everyday language (Leisen 2013: 39) and mostly used orally, the concept of CALP is described as an educational language, which is 'an academic language' (Carnevale/Wojnesitz 2014: 8) and differs from everyday language in terms of abstract content and written language. The teaching of CALP therefore requires special attention and systematic support (Busse 2019: 6). Regardless of their first language(s), students can have difficulties acquiring CALP. It should be mentioned that the concept of 'academic language' is also criticized, for example, by García et al. (2021) who associate this term with skills of socially dominant, white, middle-class learners. To categorize minority language students as 'deficient' in academic language is a kind of structural linguicism that embeds privilege and places students from minority backgrounds at a disadvantage. With the concept of 'integrative language learning' teachers could meet these challenges, because CALP still remains essential in the educational system. So we have to train language skills in all subjects. To achieve this, more attention needs to be paid to the topic in teacher education (Danilovich/Putjata 2019: 5f.). However, this assumption is already well discussed by researchers, because the systematic promotion of CALP, for example in the planning and design of lessons, is inadequately realized in lessons (Riebling 2013 quoted from Rank et al. 2016: 2), which corresponds to the phenomenon of the 'hidden curriculum', where the acquisition of CALP skills is presumed and not explicitly taught during subject learning (Kleinschmidt 2017: 117). This inevitably creates a form of inequality between those who have already acquired the register of CALP elsewhere and those who have not had these opportunities. It is up to teachers to recognize the need for language-sensitive lessons where language and subject learning take place at the same time. This is what 'integrative language learning' is all about and supports mastering CALP as the basis for educational success, for all students (Fürstenau/Gomolla 2011: 108). If the teacher does not explicitly address the register of CALP, this could lead to an educational disadvantage as already mentioned as well as to a reduced self-esteem of students, regardless of their first language (Danilovich/Putjata 2019: 4). Integrative language learning can thus help to compensate for social injustice.

In their study on the linguistic beliefs of candidate teachers, Fischer et al. found a lack of research dealing with linguistic diversity in teaching (2018: 158). In addition, the missing knowledge of the concept of 'integrative language learning' in teacher education in Germany is also mentioned.

To fill the gap, the Ministry of Education in Austria is currently making efforts to propagate the didactic tools of 'integrative language learning' in voluntary teacher training.

## Definition of Concepts

The following example is intended to clarify the concept of integrative language learning: Mathematics lessons seem to be a particular challenge for many students, regardless of their first language. If the language of instruction is not understood, the content cannot be understood either. With the concept of integrative language learning, language will be discussed and trained in mathematics lessons so that content can be understood and CALP is no longer presumed.

The need to combine language learning with content learning seems to be inevitable in any subject-related didactics to close the educational gap. Language learning is always included in the subject (Leisen 2011: 17). In the concept of integrative language learning, language functions as a tool to understand the content (ibid. 5). For this method, the teacher needs to have sufficient knowledge of language requirements and difficulties. Leisen emphasizes that in classrooms, language support may not be everything, but without language support everything is nothing (Leisen 2015: 137).

To achieve this goal, 'integrative language learning' must consistently take place in all subjects, include all students (Becker-Mrotzeck/Roth 2017: 30) and every teacher should be able to provide 'language-sensitive' teaching. Leisen (2011) describes the sensitivity as the way in which linguistic issues in non-language subjects are dealt with. In this form of teaching, language is the matter of subject (Nolte 2016: 40).

Dirim/Mecheril (2018) criticize the term 'integrative language learning' because 'language' is equated with 'German'. The term 'integrative multilingual learning' takes into account, appreciates and promotes all languages of students in the classroom. Gogolin/Lange (2010) also take this aspect of integrative multilingual learning into account, together with the knowledge that languages of origin should be viewed as a valuable resource for educational processes. Therefore, Tajmel underlines the importance of a resource-oriented rather than a deficit-oriented perspective (2017: 73).

Due to the fact that everyone is trained in language, not only students with other languages than German get in the centre of the need for support and so, the associated stigmata fade. In this sense, a connection between 'integrative language learning' and 'inclusion' can be seen. The commonality of both terms is shown by the equal social participation of all people, granting every person the necessary help (Rödel/Simon 2017a cited from Rödel 2019: 253).

## Differences of the CLIL-Method

'Content and Language Integrated Learning (CLIL) is a dual-focused educational approach in which an additional language is used for the learning and teaching of both content and language' (Coyle et al. 2010: 1). The main goal is to extend the vocabulary in a foreign language. However, the concept of integrative language learning strengthens language skills in the language of instruction (surrounding language) to improve content understanding.

While both CLIL and the concept of 'integrative language learning' help to acquire educational language skills by means of various methods (e.g., scaffolding). The concept of 'integrative language learning' should be expanded to 'multilingual learning', which takes first languages into account.

## Methods

### *Aims of the Present Study*

The primary goal of this mixed methods study is to research to what extent the concept of 'integrative language learning' has been implemented in primary schools. The results should present an actual state of 'integrative language learning' in the surveyed areas and bring the topic more into the focus of researchers. The results are also intended to offer opportunities for advanced training and further education of teachers.

### *Research Design*

A mixed methods design enables a multi-perspective view and provides a better understanding of a complex problem (Kuckartz 2014: 53). With a quantitative survey, a large number of responses are shown in numbers. To investigate in more depth at the same time, guideline interviews with primary school teachers were carried out so that personal attitudes and opinions can be explored and new perspectives can be opened up.

As part of the parallel design, according to Kuckartz, the data collection of both methods takes place at the same time. The results are brought together in a final step (2014: 129). To develop research methodological skills, students in teacher education were included in this study under the direction of the author in the Winter term of 2020/21.

Quantitative analyses are carried out via SPSS. The Qualitative Content Analysis (QCA) by Kuckartz (2014) is used for the interpretation of the interviews.

### *Research Question for This Study*

The main research question for the study aims to clarify to what extent the concept of 'integrative language learning' is already implemented in primary schools in Vienna and Lower Austria. This chapter focuses on answering the following subordinate questions: Which actions and beliefs of primary school teachers in instruction make it clear that they are responsible for integrative language learning in non-language subjects? Is there a connection between the number of multilingual students and the intensity of these actions and beliefs? The study sees the following categories to be operationalized for the quantitative and qualitative data analysis to answer the main research question:

1. Language-sensitivity teaching in non-language subjects;
2. Responsibility of teacher for teaching language in non-language subjects;
3. Teachers' attitude to language.
4. Language didactic measures in non-language subjects.

As an analysis of all categories would go beyond the scope of this chapter, the focus will be on the results of Category 2.

## *Hypotheses*

1. The sooner teachers see their non-language subjects as language lessons, the more likely they are to think about special vocabulary in advance.
2. The sooner teachers see their non-language subjects as language lessons, the more likely they will be to address the differences between BICS and CALP in non-language subjects.
3. The sooner teachers see their non-language subjects as language lessons, the more likely they are to recognize that language can produce discrimination.
4. The more students with a non-German first language in the class, the more teachers see their non-language subjects as language lessons.

## *Theoretical Foundation of Category 2*

It is the responsibility of teachers to make language learning possible in non-language subjects. The question is how primary school teachers feel responsible to train language in non-language subjects to challenge discrimination. Michalak et al. emphasize the permanent change between BICS and CALP in the classroom and the need to discuss the changing of these registers (2015: 11). It is recommended not primarily to simplify the content, but to offer opportunities to train CALP (Carnevale/Wojnesitz 2014: 12). Finally, the teacher has to be a linguistic role model in the use of CALP in the classroom (Fuchs et al. 2015: 23).

CALP can be achieved by regular repetitions, increased demonstrations of contents and so on (Schröder/Ritterfeld 2014: 64). Even in the case of linguistic errors, a correction in the form of an implicit repetition of the statement may have positive effects on language learning. This approach favours the self-confidence of students, who thus experience a positive error culture (Fuchs et al. 2014: 10).

The leitmotif of representatives of integrative language learning, 'Every lesson is a language lesson' (Fuchs et al. 2014: 7), is also relevant, especially when language can produce discrimination. In accordance with the UN Convention on the Rights of the Child, Article 28 (the right to education), the concept of 'integrative language learning' needs to be considered as a task of the teachers to make their lessons non-discriminatory and understandable for everyone (Tajmel 2017: 267).

## Sample

The decision was made to question primary school teachers in active service as a non-probabilistic sample. This is a common procedure in quantitative academic social research (Döring/Bortz 2016: 305) since the planning of the sampling is less complex. However, the disadvantage is that the results might not be representative (Bühner/Ziegler 2009: 745). The sample of the quantitative survey consisted of 310 primary school teachers. The dissemination of the online questionnaire was carried out mainly by the students, to the previously defined sample. The sample was recruited through gatekeepers, the snowball sampling and self-activation of the sample in social media. At 92 per cent, a significantly higher number of female teachers participated in the study. The mean of the years of service was 12.81, with a wide spread of SD = 11.35. The range was from a minimum of <1 to a maximum of 40 years of service. There is an equal distribution of school location: approximately 53 per cent taught in an urban (> 200,000 inhabitants) environment. A total of 89 per cent of the respondents were employed at a public school. Approximately 5 per cent of the respondents spoke a migration language or a minority language in Austria.

The sample of the qualitative survey consisted of forty-five primary school teachers. Again, at 96 per cent, there was a high participation of female teachers. The mean of the years of service (M = 10.55; SD = 10.33) as well as the range are comparable to the quantitative survey. The interest of the participants was rated with an average of 4 on a scale of 1 to 5. Approximately 15 per cent of the respondents spoke a migration language or a minority language.

## Survey Instruments

### *Online Survey*

The items were formulated based on theory (especially Leisen 2011; Tajmel 2017; Fuchs et al. 2014, 2015). In addition, items from previous studies such as Jost et al. (2017) and Thürmann/Vollmer (2011) were adapted. The items were defined as statements and mostly presented by a four-point Likert scale (1 to 4 = rejection to strong agreement) to avoid a tendency towards the middle. Demographic data was collected at the end of the questionnaire. To test the questionnaire, an online pre-test was created by the author and tested by colleagues and students. The online questionnaire was sent out mainly by students.

### Protection of Data Privacy

All participants were informed about the purpose of the survey, the duration of the data storage (maximum 24 months) and the use of the data. Before starting the questionnaire, participants were asked to click a checkbox. In the event of rejection, this person did not take part in the survey. The following personal data was collected in the survey: gender, years of employment, spoken language(s), school-specific information (public vs. private) and school location (urban vs. rural areas).

### Interviews

The interviews were carried out by instructed students. Due to the pandemic situation, some interviews were online. The interview had to be documented afterwards to capture any disturbances or peculiarities that arose during the conversation to counteract any risk of bias in the data collection.

## Results

### Results of the Quantitative Survey

The descriptive analysis shows a highly positive tendency in the feedback for the following items. A total of 81 per cent of the respondents partially or very much recognized that a non-language subject is also a language lesson. Also, 100 per cent described themselves partially or very much as a language role model for their students. A total of 81 per cent agreed partially or very much to repeat difficult subject matter in every lesson so that the students understand it better. And 83 per cent thought (very much) about the subject-related vocabulary in advance.

Significantly, lower approval values were found for items such as the distinction between BICS and CALP. Only 16 per cent pointed out differences between the two registers to their students in every lesson and only 47 per cent sometimes paid attention to addressing differences.

Only 25 per cent of the respondents fully or partially recognized that language can produce discrimination. And 63 per cent of the respondents stated that they simplify their language (very much) when communicating with their students.

In urban areas (> 200,000 inhabitants), as expected, more students with a non-German first language were represented in the classes. The t-test results show a comparison of the means: urban 3.29 (SD = 0.98) vs. rural 2.35 (SD = 0.88). The scale ranges from 1 = only German first language to 5 = all students with a non-German first language. Overall, only twenty-one out of 310 teachers surveyed stated that no first language other than German existed in the class. The knowledge of the rest of the teachers about which languages other than German were spoken in the classes was remarkably positive. Another 73 per cent were very much aware of the children's languages. Another 16 per cent were mostly certain that they knew which languages were spoken.

## *Review of the Hypotheses*

### Thoughts in Advance about Subject-related Vocabulary

The first bivariate correlation shows a highly significant ($p < 0.001$) relationship ($r = 0.220$) between the thoughts that a teacher has in advance about the subject-related vocabulary in the lesson planning and his or her opinion as to whether a non-language subject is also a language lesson. H1 is thus confirmed.

### Discussion of the Differences between BICS and CALP

The second bivariate correlation also shows a highly significant ($p = 0.001$) relationship ($r = 0.185$) between whether a non-language subject is also seen as a language lesson by the teacher and the intensity of how often the differences between BICS and CALP are discussed during lessons. H2 is thus confirmed.

### Language Can Produce Discrimination

The third bivariate correlation shows no significant ($p = 0.150$) connection between the belief that a non-language subject is also a language lesson and the idea that language can produce discrimination in the classroom. H3 can therefore be rejected.

### Multilingual Students

The last bivariate correlation highly significantly ($p < 0.001$; $r = 0.238$) confirms hypothesis 4. The more multilingual students are taught, the more a teacher recognizes non-language subjects as language lessons.

## *Results of the Qualitative Survey*

In the context of individual interviews, the items of the online questionnaire were dealt with in more depth by designing a guideline that included the different categories of the quantitative survey. The following section will discuss and analyse two questions or statements which address the responsibility of the teacher for integrative language learning in non-language subjects as well as the inclusion of (home) languages of students.

### My Non-language Subject Is Also a Language Lesson

A 100 per cent approval by the teachers could also be determined when it came to the question of whether they agreed that a non-language subject was always a language lesson. The respondents justified the need for integrative language learning by

- arguing that due to the Austrian dialect of their region of origin, students had difficulties mastering CALP:

    *Well, I can only confirm this expression because more and more (kids) [. . .] come to us at the beginning of their school career with language deficits [. . .] or with little knowledge of the written language. And that is especially true in rural areas. [. . .] These students often speak in a dialect and then of course firstly, they have to familiarize themselves with Standard German. (1_10, Z 15–19)*

- arguing that students had insufficient knowledge of the German language due to their non-German first language, which made it necessary to explicitly teach language in non-language subjects:

    *. . . especially with children whose mother tongue is not German [. . .] it is really [. . .] challenging to explain these basic terms to the children [. . .] so that one can [. . .] even teach . . . (2_8 , Z 11–14)*

- emphasizing the importance for all students to understand language before understanding the content: *Children must first acquire linguistic resources [. . .] so that they can understand content. (2_22, Z 19–21)*

    *I would say the language is something that is always present in our everyday life at school in all subjects in my opinion. (2_5, Z 7–9)*

    *Yes, I would definitely agree with the statement [. . .] because I always think about it in advance, so in every subject [. . .] German, mathematics, non-language subjects also in physical education [. . .] which words are used to make it understandable to everyone . . . (2_17, Z 17–20)*

> . . . to ensure fair and equitable education for everyone, the promotion of CALP in German in all subjects naturally also has an important function, because first of all, learning in school takes place through language. (2_29, Z 11–14)

Both the qualitative and the quantitative results make it clear that teachers recognize the special importance of German language in subject teaching.

## Inclusion of the First Language(s) in Non-language Subjects

In the individual interviews teachers were asked if and how they integrate non-German languages of the students into the non-language subject. The inclusion of the home languages in kindergarten and school fulfils an important psychosocial function for those affected. It confirms students' self-image and their sense of belonging (Krumm 2009: 239).

*In contrast to the first question, fewer respondents stated that they integrate their students' non-German language(s) in non-language subjects. The examples given have been categorized as follows:*

- Opportunity to converse in the first language:

  '. . . if now [. . .] a Turkish child sits next to a Turkish child, for example [. . .] they are allowed to [. . .] have a short conversation in their own language . . .' (1_1, Z 91–3)

  '. . . if a child actually does not understand and I know there may be a second Turkish-speaking child who understands better then I would like to have it summarized again in Turkish . . .' (1_9, Z 70-72)

  '. . . Yes, so the children are allowed to use their first language if they have no clue and don't know what to do. They are allowed to talk to other students who speak the same language . . .' (1_14, Z 73–5)

- Possibility to Solve Work Assignments in the First Language:

  'Yes, I had a student who had very big problems [. . .] But in maths class I had the feeling [. . .] that it was much easier for him in Turkish [. . .], it was completely okay for us if the [. . .] result was correct . . .' (1_13, Z 55–62)

  A student, for example, always did all the calculations [. . .] in his native language [. . .] in his head [. . .] but always answered in German; at an incredible speed . . . (2_16, Z 90–8)

- Linguistic Comparison in Non-language Subjects:

  'You can always integrate the first language by asking the children how the term is translated into their mother tongue.' (1_14, Z 79–80)

'... sometimes a child who has a different language can also teach the other children.' (1_18, Z 112–13)

'The children [. . .] who are not so good at German could then show what they can say in their language. [. . .] In any case it would be an idea, I have not yet carried it out but it sounds exciting.' (2_24, Z 343–6)

'... the good thing is that I have a different language myself [. . .] then I say: 'Oh and you know what? Apple, for example, is x in my language. And then the Serbo-Croatian children immediately [. . .] say: 'Ah, in my language it sounds so similar. And then it comes from all sides.' (2_25, Z 98–101)

- **Organizing Events**

'... you would probably have to somehow do an extra project or an extra day [. . .] when Corona is over, maybe also invite people or parents.' (2_18, Z 88–92)

'Or once I started a project where the children gave lectures about their countries of origin [. . .] about their famous dishes, stars, traditions or the country, yes.' (1_14, Z 81–3)

In addition to the categories presented, it was found that children who were given the opportunity to talk in their first language were particularly proud of it:

'The children feel very good about it and they are also proud . . .' (1_21, Z 75)

'And the children are so proud.' (1_24, Z 350)

'The children are happy [. . .] when I ask [. . .] 'what is that called in your language . . . ?' (2_8, Z 102)

'That is also very motivating when the children are allowed to act as teachers [. . .] that means I ask them then [. . .] "how do you say: to this and that in your language?" [. . .] or also 'how do you celebrate Christmas at home?' (2_8, Z 103–7)

'The children are happy when they say it in their mother tongue . . .' (2_15, Z 131)

'And you can easily see how it is good for the children that their language is also noticed and valued.' (2_28, Z 114–15)

... especially when the teachers know a few words in the home languages

'And then I tell them, for example, Ah: 'The dog is called Köbek (in Turkish), isn't it?' [. . .] Then they are amazed that I know a few words in their language and are motivated . . .' (1_12, Z 110–13)

'... we also made great progress on the relationship level and it impressed him (the student) very much and he made progress because of it, because he then had a lot more fun while learning, because of course [. . .] he enjoyed teaching the teacher Turkish words.' (1_13, Z 65–9)

Despite the commitment of the teachers, there are signs of othering and language bans that require closer examination in the following discussion.

## Discussion

The results of the online survey only partially illustrate an awareness of the responsibility of the teacher for providing language training outside of language subjects. Especially the responsibility for addressing the differences between BICS and CALP seems to be less pronounced. For this reason, the high level of agreement that teachers consider themselves to be linguistic role models for students should be questioned critically because the language of the teacher in the class should consistently address the change of register. A consistent distinction between the two registers, BICS and CALP, is also necessary to, for example, build up the vocabulary of students in CALP. Also, the tendency to simplify the language of instruction refers to a lack of training options for the language, such as scaffolding.

The lack of belief that language can have a discriminatory effect also shows that teachers take less responsibility for integrative language learning in teaching. Only 25 per cent seem to be (very) aware that language barriers may hinder and thus exclude students in their comprehension and participation from understanding. The significance tests of the hypotheses show a lack of awareness that language can produce discrimination, even if teachers recognize the importance of integrative language learning in all subjects. According to this, the connection between discrimination and language might not be visible for teachers. More information on these issues is needed in teacher education and training.

The qualitative results confirm the lack of awareness that language can produce discrimination. Even if there is a strong agreement that subject teaching should always be language teaching, all respondents automatically associated German with language. Other languages of students were not mentioned, which Dirim/Mecheril (2018) criticize with regard to the lack of plurilingualism among students. Therefore migration languages seem to be often invisible in the Austrian education system. Consequently, it is not surprising that interviewees were mostly reluctant to answer if and how the students' first language(s) can be integrated in classes.

For this reason, the high knowledge of which migration language(s) are present in the classroom becomes irrelevant if these languages are insufficiently used. The mentioned one-off events contribute little to the inclusion of other languages. On closer inspection, the phenomenon of 'othering' can be observed when teachers try to refer to 'their language, their culture . . .'. This separation between 'we' and 'they' reinforces the function that language can produce discrimination. In addition, there are indications of language bans in the interviews due to the 'permission' that teachers give their students to use their other languages briefly to help other classmates to understand. This 'permission' is to be questioned critically if all languages should experience the same appreciation and if linguistic rights are part of human rights (UNESCO). Otherwise, only certain languages seem to be 'worth' learning. We need to keep in mind that migration languages are 'the key to success' in a double sense. On the one hand, their appropriate development is the basis for the development of the surrounding language (especially for the development of CALP). On the other hand, a good command of migration languages is currently and in future more than necessary on the job market. Prestigious languages such as French have become a 'nice-to-have' in many areas. Therefore all languages should be everyone's languages and their consistent use in all subjects should be normal (see the concept of 'Translanguaging' by Ofelia García). After all, teachers seem to recognize the joy and pride of students when they are 'allowed' to use their first language(s).

To move minority languages from their marginal position into the centre of attention, more multilingual teachers are needed and/or topics like plurilingualism and integrative language learning should be treated as mandatory and more deeply in teacher education. In line with this, 38.1 per cent of those surveyed stated that they had received little or no preparation for language-sensitive teaching during their studies. Another 18.4 per cent can no longer remember the contents in this topic.

The knowledge and implementation of integrative multilingual learning can help to design lessons that are free from language barriers and discrimination and thus contribute to more equal opportunities. The potentials of multilingual students and their resources must be included in school. The results show a commitment of primary school teachers to realize the concept. Advanced training for teachers must provide them with the necessary tools for instruction. Thus, this study is above all a call for (more) 'language' in teacher education (worldwide).

Finally, to answer the question how modern languages can be taught so that they challenge rather than reinforce social inequalities, language teaching should take place not only in language lessons. To take action against social injustice, teachers of all subjects and school types must contribute to ensuring that a lack of language competences doesn't hinder the understanding of the content in order to guarantee non-discriminatory teaching. This approach corresponds to the concept of integrative language learning and also to the SDG4 of the United Nations. A long-time goal of all responsible stakeholders should be the integration of this concept in teacher education and training so that students can critically question existing structures and counteract inequalities in teaching. Hence, suitable teacher instructors are needed. In addition, we need to ask the question if future teachers have experienced their own plurilingualism as valuable or whether they are struggling with social injustice and excessive linguistic demands in their studies for teacher education. These thoughts make it clear that this study has only started the discussion of the problem whose roots are deeper than it might seem at first sight.

# References

Becker-Mrotzek, M., and H.-J. Roth. (2017), 'Sprachliche Bildung – Grundlegende Begriffe und Konzepte', in M. Becker-Mrotzek, H.-J. Roth, S. Bredthauer, and C. Lohmann (eds.), *Sprachliche Bildung – Grundlagen und Handlungsfelder*, Münster: Waxmann.

Busse, V. (2019), 'Sprachbildung im Musikunterricht? Umgang mit Mehrsprachigkeit und sprachsensibler Unterricht aus pädagogischer Sicht. Ein einführender Überblick', in M. Butler and J. Goschler (eds.), *Sprachsensibler Fachunterricht: Chancen und Herausforderungen aus interdisziplinärer Perspektive*, 1–33, Wiesbaden: Springer Press.

Bühner, M., and M. Ziegler. (2009), *Statistik für Psychologen und Sozialwissenschaftler*, München: Pearson Press.

Carnevale, C., and A. Wojnesitz. (2014), *Sprachsensibler Fachunterricht in der Sekundarstufe Grundlagen – Methoden – Praxisbeispiele*, Graz: ÖSZ.

de Cillia, R. (2013), 'Integrative Sprachenbildung an österreichischen Bildungsinstitutionen und SprachpädagogInnenbildung', in E. Vetter (ed.), *Professionalisierung für sprachliche Vielfalt: Perspektiven für eine neue Lehrerinnenbildung*, 5–20, Baltmannsweiler: Schneider-Verl. Hohengehren.

Coyle, D., P. Hood, and D. Marsh. (2010), *CLIL: Content and Language Integrated Learning*, Cambridge: Cambridge University Press.

Cummins, J. (2008), 'BICS and CALP: Empirical and Theoretical Status of the Distinction', in B. Street and N. H. Hornberger (eds.), *Encyclopedia of Language and Education*, 71–83, New York: Springer Science + Business Media LLC.

Danilovich, Y., and G. Putjata, eds. (2019), *Sprachliche Vielfalt im Unterricht: Fachdidaktische Perspektiven auf Lehre und Forschung im DaZ-Modul*, Wiesbaden: Springer Press.

Dirim, İ., and N. Khakpour. (2018), 'Migrationsgesellschaftliche Mehrsprachigkeit in der Schule', in İ. Dirim and P. Mecheril (eds.), *Heterogenität, Sprache(n), Bildung: Eine differenz – und diskriminierungstheoretische Einführung*, 201–25, Münster: UTB.

Dirim, İ., and P. Mecheril, eds. (2018), *Heterogenität, Sprache(n), Bildung: Eine differenz – und diskriminierungstheoretische Einführung*, Münster: UTB.

Döring, N., and J. Bortz. (2016), *Forschungsmethoden und Evaluation in den Sozial- und Humanwissenschaften*, Berlin: Springer Press.

Drumm, S. (2017), 'Gemischte Zeichenkomplexe verstehen lernen: Arbeit mit Sachtexten im Fach Biologie', in B. Ahrenholz, C. Schmellentin-Britz, and

B. Hövelbrinks (eds.), *Fachunterricht und Sprache in schulischen Lehr-/Lernprozessen*, 37–55, Tübingen: Narr Francke Attempto.

Fischer, N., S. Hammer, and T. Ehmke. (2018), 'Überzeugungen zu Sprache im Fachunterricht: Erhebungsinstrument und Skalendokumentation', in T. Ehmke, S. Hammer, A. Köker, U. Ohm, and B. Koch-Priewe (Hrsg.), *Professionelle Kompetenzen angehender Lehrkräfte im Bereich Deutsch als Zweitsprache*, Münster: Waxmann.

Fuchs, E., C. Haberfellner, and K. Öhlerer. (2014), *Sprachsensibler Unterricht in der Grundschule – Fokus Mathematik*, Graz: ÖSZ.

Fuchs, E. (2015), *Sprachsensibler Unterricht in der Grundschule - Fokus: Sachunterricht*, Graz: ÖSZ.

Fürstenau, S., and M. Gomolla, eds. (2011), *Migration und schulischer Wandel: Mehrsprachigkeit*, Wiesbaden: Verlag für Sozialwissenschaften.

García, O., N. Flores, K. Seltzer, L. Wei, R. Otheguy, and J. Rosa. (2021), 'Rejecting Abyssal Thinking in the Language and Education of Racialized Bilinguals: A Manifesto', *Critical Inquiry in Language Studies*, 18 (3): 203–28.

Gogolin, I. (2008), *Der monolinguale Habitus der multilingualen Schule*, Münster: Waxmann.

Gogolin, I., and I. Lange. (2010), *Durchgängige Sprachbildung: Eine Handreichung*, Münster: Waxmann.

Jost, J., E. Topalović, and B. Uhl. (2017), 'Sprachsensibler Mathematikunterricht in Hauptschulen. Sprache im Fach aus Sicht von Sprachfördercoaches, Lehrkräften und Lernenden in einem BiSS-Projekt', in B. Ahrenholz, C. Schmellentin-Britz, and B. Hövelbrinks (eds.), *Fachunterricht und Sprache in schulischen Lehr-/Lernprozessen*, 161–85, Tübingen: Narr Francke Attempto.

Kleinschmidt, K. (2017), 'Die an die Schüler/–innen gerichtete Sprache als Spiegel transitorischer schulsprachlicher Normen', in B. Ahrenholz, C. Schmellentin-Britz, and B. Hövelbrinks (eds.), *Fachunterricht und Sprache in schulischen Lehr-/Lernprozessen*, 117–37, Tübingen: Narr Francke Attempto.

Krumm, H.-J. (2009), 'Die Bedeutung der Mehrsprachigkeit in den Identitätskonzepten von Migrantinnen und Migranten', in I. Gogolin and U. Neumann (eds.), *Streitfall Zweisprachigkeit – The Bilingualism Controversy*, 233–47, Wiesbaden: Verlag für Sozialwissenschaften.

Krumm, H.-J., and H. H. Reich. (2011), 'Curriculum Mehrsprachigkeit'. Available online: http://oesz.at/download/cm/CurriculumMehrsprachigkeit2011.pdf (accessed 30 October 2021).

Kuckartz, U. (2014), *Mixed Methods: Methodologie, Forschungsdesigns und Analyseverfahren*, Weinheim: Springer Press.

Leisen, J. (2011), 'Praktische Ansätze schulischer Sprachförderung – Der sprachsensible Fachunterricht'. Available online: http://www.hss.de/download/111027_RM_Leisen.pdf (accessed 11 November 2021).

Leisen, J. (2013), 'Kinder zur Sprache im Sachfach führen', *Grundschule Deutsch*, 39: 39–42.

Leisen, J. (2015), 'Fachlernen und Sprachlernen!', *Der mathematische und naturwissenschaftliche Unterricht*, 68 (3): 132–37.

Luchtenberg, S. (2009), 'Vermittlung interkultureller sprachlicher Kompetenz als Aufgabe des Deutschunterrichts', in P. Nauwerck and I. Oomen-Welke (eds.), *Kultur der Mehrsprachigkeit in Schule und Kindergarten: Festschrift für Ingelore Oomen-Welke*, 277–88, Freiburg im Breisgau: Fillibach Verlag.

Michalak, M. (2008), 'Fördern durch Fordern – Didaktische Überlegungen zum Förderunterricht Deutsch als Zweitsprache an Schulen', *Fachzeitschrift Deutsch als Zweitsprache*, 3: 7–17.

Michalak, M., V. Lemke, and M. Goeke. (2015), *Sprache im Fachunterricht: Eine Einführung in Deutsch als Zweitsprache und sprachbewussten Unterricht*, Tübingen: Narr Francke Attempto.

Nolte, M. (2016), 'Sprache und Sprachverstehen in mathematischen Lernprozessen aus einer mathematikdidaktischen Perspektive', in U. Stitzinger, S. Sallat, and U. Lüdtke (eds.), *Sprache und Inklusion als Chance?! Expertise und Innovation für Kita, Schule und Praxis*, 37–44, Idstein: Schulz-Kirchner Verlag.

OECD. (2019), 'Where All Students Can Succeed'. Available online: https://doi.org/10.1787/b5fd1b8f-en (accessed 22 October 2021).

Office of National Statistics. Available online: https://www.ons.gov.uk/peoplepopulationandcommunity/culturalidentity/language/articles/detailedanalysisenglishlanguageproficiencyinenglandandwales/2013-08-30 (accessed 13 November 2021).

Rank, A. et al. (2016), 'Sachunterricht – Der geeignete Ort zur Förderung von Bildungssprache?' Available online: www.widerstreit-sachunterricht.de (accessed 18 October 2021).

Rödel, L., and T. Simon. (2019), *Inklusive Sprach(en)bildung: Ein interdisziplinärer Blick auf das Verhältnis von Inklusion und Sprachbildung*, Klinkhardt.

Schröder, A., and U. Ritterfeld. (2014), 'Zur Bedeutung sprachlicher Barrieren im Mathematikunterricht der Primarstufe: Wissenschaftlicher Erkenntnisstand und Reflexion in der (Förder-)Schulpraxis', *Forschung Sprache*, 1: 49–69.

Tajmel, T. (2017), *Naturwissenschaftliche Bildung in der Migrationsgesellschaft: Grundzüge einer Reflexiven Physikdidaktik und kritisch-sprachbewussten Praxis*, Wiesbaden: Verlag für Sozialwissenschaften.

Thürmann, E., and H. Vollmer. (2011), 'Checkliste zu sprachlichen Aspekten des Fachunterrichts'. Available online: http://www.unterrichtsdiagnostik.info/media/files/Beobachtungsraster_Sprachsensibler_Fachunterricht.pdf (accessed 13 March 2023).

Statistik Austria. (2021), 'Migration und Integration'. Available online: https://www.integrationsfonds.at/fileadmin/content/AT/Fotos/Publikationen/Statistikbroschuere/OEIF_Statistisches_Jahrbuch_2021.pdf (accessed 12 November 2021).

# CHAPTER 13

# English for Creative Resistance

# Critical Pedagogy in a Teacher Education Programme in Palestine

*Maria Grazia Imperiale*

## Introduction

This chapter presents two specific vignettes from a teacher training course, in which trainees/participants challenged me as their educator. As part of a piece of practice-led research, I developed a study on critical and creative pedagogies for language education in the context of the Gaza Strip (Palestine). I worked together with trainees to explore and foster their knowledge and practices of critical and creative pedagogies for English language teaching.

The Gaza Strip (Palestine) is a context of protracted crisis. It has been under blockade since 2007, which means that people cannot freely move in and out of the Strip. High poverty, high unemployment rates and a highly dense population make the Strip an 'unliveable place' (UN 2017). In addition, frequent military operations have hit the Strip in the last decade, destroying the already weak infrastructure, and causing several thousands of deaths, and injuries to people.

Within this context of protracted crisis and emergency, education is a potent tool to nurture individuals' well-being. English has an important role as it enables the creation of counternarratives before the international community (Imperiale 2017, 2018, 2021). English language education can therefore represent the opportunity for learners to nurture critical, creative and peaceful resistance. In order to develop and nurture critical approaches to language education, I argue in this chapter, it is important that we, as educators, are ready to be challenged and to be inspired by our students, celebrating a teaching that enables transgression (hooks 1994). Drawing on critical pedagogy, in this chapter I celebrate how trainees nurtured their critical voice, also by challenging me and re-appropriating and re-interpreting the inputs that they were given.

This chapter is structured as follows: in the next section I present some key critical approaches to language education, including a discussion of the Palestinian Arts of Resistance. Then, I briefly present the teacher training course I developed, with its aims and course participants. I move on to the two vignettes I use to illustrate how participants challenged me as their educator: the first one is entitled 'I really liked this activity, but . . .'; the second vignette, the 'simple drama' shows how participants resisted my input on drama pedagogy during their teaching practice. Finally, I present a section reflecting on whether we should talk about language education for resilience or for resistance, and I argue that within the Palestinian context, English education can unlock creative and peaceful resistance.

## Critical and Contextualized Art-Based Pedagogies in Language Education in the Gaza Strip

The critical turn in applied linguistics has become popular in the recent decades. Some scholars have maintained that language and language education are never neutral, and inspired by critical theory and postcolonial studies, the critical turn has seen discussions around language ownership and critical approaches to language policies and practices (Phillipson 1992; Pennycook 1994, 1998, 2001a, 2001b, 2007; Holliday 2005; Canagarajah 2003, 2005; Canagarajah and Said 2013).

The term *critical,* as used by those authors and as used in this chapter, emphasizes the connection between language and broader social constructs such as ideology, politics and discourse. Highly influenced by critical literacy and critical pedagogy (Freire 1976, 1996), Pennycook (2001a) was probably one of the first proponents of the integration of critical pedagogy in applied linguistics, suggesting that the field needed reflexivity, through which it could problematize practice and aim for the improvement of society.

According to Pennycook (2007), *critical* applied linguistics rests on principles of performativity, contextuality and transgression. Performativity refers to the work of Judith Butler (1990), which goes beyond a framing of identities as static and focusing, rather, on the contingency of the encounter; language is constantly reshaped and performed in the encounter. Contextuality refers to adopting a localized understanding of social and political issues which encourages the development of contextualized practice and intervention formulated in collaboration with local communities. Finally, a transgressive approach refers to resisting mainstreaming thoughts and politics which are shaped in language, opening up a space for language and language education to enable the construction of counter-hegemonic narratives and practices.

Pennycook's argument on the adoption of critical pedagogy in English language education is firstly underpinned by an understanding that English embeds, and is related to, colonial discourses (Pennycook 1994, 1998). On the other hand, English can also be a site of resistance since it opens up possibilities for the creation of counter-discourses within the language classroom. He writes:

> I would suggest that counter-discourses can indeed be formed in English and that one of the principal roles of English teachers is to help this formulation. Thus, as applied linguists and English language teachers we should become political actors engaged in a critical pedagogical project to use English to oppose the dominant discourses of the West and to help the articulation of counter-discourses in English. (Pennycook 2001b: 87)

Inspired by the critical pedagogue bell hooks (1994) and her seminal work *Teaching to Transgress*, he provocatively wonders whether language teachers would enable teaching to transgress, teaching to be resisted:

> How can we teach English in a way that both acknowledges the colonial and neo-colonial implications of ELT yet also allows for an understanding of the possibilities of change, resistance, and appropriation? Can we teach in order to be resisted? (Pennycook 2007: 22)

bell hooks' book (1994) further developed Paulo Freire's critical pedagogy, to argue for what she called 'engaged pedagogy', which also encompasses embodiment and well-being. hooks focuses on the well-being of students – and especially of those who have a difficult past. Drawing on the philosophy of Thich Nhat Hanh, hooks embraces a view of pedagogy that engages with wholeness, encompassing the mind, the body and the spirit. The teacher is not to be considered as a healer, but she believes in the healing purpose of education:

> I do not think that they [students] want therapy from me. They do want an education that is healing to the uninformed, unknowing spirit. They do want knowledge that is meaningful. (Ibid.: 19)

In this study I was inspired by both critical engaged pedagogy (hooks 1994) and by the critical turn in applied linguistics (Pennycook 1994; Canagarajah 2003). I found a strong nexus between criticality and embodiment thanks to art-based pedagogies. Art-based pedagogies are often considered beneficial so as to let students' positions of 'plenty' to emerge in language encounters and relationships (Frimberger 2016). Several scholars use art-based pedagogies in language education, especially for their focus on embodiment, playfulness and creativity, without necessarily encompassing a critical dimension. Given that in the context of this study, critical approaches to language education and critical pedagogy more broadly were key, I focused on developing and co-constructing localized critical and creative approaches that could be used in English language teaching. I therefore developed a teacher training course titled 'Using the Palestinian Arts of Resistance in English Language Teaching'.

What is the Art of Resistance? James Scott, in his book *Domination and the Arts of Resistance* (1990), unpacks how subordinate groups perform resistance strategies against the subjugating powers in their everyday life – in both organized and spontaneous ways. Scott argues that resistance consists of everyday acts often characterized by 'spontaneity, anonymity and lack of formal organization', which 'then become the enabling modes of protest' (Scott 1990: 151). Subordinate groups create dissonant, and often hidden, *cultures*, which he calls 'hidden transcripts' (Ibid). When hidden transcripts become visible and enter the public spaces, they become recognized and as recognizable forms of protest, they carry political impact (Ibid.: 18–19). The arts are used as a multimodal, multi-genre way of protesting injustice. This is what the Art of Resistance does, with its multiple genres.

In the context of Palestine, Charles Tripp (2012) conducted research on the politics of resistance in the Middle East – be it against foreign military powers, internal dictatorships, economic powers or any other subjugating force. He noticed that artistic expression was widely used in spontaneous and anonymous ways, as well as being used by leading intellectuals. For example, he analysed the use of posters, of street-art graffiti – especially the ones that appeared on the wall built by Israel within the Occupied Territories – and of political cartoons as forms of visual resistance (Tripp 2012). One of the icons of the Palestinian resistance became, for instance, the character created by the cartoonist Naji al-Ali, Handala. Handala is a child who appears in al-Ali's cartoons with his back turned, eternally ten years old, often pictured in Palestinian refugee camps. The cartoonist became famous only when Ghassan Kanafani, one of the most prolific and important Palestinian writers and politicians, published al-Ali's drawings in the magazine he edited, *Al-Hooryya* (English translation: freedom). al-Ali's work, from being a hidden transcript, therefore became part of the public domain and his 'voice' reached way beyond the checkpoints of that camp (Hamdi 2011).

The Palestinian arts of resistance, whether visual arts, comics, political cartoons, literature or drama, to my knowledge, have never been explored in relation to language education; that was also one of the reasons that motivated me to develop a teacher training course on using the Palestinian arts of resistance in English language teaching.

## *The Teacher Training Programme*

The online teacher training course consisted of an experimental, optional and uncredited series of workshops involving thirteen pre-service English teachers from the Gaza Strip, who had enrolled at – or recently graduated from – the Islamic University of Gaza. The course focused on 'Using the Palestinian Arts of Resistance in English-language teaching', and it aimed at exploring and developing localized, critical and creative approaches in teaching English in the Gaza Strip.

The teacher training course was developed as part of a broader research project (Imperiale 2018). The research methodology was inspired by participatory approaches (Kemmis et al. 2014) and decolonizing methodologies (Tuhiwai Smith 2006), and made use of critical participatory action research: the course, therefore, was not only developed for pedagogical purposes but it was also the main object of this piece of practice-led research. The priority of my research study was to – or at least to try to – make a positive difference for the participants I was working with. The aim of the research study was to engage in a process of knowledge co-production and radical listening (Siry et al. 2016).

By the end of the teacher training programme, the participants/trainees would be able to:

(a) acquire an introductory subject knowledge on adopting creative methods in language teaching, exploring drama pedagogy and the use of comics and political cartoons in class;

(b) experiment with creative teaching techniques through interactive workshops;

(c) reflect on the teaching materials in use in the Gaza Strip (*English for Palestine, Grades 8–9*) and on how certain units could be supplemented with the inclusion of creative methods;

(d) apply their learning in a teaching context;

(e) strengthen and create an active network of pre-service English teachers in the Gaza Strip.

The format of the course was highly interactive, structured as a series of workshops rather than a series of lectures. It included input sessions, interactive activities, discussions, peer learning, peer observation, lesson planning and teaching practices in which the trainees planned, developed and delivered simulated English lessons by teaching to their peers. The course ran in April and May 2015, for a total of twenty-four hours. The research study was approved by the Ethics Committee of the College of Social Sciences at the University of Glasgow.

In the next sections, using two vignettes, I explore how trainees challenged me as their teacher trainer, showing how they were able to re-appropriate English pedagogy in a critical and creative way that would make their learning meaningful, and suitable to their own context.

## Vignette 1: 'I Really Enjoyed the Session, But . . .'

I present here a vignette about an activity that was developed during one of the workshops, which focused on drama pedagogy. The workshop was planned and developed in collaboration with a GRAMNet (Glasgow Refugee Asylum and Migration Network) artist in residence, Tawona Sithole, who is an expert in drama-related activities. During that session, participants were encouraged to experience multimodality and drama-pedagogy-related activities for language education, for example using playful sketches and improvising role-plays.

Participants, for example – divided into smaller groups – were invited to share some recipes that have value to them, and to mime the procedure of preparing the dish. These activities led to playful moments and created a very relaxed atmosphere. This is an extract from an exchange – during the break – that followed the activity of miming a recipe. The extract exemplifies the playfulness and curiosity that brought the participants and me closer:

> S.: Grazia, do you know how to cook?
> Grazia: Of course, girls!
> A.: Do you know how to cook Palestinian dishes?
> Grazia: Only Molokhyya. But the other dish that you mentioned seem delicious . . .
> S.: Ohh . . . you know how to prepare molokhyya!?! – Girls, Grazia knows to cook molokhyya! Ahah [laughing]!
> Grazia: Ah, molokhyya djaja [*Yes, Molokhya with chicken*].
>     [A., turning her head to talk to the other students] Wait . . . ehm, you cook molokhyya like that? (showing a picture on the screen).
> Grazia: No no, mine is more ehm liquid . . . less thick.
> A: [Laughing] Maybe you *think* you know how to cook molokhya . . . [laughing].
> Grazia: [laughing] yes, maybe you are right . . .

During this brief distilled extract, after the task of describing and miming recipes, participants spontaneously asked me some questions related to my own cooking skills. After this extract, we continued this discussion providing each other detailed recipes: I asked for a link to a blog, and A. stated that she would have tried cooking a dish of pasta in the way that – as I confirmed – 'Italians do'. In the discussion that followed we addressed the untranslatability of some context-specific and culturally related words, and the strategies adopted to convey and construct meaning when the interlocutors do not share the same cultural background.

The workshop was very well received by participants, as these extracts show:

> What I liked the most today is talking about one of our recipes. We had much fun describing our recipes, and trying to get the suitable words for them. We do it in passion since this is a thing that we love, it is part of our traditions, talking about a traditional Palestinian dish. (S., reflective journal)

> Using this activity would build harmony among them [students] and English language, in particular our students and us have no access to be in contact with other people abroad so we can talk about things that we know and we love, but in English. It was fun to hear about Italian recipes too and not in books! (N., reflective journal)

N. and S. emphasized that during the activity they addressed something that they loved and valued. They appreciated the entertainment of the workshop, and as also other participants stated, recognized the value of ludic pedagogies. N. also clearly stated that she appreciated the chance to discuss Italian dishes with me, rather than reading them in recipe books as she had done before. She also focused on the 'harmony' that the embodied intercultural encounter could foster. The participant perceived the relationship with English in terms of an emotional and embodied connection nurtured in intercultural encounters and facilitated through creative art-based pedagogies. N. hoped for a harmonious relationship between herself, her students and English. These excerpts show an implicit understanding of language as socially, relationally and contextually created *in situ*, which places the human encounter rather than the 'culture type' at the heart of any language- and culture-producing act. For it to be meaningful, the experience needs to nurture and develop encounters with cultural others, rather than with other cultures: the individual's positions and attitudes are central in such an intercultural situation.

However, even though eleven participants among thirteen praised the session, two trainees reported:

> The session was nice but I didn't understand how and why it was connected with our Arts of Resistance and with our context. Even if we did Palestinian recipes and it is true that there are arguments about where

these recipes are from etc. I still didn't find this session very meaningful for me. [Y. reflective journal]

I really enjoyed the session, but why did we have to mime a recipe? Role-plays about some real situations maybe are more effective than just a recipe. This felt too much easy and maybe not very related to our cause. [F. reflective journal]

Y. and F. questioned the activity as they felt it was not completely connected to their cause, to the Arts of Resistance, and, overall, to their expectations. F. perceived it as 'too easy', Y. said it was not very 'meaningful'. I cherished their reflections on the session, and I was very pleased to see that those two young women, even though it was only the second time we were meeting, were already ready to challenge my choices. It was thanks to those brave trainees that we started to enact critical engaged pedagogy, and that – as confirmed by the participants – both the participants and I felt that we were starting to co-create knowledge in praxis.

In follow-up in-depth interviews, both with Y and with F, we reflected on the importance of developing a playful atmosphere in class, since it allows to create a safe space where difficult, poignant, challenging conversations can be held. The activity was recognized as meaningful since it brought us closer through its playfulness. However, my understanding of the participants' comments was that the activity, even though meaningful, was not *critical*. It did not empower them, it did not challenge relationships or power dynamics, it did not help make their critical voices visible. In contrast, other activities I described in other studies were more explicitly critical (see Imperiale et al. 2017, Imperiale 2021; Imperiale et al. 2021; Imperiale 2018).

However, what I would like to point out here is that criticality was still embedded in the act of those two participants writing their reflections and sharing them with me. They critically engaged with the input I gave them and felt free to challenge me through their texts: they understood that what we were doing did not have a strong critical component, and as such they were ready to challenge their educator in a respectful and also powerful way, in text. In the next vignette, I present how other participants 'resisted' my inputs in *practice*.

## *Vignette 2: The 'Simple Drama'*

During the teacher training course, participants were invited to develop teaching practices which would be delivered as simulated, to their peers. Participants were divided into small groups and each group chose a lesson. As a reference they used the textbook used in most schools in Gaza, and altered and re-adapted the chosen lesson, integrating it with any creative methods that would fit the session.

One group chose a lesson from the English for Palestine Grade 9 textbook, entitled 'The World with Its Countries', and they changed the title to 'The World with Its countries . . . in the Palestinian way'. I discussed some activities from this teaching practice in another publication (Imperiale 2017), in which I focused on how participants nurtured their capability of voice and agency during this lesson. I want to focus here on an activity they developed that they called 'a simple drama'.

The 'simple drama' consisted of a brief sketch that the group of trainee teachers had prepared for the class, adopting drama pedagogy: three of them acted out the script that they themselves wrote, while the fourth one played the soundtracks they had chosen for the performance. The performance was held towards the end of the teaching practice, in English. It was about the plight of an old lady in exile, who remembers the 'old days' in Palestine and the places she is now prevented from visiting. The script of the short 'play' that the four of them wrote is reproduced here:[1]

> The mother, Um Saeed, was sitting on the table, contemplating at her past days. Suddenly, her daughters, Lara and Mariam get to the home suddenly, and greet their mum. The daughters ask their mother: Oh mum, how it's going? The mother replied with a sick voice: 'Not so good'. The daughters start wondering: 'oh why? What's wrong with you?' The mum releases her thoughts related to the past days saying:
>
> 'I do miss that days'. Lana and Lara start wondering: 'Oh, what days do you miss mum? Tell us!' Um Saeed starts to narrate her story saying: 'That time when the roses sway along the bay,
>
> It was a time when we were gathering beside the lake,
>
> It was a time when we were crossing the rivers, diving highly deep in the sea, playing around the trees and smelling the lovely breeze,
>
> It was a time when doves were knitting their nests up the mountain,
>
> It was a time when children were singing for freedom and say: we are free,
>
> It was a dream, but I waked up to see how roses withered, how rivers besieged, how doves where chased, so they far away fled'.
>
> The daughters got too much sad over that speech dismal. They feel how much they are deprived from their least rights which everyone should own as a human body, which is to enjoy the air and the natural views of their country, Palestine.
>
> Lara replied: 'Oh, mum how harmful to live in this open prison!! when I want to watch any place from our country, we google and

search for it to see just a pictures, yes, we watch nothing, but a picture which can't be touched!!'.

Lana replies: 'but we will struggle and fight,' Lara continues: 'we will strive', the mum happily ends the conversation: 'and survive'.

A. played the role of the mum L. played the role of Lara

R. played the role of Lana.

The script and its pedagogical use present an opportunity for reflection. The trainees performed this sketch without setting tasks for the students. The trainees, in doing so, re-appropriated drama pedagogy. While during our session on drama pedagogy we always presented activities that could have involved students in an active and engaging way; the participants chose not to use drama pedagogy in that way, but they, rather, made use of it to create a moment of contemplation and admiration during the teaching practice, as they themselves confirmed. Pedagogically, it was a moment of rupture. In doing so, they activated a careful negotiating process: pedagogies that were introduced during the workshop series (as drama pedagogy) were not unproblematically received by the trainees, but were, rather, appropriated and re-interpreted according to the trainees' needs and vision.

It must be acknowledged that my virtual presence – as I was online observing their teaching practice – probably affected the way in which trainees made use of drama pedagogy: for instance, when I was sent the script of their play, I found I was included as a spectator:

> This is our simple drama that we did during our lesson on Saturday, hope you liked it, Grazia. (A. W., email)

The script of the performance itself is worth reflecting upon. Written by the participants, the script combines symbols of the traditional Palestinian literature of resistance such as checkpoints, passports, walls, keys of destroyed homes and so on, with new symbols that do not belong to this tradition: for instance, the daughters add to the mother's memories that they use Google now, to search for beautiful pictures of their land. Adding the technological dimension to the reality of immobility is an interesting choice, as it breaks with the Palestinian aesthetic regime, and introduces a component of modernity. As Salih and Richter-Devroe write, traditional symbols risk normalizing Palestinians as victims of the past before the international audience (Salih and Richter-Devroe 2014: 21). Conversely, the participants replaced those codified symbols of olives, oranges, barbed wires, olive tree, and replaced some of them with roses, birds, rivers, sea, lakes (uncommon symbols within the Palestinian tradition) and technologies: they affirmed their subjectivities as writers and agents and as young people engaging with contemporary challenges and opportunities. They appropriated English to rewrite narratives, altering both a sense of beauty and the power structures of established regimes, including aesthetic regimes.

With this vignette, I am reminded of the work of the philosopher Jacques Rancière, who wrote extensively about the 'aesthetic regime of art' and the relation between politics and aesthetics (Rancière 2004, 2010). The aesthetic regime of art is a system that provokes a *rupture* among the given orders of norms and representation (i.e., the system of representation), shaking hegemonies and hierarchies and allowing heterogeneities and subjectivities to be valued and to emerge. Rancière interprets 'aesthetic acts' as configurations of experience that create new modes of perception and induce novel forms of 'political subjectivity' (Rancière 2004: 9). The aesthetic regime of art, as intersection between aesthetic and politics, is grounded in 'dissensus' (Rancière 2010). Dissensus – as the opposite of consensus – is at the heart of the aesthetic–political nexus: politics started when people in the domains of the domestic and invisible 'territory of work and reproduction' started to manifest their voice and 'dissensual commonsense' (Rancière 2010: 139). Similarly, this aesthetics creates new configurations and sensory experiences in unanticipated ways, breaking with predetermined regimes (Rancière 2010).

I interpreted the 'simple drama' as a gift to me – who, given my role as spectator, became actively engaged in the process of witnessing trainees' dissensus. Trainees challenged at the same time: (i) my role as a trainer, (ii) the input they were given on possible uses of drama pedagogy; and (iii) the canonical and classical Palestinian aesthetics. Their performance was an aesthetic piece of critical art, without the intention to be used as such: it did not have a pedagogical motive attached to it other than contemplation and admiration, and trainees could not have anticipated what my response would have been. They just 'hoped that I liked it'. In doing so, they actually stimulated my curiosity, and provoked a reaction in me, which configured my willingness to write about that. This is what critical art does: it stimulates reactions in the spectator who is moved to respond and to continue the work initiated by the art piece (Rancière 2004, 2010).

I believe there was something quite extraordinary in this 'simple drama', as it embodied critical engaged pedagogy and the ruptures that critical pedagogy can create. It embodied resistance on different levels, and it unlocked participants' creative *resistance*.

# Final Reflections: English for Resilience or Resistance?

In studies on language education with refugees we often encounter the idea of language for resilience. For instance, the British Council developed a highly successful strand of work entitled *Language for Resilience*, which mainly focused on refugees in the Middle East, but was also piloted with refugees in Ethiopia (see Capstick and Delaney 2016). Within this strand, language and language education can enable resilience on different levels, as learners also learn to cope with their difficult realities through a contextualized approach to language education.

The concept of resilience is key when working with oppressed populations. In a post-war context, and in the context of being under siege and the forced immobility of the Gaza Strip, coping with the detrimental conditions of everyday life has, indeed, been seen as life-saving. Chandler (2012: 217) defines resilience as 'the capacity to positively or successfully adapt to external problems or threats'.

Contexts of despair caused by human-made disasters and injustice are also often analysed through the lens of *resistance*. 'Resistance' could be considered a contested term, especially when referring to the Palestinian context, where it might be associated with violent uprisings. In this chapter, instead, I point at the creative tension that *peaceful resistance* enables. Resistance, in the Palestinian context, is embedded in the term *sumoud*, which is meant to signify a disposition of actions of everyday resilience. *Sumoud* could be translated as 'perplexity, sadness, resilience and weary endurance' (Shehadeh 2015: 76) and is specific to the Palestinian habitus after decades of occupation, after a forced diaspora, and family separations. Ryan (2015) defines *sumoud* as 'resilient resistance', which primarily consists of rejoicing in Palestinian culture, traditions and in life in general, despite the harsh living conditions, also developing a site to challenge those conditions. Ryan (2015) also argues that Palestinians themselves prefer to point at *resistance* (Ryan 2015) rather than resilience, since they not only adapt to their living conditions, aiming at survival, but also find ways to protest the conditions in which they live, through violent uprisings, artistic work or in language.

In the literature on applied linguistics, *linguistic resistance* consists of the appropriation of both English, to write counternarratives and alternative epistemologies (Pennycook 1994, 1998; hooks 1994), and of critical, creative and localized English language pedagogies, to counter English language imperialism (Imperiale 2018; Canagarajah 2003). Language, as owned by each speaker, is an egalitarian tool and it can be a site of resistance.

Drawing a parallel to Rancière's theories on politics and aesthetics, I argue that linguistic and cultural resistance practices embody dissensus, much in the same way that aesthetics and politics are related: within an aesthetic regime of art, linguistic and cultural resistance can be interpreted as art which reconfigures what is visible and what is invisible and what is speakable and unspeakable. The participants in this study, with both their textual-artistic productions and their everyday resistance practices, developed their individual political subjectivities and produced counternarratives that carry political meaning.

The participants, writing about what Arts of Resistance means to them, stressed that it is both critical art and the aestheticization of their lived experiences, as the extracts below demonstrate:

> Art of resistance is a language of silence and pains by artists, poets, painters, etc. who use it to show how much they love their country as well as it's a way to present their own pains that cannot easily be shown. They are trying to hide the pains which are so close to their hearts, lives, and souls defying their dignity. Art of resistance is a sign of silence that is a result of continuing pains people still suffer from, so keeping silent and talking by their drawings, poems, words, music surely are the language that those artists would like to come through showing their own tears and pictures of love and smiles. (N., written assignment)

In this poetic extract, N. relates Arts of Resistance to Palestinian artists' voice and agency, who, suffocated by the conditions in which they live, produce works of art to express their distress and to protest the injustice they are subjected to. The participant also poignantly describes the place of silence in unspeakable traumas, which, for artists, is replaced by other symbolic forms of representations, for example by music, paintings and poetic productions. Their expressions are not always manifested in linguistic form. The 'simple drama' that the participants created serves as a critical work of resistance. N. implicitly posits that the content of artists' work of resistance is not only tears and distress, but also 'pictures of love and smiles'. Through the arts, Palestinian artists return to beauty and produce something beautiful with their sufferings, longing for justice.

Forms of dissensus, being it cultural, linguistic, and aesthetic, are found in participants' everyday lives as *language teachers*. Their resistance against the system in which they live clearly emerges in the next extract:

> When you see a teacher having unhealed wounds teaching his children to be patient, determined, and painstaking, you should realize that this is art of resistance in Gaza. [. . .] the people of Gaza try their best to overcome the situation and prepare a generation that defend their identity. (A., written assignment)

This participant relates resistance and its arts to her own living experience, and reflects on the art of living of teachers in the Gaza Strip, who despite their own distressful and traumatic experiences caused by the siege, teach their students values like hopeful patience and determination.

It is within this context, and after these considerations, that I argue that English and the English language classroom should not contribute only to makng people more resilient, but should also enable a critical, *creative resistance*. The pedagogy of resistance stimulates students to transgress, and to celebrate transgression as opposition against the *status quo* and the conditions in which they live, in an overall celebration of their own dreams and aspirations. It stimulates students to go beyond the boundaries that are imposed on them, limiting their freedom. It also stimulates a peaceful and creative way of responding to the social injustice that individuals suffer from, providing a meaningful education that reaches beyond the classroom.

## Conclusion

In this chapter, I discussed how pre-service English teachers in the Gaza Strip (Palestine) challenged me as a teacher trainer during an online teacher training programme. I reflected on how pre-service teachers transgressed and resisted inputs I gave, re-appropriating English language teaching in a way that would suit their needs, values, hopes and aspirations.

I presented two vignettes to ground my discussion: in the first one, during a drama pedagogy training session, pre-service teachers participated in an activity on presenting a recipe, miming it and developing a role-play around it. While they actively participated and engaged with it, in their post-workshop reflections, some of them wrote that although the exercise touched upon affectivities and embodiment and it was linked with their identity as Palestinians, it did not stimulate their critical approach in the way they would have hoped. In the second vignette, I discussed how they re-interpreted drama pedagogy in their teaching practice – by creating a 'simple drama' for students to watch and listen to – without developing further exercises. This was a way to allow for a space of contemplation and self-reflection that challenged the idea of needing to perform a task, and also challenged the input/instruction that they were given. I argued that this was an extraordinary moment, where trainees celebrated a teaching that enables transgression.

I concluded by reflecting on the terms 'Resilience' and 'Resistance', since in recent literature, within English language teaching and language education more broadly, 'resilience' is becoming increasingly popular, especially when working with groups living in vulnerable and challenging conditions. I argue that when language pedagogy aims to transform, make a change, transgress, that is, when we aim to achieve a critical education in hope (Freire 1992), we, as educators, should not be afraid of framing our work within a 'resistance' agenda, and should also be prepared to be resisted and challenged. In fact, we should encourage our students and early-career teachers to do so, to ultimately make their own teaching meaningful in a way they value.

As educators, if we are to work within a critical paradigm and if we are to promote our students' well-being and to contribute to our society, then we should not be afraid of promoting these kinds of resistant pedagogies, but, rather, embrace them, valuing the critical moments when our students are challenging us within and beyond the classroom. This perhaps requires some humility at our end, and also being brave enough to let go of our control of the classroom, welcoming challenges and critiques. This is not an easy task, but perhaps it is the one that could

> celebrate teaching that enables transgressions – a movement against and beyond boundaries. It is that movement which makes education the practice of freedom. (hooks 1994: 12)

## Acknowledgements

I am grateful to the editor of this book, Dr Derek Hird, and to the reviewers for their precious advice on how to improve earlier drafts of this book chapter. I am indebted to the trainee teachers who took part in this study, for this teacher training course enriched me and improved my own pedagogical practices. This study was supported by the Arts and Humanities Research Council (AHRC Grant Ref: AH/L006936/1).

## Note

1 The script is the original and hasn't been edited.

## References

Butler, J. (1990), *Gender Trouble: Feminism and the Subversion of Identity*, New York: Routledge.
Canagarajah, A. S. (2003), *Resisting Linguistic Imperialism in English Teaching*, Oxford: Oxford University Press.
Canagarajah, A. S. (2005), *Reclaiming the Local in Language Policy and Practice*, Mahwah, NJ: Lawrence Erlbaum Associates, Inc.
Canagarajah, S., and S. Ben Said. (2013), 'Linguistic Imperialism', in J. Simpson (ed.), *The Routledge Handbook of Applied Linguistics*, 388–400, Abingdon: Routledge.
Capstick, T., and M. Delaney. (2016), *Language for Resilience: The Role of Language in Enhancing the Resilience of Syrian Refugees and Host Communities*, London: British Council.
Chandler, D. (2012), 'Resilience and Human Security: The Post-Interventionist Paradigm', *Security Dialogue*, 43 (3): 213–29.
Freire, P. (1976) (first published in 1973), *Education, the Practice of Freedom*, London: Writers and Readers Publishing Cooperative.

Freire, P. (1992), *Pedagogy of Hope: A Reencounter with the Pedagogy of the Oppressed*, Rio de Janeiro: Paz e Terra.

Freire, P. (1996) (first published in 1970), *Pedagogy of the Oppressed*, London: Penguin Books.

Frimberger, K. (2016), 'Towards a Well-Being Focussed Language Pedagogy: Enabling Arts-Based, Multilingual Learning Spaces for Young People with Refugee Background', *Pedagogy, Culture & Society*, 24 (2): 285–329.

Hamdi, T. (2011), 'Bearing Witness in Palestinian Resistance Literature', *Race and Class*, 52 (3): 21–42.

Holliday, A. (2005), *The Struggle to Teach English as an International Language*, Oxford: Oxford University Press.

hooks, b. (1994), *Teaching to Transgress: Education as the Practice of Freedom*, New York: Routledge.

Imperiale, M. G. (2017), 'Language Education in the Gaza Strip: 'Planting Hope in a Land of Despair", *Critical Multilingualism Studies*, 5 (1): 37–58.

Imperiale, M. G. (2018), *Developing Language Education in the Gaza Strip: Pedagogies of Capability and Resistance*, Unpublished PhD thesis, University of Glasgow.

Imperiale, M. G. (2021), 'Intercultural Education in Times of Restricted Travel: Lesson from the Gaza Strip', Special Issue 'Intercultural Communicative Competence and Mobility: Perspectives on Virtual, Physical, and Critical Dimensions'. *Intercultural Communication Education*, 4(1): 22–38. doi: 10.29140/ice.v4.n1.446.

Imperiale, M. G., A. Phipps, N. Al-Masri, and G. Fassetta. (2017), 'Pedagogies of Hope and Relationship: English Language Education in the Context of the Gaza Strip', in E. Erling (ed.), *English Across the Fracture Lines: The Contribution and Relevance of English to Security, Safety and Stability in the World*, 31–8, London: British Council.

Imperiale, M. G., A. Phipps, and G. Fassetta. (2021), 'On Online Practices of Hospitality in Higher Education', *Studies in Philosophy and Education*. http://dx.doi.org/10.1007/s11217-021-09770-z.

Kemmis, S., R. McTaggart, and R. Nixon. (2014), *The Action Research Planner: Doing Critical Participatory Action Research*, London: Springer.

Pennycook, A. (1994), *The Cultural Politics of English as an International Language*, New York: Longman Group Limited.

Pennycook, A. (1998), *English and the Discourses of Colonialism*, London: Routledge.

Pennycook, A. (2001a), *Critical Applied Linguistics: A Critical Introduction*, New York: Routledge.

Pennycook, A. (2001b), 'English in the World/The World in English', in A. Burns and C. Coffin (eds.), *Analysing English in a Global Context*, 78–88, London: Routledge.

Pennycook, A. (2007), 'ELT and Colonialism', in J. Cummins and C. Davison (eds.), *International Handbook of English Language Teaching*, 13–24, New York: Springer Science + Business Media.

Phillipson, R. (1992), *Linguistic Imperialism*, Oxford: Oxford University Press.

Ranciere, J. (2004), *The Politics of Aesthetics: The Distribution of the Sensible*, London: Continuum International Publishing Group.

Ranciere, J. (2010), *Dissensus: On Politics and Aesthetics*, London: Continuum International Publishing Group.
Ryan, C. (2015), 'Everyday Resilience as Resistance: Palestinian Women Practicing Sumud', *International Political Sociology*, 9: 299–315.
Salih, R., and S. Richter-Devroe. (2014), 'Cultures of Resistance in Palestine and Beyond: On the Politics of Art, Aesthetics, and Affect', *Arab Studies Journal*, XXII (1): 8–28.
Scott, J. (1990), *Domination and the Arts of Resistance*, New Haven, CT: Yale University Press.
Shehadeh, R. (2015), *Language of War, Language of Peace: Palestine, Israel and the Search for Justice*, London: Profile Books.
Siry, C., M. Brendel, and R. Frisch. (2016), 'Radical Listening and Dialogue in Educational Research', *The International Journal of Critical Pedagogy*, 7 (3): 119–35.
Tripp, C. (2012), 'The Art of Resistance in the Middle East', *Asian Affairs*, 43 (3): 393–409.
Tuhiwai-Smith, L. (2006) (First published 1999), *Decolonizing Methodologies*, Dunedin: The University of Otago Press.
UN (2017), *Gaza Ten Years Later*. Retrieved from https://unsco.unmissions.org/sites/default/files/gaza_10_years_later_-_11_july_2017.pdf

# INDEX

ableism 5
Abourehab, Y. 109, 110
abyssal thinking 153–4, 205
Academic Service Learning (ASL) 88
aesthetic acts 245
*The Age of Ideology: The 19th Century Philosophers* (Aiken) 32
Aiken, Henry D. 32
*Airbus*, language policies by 93, 99
Alaa 111–12
al-Ali, Naji 238
Alim, H. Samy 3, 137
Al Masaeed, K. 107, 109–10
Almodóvar, Pedro 126–7
Alshobaki, Sahar 10–11
Altmann, Howard 202
*Ammiyyah* 106
anthropological linguistics 152
anti-intercultural conflicts 25
anti-oppressive education, theory of 12, 166
anti-racist pedagogy, for ELT classroom 15, 130–1, 135, 139, 143, 145
anti-racist practices 150
Anya, Uju 11, 128, 151
Appadurai, A. 30
applied linguistics 4–6, 15, 47, 51, 87–8, 107–8, 236–8, 246
art-based pedagogies 236–8
ASL, *see* Academic Service Learning (ASL)
asset-based pedagogies of translingualism 89, 91, 100
Austrian Federal Ministry of Education, Science and Research 202
Austrian primary teacher education, translanguaging in

abyssal thinking, impact of 205
Austrian Primary Curriculum 202
interaction 206
multilingualism in curricula 202–3
multilingual magazines 207
(neo-)linguistic exclusion 204–5
peer-interaction 206
plurilingualism, advantages 202, 204
pupils' abilities 207
skills 205–7
spontaneous translanguaging 204
*sprachliche Bildung*, concept of 202
teacher education programmes 206
Ubuntu translanguaging pedagogy (UTP) 205
voXmi 202
authochthonous minority languages 202
Azaz, M. 109–10
Azimova, N. 165, 187

Balosa, David 8–9, 23, 25–7, 31, 34–5, 37
Bantu languages 151
Basic Interpersonal Communications Skills (BICS) 220
Bateson, G. 26
Beck, U. 29
Beijing Language and Culture University Press 187
Beijing Mandarin pronunciation 145
Belgium, gender and LGBTQ+ in textbooks 169, 178
bell hooks 237
biculturality 95
Bidisha 10, 67, 74–9, *see also* Defoe and Bidisha (case study)

*Bienvenue chez les Ch'tis* (French comedy)   98–9
bilingualism   90, 95, 152
BIPOC   127, 133
Black Lives Matter   1
Brazil, language and racism in   150–2
　abolition of slavery   151
　African American Vernacular English   152
　Afro-Brazilian/African culture and history law   150
　anthropological linguistics   152
　bilingual education among black learners   151
　colour-blind ideologies   151
　racial equity legislation   150
　self-identification   150
Briggs, Charles L   135
Bromseth, J.   168, 171
Bron-Wojciechowska, A.   168
Brown, Richard Harvey   24
Bucholtz, M.   37–8
Butler, Judith   140, 237
Byram, M.   87, 96

Camargo, M.   151
Canclini, García   24
capitalism   7, 153
CASNAV (*centre académique pour la scolarisation des enfants allophones nouvellement arrivés et des enfants issus de familles itinérantes et de voyageurs*)   99
Celier, Paul   34
Cenoz, J.   108, 203
Center for Civic Learning and Action at Dickinson College   94, 100
Chandler, D.   246
Cheng Zhanlu   141
China National Office for Teaching Chinese as a Foreign Language (NOTCFL)   187
China Visual Arts Project, Westminster's   194, 196 n.4
Chinese-language textbooks
　2016 animation *Have a Nice Day*   190
　authentic Chinese-language texts   188, 193–5
　combining language and culture teaching   187
　cultural classes by research-active staff   185
　discourse 1: historical change   189–91
　discourse 2: women's status   191–3
　discourse 3: cultural practices   193–5
　discourse of 'leftover women'   192, 195
　family planning policy   192
　Integrated Chinese (IC)   188
　language and culture teaching   184–7
　language core modules at Westminster in 2016/17   185
　lecture and textbook learning, link between   188–9
　modern languages teaching   184–5
　Nanjing   189–91, 193
　New Practical Chinese Reader (NPCR)   188
　NOTCFL   188
　one-child policy   192
　one-hour tutorial in small groups   186
　PRC dominant, Han-centric heteronormative system   184
　proficiency in a language   186
　'Reform and Opening Up'   191, 196 n.3
　textbooks   187–9
Chinese modern languages classroom
　critical anti-racist pedagogy, Kubota's   139
　epistemological racism   140
　gender pedagogy (*see* critical gender pedagogy)
　Han race (*see* Han Gaze)
　imposition of Putonghua   140
　linguistic performativity   139–40
　metadiscursive regimes   135–6
　misgendering   140
　patriarchy and linguistic sexism   135, 137–9
　third-person pronouns   141–3

'Chineseness' 194
Chinese studies 184, 188, 190, 192, 196, *see also* Chinese-language textbooks; Chinese modern languages classroom
City University of New York's New York State Initiative on Emergent Bilinguals (CUNY-NYSIEB) 207
Classical Arabic (CA) 10, 106
classism 4
climate emergency protests 1
co-creation of knowledge 11, 126, 132
Coetzee 67
Cognitive Academic Language Proficiency (CALP) 14–15, 220–1, 223, 225–8, 230–1
Cohen, W. 64
communal critical self-consciousness 31, 33
communication, styles 23–4
Community-Based Service Learning (CBSL) 90
comparative intertextuality 64–7, *see also* upper secondary schools, pedagogical stylistics
Confucianism 137, 140
Conrod, Kirby 139–40
Content and Language Integrated Learning (CLIL) 14, 221–2
contextuality 237
*Continua of Biliteracy: An Ecological Framework* (Hornberger) 25
cosmopolitanism 63, 79
creative resistance 243, 245–9, *see also* Palestine (Gaza Strip), critical pedagogy in teacher education
critical antiracist pedagogy 15, 130–1, 135, 139, 143, 145
critical engaged pedagogy 15, 238, 242, 245
critical gender pedagogy 143–4
  critical decolonization 144
  decolonizing antiracism 144
  de-essentialising racism 143
  de-silencing anti-racism 144
  de-simplifying racism 143

multilayerism 143–4
open discussion 144
reflexivity 144
criticality 4–5, 7–10, 186, 238
critical pedagogy in modern language classroom 88–91
  ASL 89–90
  CBSL 90
  CSP 89
  DAE 89
  First-Year writing programme 90
  issues of social justice 89
  practitioners and researchers 6
  principles of access and representation 88
  shift in language attitudes 89
critical race pedagogy (CRP) 128, 131
critical race theory (CRT) 11, 128, 131
cultural dependence 24–5, 34
cultural globalization 29
cultural humility 123, 127–8
Culturally Sustaining Pedagogies (CSP) 1, 3, 89
cultural studies 5, 13, 54, 145, 185–90, 196
  Chinese 183, 187–8, 192
  lectures 188–9, 194–5
culture of dignity for all languages 26, 28, 32–3, 37, *see also* existential literacy
Cummins, Jim 220
Curran, M.E. 90
Curtis 90

Darj, F. 168
da Vinci, Leonardo 177
de Boise, S. 168
decanonization 1, 16 n.1
De Cillia, R. 219
decolonial pedagogies 151
decolonization 1, 4–5, 7–11, 15, 25, 35, 144–5
  and existential literacy (*see* existential literacy)
Defoe, Daniel 10, 67, 70–1, 74, 78–9, *see also* Defoe and Bidisha (case study)

Defoe and Bidisha (case study)  67–78
  digital processing of the passage  72
  first-person subject pronoun 'I' and transitive use of verbs  73
  frequency of third-person and first-person pronouns  72
  intransitive verbs referred to 'He'/Friday  73
  NRS/TA strategy and use  69–70, 78
  *Robinson Crusoe*  10, 67, 71, 79
  use of descriptions  70–2
  *Venetian Masters: Under the Skin of the City of Love*  10, 67, 74–9
de Sousa Santos, Boaventura  7, 12, 153
De Souza, L.T.M.  151
Dewey, John  28, 34
dialogue, Gadamer's paradigm on  69
diglossia  105–6
DILAMI (*Dispositif d'Accueil des Immigrés* - reception system for migrants)  99
director culture/society  27
Dirim, I.  204, 221
discrimination  1–2, 10–11, 32, 92, 98–9, 129, 140–1, 144, 174, 191, 223–4, 226
  gender  191
  and language  224, 226, 230–1
  linguistic  10, 92, 98, 140
Dominant American English (DAE)  89
*Domination and the Arts of Resistance* (Scott)  15, 238
Dragon Boat Festival  193
Duperron, Lucile  10
Dutch as foreign language  166, 168, 172, *see also* gender and LGBTQ+ in textbooks
Dutch textbooks  172–4
  LGBTQ+ and heterosexual relationships  173
  women, men and non-binary  172–3

ecological globalization  29
educational linguistics  6, 26–9

Employment Skills Center (ESC)  92
engaged pedagogy  237–8, *see also* critical engaged pedagogy
English Language Learning (ELL) classes  92
English language teaching (ELT)  12, 46, 149
  Anglophone perspectives in  47–8
  critical anti-racist pedagogy in  135, 145
  racism in (*see* racism in ELT, racially relevant pedagogies)
  UK and US domination of  58
Erskine, John  30
Espinosa, C.M.  207, 210
European Charter for Regional or Minority Languages  98
*Exercises for Rebel Artists: Radical Performance Pedagogy* (Gómez-Peña)  125
*The Existential Background of Human Dignity* (Marcel)  32
existential justice  25–6, 34, 38–9
existential literacy
  communication, styles  23–4
  critical pedagogy and existential sociolinguistics  31, 39
  cultural globalization  29
  decolonization and decolonizing mind on language issues  37
  first language use in teaching French conjugation  37
  homogenization of cultural and linguistic diversity  38
  miscommunication  38
  in modern foreign language classrooms  35–8
  notion of linguistic difference  36
  oppressive linguistic diversity treatment  37
  social and human justice  35
  definition  25–7
  ecological globalization  29
  educational linguistics  29
  experience and education  28
  globalization and critical pedagogy  29–30

intercultural or humane practices, promotion of   24
language classroom strategies   33–4
mentorship   33, 39
research method, of philosophical reflection   32–3
role of (re)education, (re)construction and (re)adjustment   24
SEIM   24
socio-philosophical educational approach   27–9
support for critical pedagogy   39
sustainable existential intercultural mindset (SEIM)   24
theoretical framework   31–2
existential sociolinguistics   30–1

Fairclough, N.   165
Fanon, Frantz   12, 35, 152–4
Felten, P.   34
feminist critical discourse analysis (FCDA)   12, 139, 145
Ferguson, C.   105–6
Ferreira, A.J.   149, 151
Filhon, A.   99
first-year seminar (FYS)   93–6
  ASL course design   94
  bilingualism and biculturality   95
  FYS and the ELL programmes   94–5
  FYS compare-and-contrast paper   95
  leadership skills, development of   96
  local communities and students   94
  poster exhibition opening event   96
  Proposition 227 campaign   95
  simulation of a local school district   95
  writing assignments and goals of FYS   95–6
Fischer, N.   220
Flores, N.   89, 152
Foreign language educators   30, 38
*Francophonie*   92
Frankfurt School   7
Freire, Paulo   3, 7–8, 12, 27, 28, 34, 166, 237

French and Francophone studies   90, *see also* linguistic diversity in college classroom
French Revolution   97, 98
French Senior-Year Seminar
  attitudes towards pronunciation   99
  effects of official monolingualism   99
  goals   96
  immigrant languages of France   99
  language policies and planning in France   96–8
  rise of Global English   99–100
  standardization forces   98
  status of Occitan   97
Fromm, Erich   7
frustration   38
Fulton, G.D.   69–70
*Fusha*   106

Gal, S.   152
García, Orfelia   24, 201, 205–7, 220
Gates, Henry Louis   151
Gates H.L., Jr.   160
Gay Pride   174
gender and LGBTQ+ in textbooks
  ambiguous/neutral relationships in textbooks   177
  anti-oppressive education, theory of   166–7
  education critical of privileging and Othering   167
  education for the Other   167
  gender-neutral pronoun *hen*   169–70
  hidden curriculum, subcategories   168
  Japanese EFL textbooks   168
  in Netherlands and Belgium   169
  representation in language teaching textbooks   168–9
  theoretical framework   166–7
  third non-binary gender   170
Gilak, Golriz   13–15
Giroux, Henry A.   31
global intercultural-intellectuality mentorship   34, 39
global intercultural mentors   33

globalization   24–5, 29–30, 47, 49, 64, 85, 88, 99, 108, 219
Global South, English teaching in
  Anglo-Atlantic leadership   47
  colonial differences   46
  critical pedagogy   48–9
  cultural superiority of Anglophone perspectives in ELT   47–8
  decolonial thinking   58
  English language in Morocco   49–50
  ethical dilemmas in ELT   46
  Inner-Circle varieties   47–8, 59 n.2
  interculturality   45, 58 n.1
  methodology
    anonymity, confidentiality and informed consent concerns   51
    assimilationist tendencies   54–5
    data collection and analysis   51–2
    English and local cultures/languages   55–6
    focus group discussions   51
    inclusion of local culture   53–4
    IT3, 'world Englishes'   54
    linguistic competence, development of   55
    Moroccan and Anglophone/international cultures, comparison   53–4
    pre-service teacher training programme modules   51
    qualitative analysis of interview data   51
    research context and participants   50–1
    results   52–3
    unclear attitude towards English teaching   54–5
    use of material references to Moroccan culture   53
  neoliberalism   47
  postcolonial contexts   45
  power imbalances   46–7
  status to native English speaker teachers (NESTs)   48
Goethe   64
Gogolin, Ingrid   14, 212, 221
Gómez-Peña, Guillermo   125
Gordon, Milton M.   25, 27
Gorski, E.   152
Gorter, D.   106, 203
grammar-translation method   123
GRAMNet (Glasgow Refugee Asylum and Migration Network)   240
Grosfoguel, R.   153
Guczogi, Theresa   13–14
Guerreiro Ramos, A.   155, 157
Gujarati, translanguage in   111–12
Gustafsson Sendén, M.   171

Han centrism   13
Han gaze   12, 136–7, 140, 142, 144
  Han Confucianism   137
  Han race   136
  Mandarin linguistic hegemony   137
  Modern Standard Chinese   136–7
  non-Mandarin languages   137
  Putonghua, varieties of   136–7
  and White gaze   137
Heller, M.   152
Helmke   225
heteronormativity   13, 183
Hird, Derek   11, 35, 40, 249
historically marginalized groups in textbooks, USA   165
Hornberger, Nancy H.   25
Hult, Francis M.   26, 29
Humanism   153, 159

ideology
  around the position of English   46
  civic   168
  inconsistency in practice and   109
  of linguistic assimilation   97
  monolingual   93, 111
*The Ignorant Schoolmaster* (Rancière)   125
immigrant languages   99, 219
Imperiale, Maria Grazia   14–15
imposter syndrome   127
inclusion
  of creative methods   239
  of the first language(s)   228–30
  in higher education   91

of local culture/perspectives 48, 53–4
Integrated Chinese (IC)–NPCR 134, 188
integrative language learning, primary schools in Vienna and Lower Austria
 BICS 220, 226
 CALP 220, 226
 category 2 223–4
 CLIL-method 221–2
 data privacy protection 225
 hidden curriculum 220
 hypotheses 223
 implementation 222, 231
 inclusion of first language(s) in non-language subjects 228–30
 integrative multilingual learning 221
 interviews 225
 language and discriminatory effect 226, 230
 'language-sensitive' teaching 221
 multilingual students 226
 non-language subject 228
 research design 222
 research questions 222–3
 sample 224
 SDG4 of the United Nations 231
 subject-related didactics 221
 subject-related vocabulary 226
 survey, online/qualitative/quantitative 224–7, 230
integrative multilingual learning 221
intercultural communication pedagogy 4
intercultural epistemology 34, 39
interculturality 9
intercultural mediation 86
interdependence 24–5, 34, 38
Irvine, J.T. 152

Japanese EFL textbooks, gender roles in 165, 168
Johnson, S. 206
Johnston, B. 165, 187

Kanafani, Ghassan 238
Kehoe, Séagh 13

Kendall, Paul 12–13
King, K.A. 98
Kleyn, Tatyana 201, 204–11
Koster, D. 168
KPH Vienna/Krems 211
KPH Wien/Krems 202
Kramsch, Claire 10, 86
Krumm, H.-J. 212
Kubota, Ryuko 12, 139–40, 143–5
Kuckartz, U. 222
Kumaravadivelu, B. 50
Kumashiro, Kevin 12–13, 166–8, 174
Kuype, L. 169

L1, use of 11, 35, 40 n.2, 131–2
L1 contextualization 11, 35, 40 n.2, 131–2
L2 Arabic curricula 106
Ladson-Billings, G. 12, 150, 157–8
Lambert, L.M. 34
Lange, I. 221
language
 bans 201, 203, 213–14, 230–1
 classroom strategies 33–4 (*see also* existential literacy)
 hierarchies and inequalities 7, 99, 108–9, 204
 issues 3, 30–1, 37
 mediation 86
 and power 2, 5, 86, 87, 128, 145, 201, 210, 214–15
 teaching 3–6, 11, 13, 15, 86, 88, 96, 108, 123, 128, 135, 144–5, 155, 168, 185, 186, 195, 211, 218, 230–1
*Language for Resilience* 245–6
Lazar, Michele 139
*lebensweltliche Mehrsprachigkeit* (plurilingualism in everyday life) 219
Lee, Jackie F.K. 168
Lee, T.S. 157
Leisen, J. 221
LGBTQ+ 12, 133
 in Belgium textbooks 169, 178
 and gender in Netherlands 169
 and heterosexual relationships 173, 175–7

*regnbågsfamiljen* (LGBTQ+ parenting) 176
   in Sweden (*see* Sweden, gender and LGBTQ+ in)
   in textbooks (*see* gender and LGBTQ+ in textbooks)
LGBTQIA 178 n.1
liberal arts 10, 91, 100
Li Lan 138
linguacultural communication 105, 110, 115, 117
linguacultural mobility 105, 115
linguistic awareness 13, 62
linguistic diversity in college classroom 1, 86
   Academic Service Learning (ASL) 88
   clarification of terms 87–8
   critical pedagogy in modern language classroom 88–91, 93–4
   Culturally Sustaining Pedagogies (CSP) 88
   Employment Skills Center (ESC) 92
   English Language Learning (ELL) classes 92
   first-year seminar (*see* first-year seminar (FYS))
   *Francophonie* 92
   French Senior-Year Seminar (*see* French Senior-Year Seminar)
   implementation model in collegiate context 91–3
   issues of social justice 89
   linguistic diversity 87–9
   linguistic proficiency and intercultural competence 92
   Metropolitan French 93
   multilingual instructor as an intercultural mediator 86–8
   power through language 87
   role of stratification 87
   Senior Seminar 91–2
   US-based view of language mediation 86
linguistic imperialism 54
linguistic justice 1, 16, 37–8
linguistic racism 12, 149

linguistic resistance 246
linguistic sexism, *see* patriarchy and linguistic sexism
Ling Yuanzheng 142
Litosseliti, L. 168
Liu Bannong 48, 141
Locke, John 135
Lunar New Year 193

Macedo, D. 35, 37
Makalela, Leketi 14, 205
Malaysia and Scandinavian countries
   English as second language 56
   textbooks produced by Anglophone institutions 56
Mao era 13, 189–91, 194
Marinaro, Isabella 9–10
Maritain, Jacques 32–3, 39
Marxist anti-capitalist class struggle 7
McCarty, T.L. 157
Mecheril, P. 221, 230
#MeToo 1
Michalak, M. 223
Mid-Autumn Festival 193
Middle East, politics of resistance in 238
Mignolo, W.D. 12, 37
Millás, Juan José 126
*Minor Feelings* (Hong) 95
minute service-learning programming 94
mixed methods study, *see* integrative language learning, primary schools in Vienna and Lower Austria
modern language pedagogy
   anti-racist pedagogy syllabus 130–1
   content 125–7
   conversations 124–5
   CRPWLT, WL research guided by CRT 128–9
   cultures of languages 129
   expertise and accumulation of knowledge 125–7
   focus on expertise 125–30
   grammar-translation method 123
   L1 contextualization 131

language, identity and bias   127–30
*Leaders Project Leaders Project*
    at Teacher's College of
    Columbia University   131
  prepositions in Spanish
    language   131
  project-based assignment   131
  radical pedagogy   124–5
  Radical Pedagogy Reading
    Group   125
  vocabulary   131
Modern Standard Arabic (MSA)   106
monoculturalism   13, 183
monolingual habitus   203
monolingual ideologies   93, 107–9
monolingualism   13, 38, 99, 183, 204, 219
Morocco, *see also* Global South,
    English teaching in
  Anglophone cultures   50
  awareness of pre-service and
    in-service teachers   50
  English's lack of colonial
    connotation   56
  linguistic dependency on
    French   50
  linguistic hybridity   46
  multilingual country   45
  power struggle between local and
    foreign languages   49
Morrison, Toni   137
Moser, D.   142
multidialectal practices   109–10
multilingualism   1, 8–10, 15, 85–8, 137, 201–2, 204, 211–12, 215
*My Freshman Year: What a Professor Learned by Becoming a Student* (Small and Nathan)   125

narrative report of speech/ thought acts (NRS/TA)   69–70, 78
Nascimento, Gabriel   11–12
Nassif, L.   107, 109
Nathan, Rebekah   125
*National Identity* (Smith)   168
national Mellon grant for civic
    engagement   93

National Museum of China   189
native speakers   5, 6, 47, 54, 92, 106–10, 112–14, 117–18, 118 n.1, 127, 131, 185, 188
  educated native speakers   92
Netherlands, gender and
    LGBTQ+   169
Neuliep, J.W.   23
Neumann, U.   212
Newman, J.O.   65
New Practical Chinese Reader
    (NPCR)   134, 187–95
NRS/TA, *see* narrative report of
    speech/thought acts (NRS/TA)

OECD   219
one-language-at-a-time   112
Ong, H.T.   85
Online Arabic from Palestine
    (OAfP)   104
  'Arabic as one' vision   106, 114
  Arabic pedagogy   106–7
  beginner AFL learners   104
  bridging languages and cultures,
    excerpts   115–17
  Classical Arabic (CA)   106
  colloquial Arabic in MSA   107
  diglossia   105
  learners' translanguaging journey
    bonding with people   111–12
    fun interactions   113
    multilingual realities   110–11
    native-speaker bias   112
    to navigate meaning among
      languages   113
    to understand   112–13
oppressive linguistic systems   2–3
Ortega   108, 112

Pakzadian, M.   47
Palestine (Gaza Strip), critical
    pedagogy in teacher
    education
  contextuality   237
  critical and contextualized art-based
    pedagogies   236–9
  critical applied linguistics   237
  engaged pedagogy   237–8
  English language education   236

linguistic resistance   246
Palestinian Arts of Resistance   15, 236, 238–9, 247
  pedagogy of resistance   247
  performativity   237
  resilience, concept of   245
  teacher training programme   239–45
    aesthetic acts   245
    follow-up in-depth interviews   242
    format of the course   239
    objectives   239–40
    participatory approaches and decolonizing methodologies   239
    pre-service teachers and role play   248
    vignettes   240–5
    workshops and teaching practices   240–1, 243
Palestinian Arts of Resistance   15, 236, 238–9, 247
Palpacuer Lee, C.   90
Paris, Django   3, 137, 157
patriarchy and linguistic sexism   135, 137–9
  characters of male and female signifier   138–9
  marginalization   137
  occupational roles   139
  patriarchal Han chauvinism   138
Paulin, M.   99
pedagogical stylistics, *see* upper secondary schools, pedagogical stylistics
*Pedagogy of the Oppressed* (Freire)   125, 166
Pennycook, A.   237
performative linguistics   145
performativity, theory of   12, 139–40, 142, 237
philosophical reflection   9, 32–3, *see also* existential literacy
Piller, I.   10, 86–8
pluralism   3, 10, 63, 79, 98, 135, 157
plurilingualism   14, 88, 201–2, 204, 207–8, 215, 219, 230–2
Pokitsch   204

politico-linguistic norms   204
polycentrism   10, 63, 79
power through language   87
PRC dominance   13
primary school, *see* integrative language learning, primary schools in Vienna and Lower Austria
primary teacher education, *see* Austrian primary teacher education, translanguaging in
Proposition 227 campaign   95

QDA Miner software   51
Qin dynasty   189
Qing dynasty   189
Qingming Festival   193
Qualitative Content Analysis (QCA)   222

racism in ELT, racially relevant pedagogies
  abyssal thinking   153–4
  in Brazil (*see* Brazil, language and racism in)
  conception of self and others   156
  culturally and racially relevant pedagogies   155–9
  culturally responsive pedagogies   157–9
  epistemologies in black lived experiences   152–5
  epistemologies of Global South   154
  narratives   149–50, 155–7
  post-apartheid contexts   155
  racially relevant pedagogies   159
  schooling practices of black teachers   158
Rancière, Jacques   125, 245–6
R'Boul, Hamza   9, 50
*regnbågsfamiljen* (LGBTQ+ parenting)   176
relationship-building   23–4, 34, 39, *see also* existential literacy
Republican era, China   137, 142, 189
resilience, concept of   15, 193, 236, 245–6, 248
resilient resistance   15, 246

revolutionary empowerment   7
Rivstart A1 + A2   171–2, 176
Rivstart B1–B2   176–7
*Robinson Crusoe* (Defoe)   67–73
Rosa, J.   89, 152
Rosenau, J.N.   38
Russian textbooks, minorities in   165
Ryan, C.   246

same-sex marriages   169, 176
SAOL, the Swedish Academy Glossary   171
Scott, James   15, 238
SDG 4   219–20, 231
second language acquisition (SLA)   107
self-decolonization   25
Seltzer, K.   206
Severo, C.G.   152
sexism   5, 129, 191
  linguistic   137–40, 143–4
Shiri, Sonia   107, 114
silence culture/alienated society   27
Silverstein, Michael   152
Skibba, Candace   11
*The Slow Professor* (Berg and Seeber)
Small, Cathy   125
Smith, Anthony D.   168
Snapp, S.D.   168, 177
social justice   3–12, 15, 34, 85–90, 100, 117, 128, 145, 154
*Society as Text: Essays on Rhetoric, Reason, and Reality* (Brown)   24
sociolinguistics   4–5, 9, 16, 29–31, 37–8, 47, 85–7, 95, 98, 105, 107, 110, 145, 149, 152
Spolsky, B.   29
*sprachliche Bildung* (integrative language learning)   13, 202, *see also* integrative language learning, primary schools in Vienna and Lower Austria
Språkporten 123   171–2, 175–7
Stamper, K.D.   98
Steger, M.B.   29
stereotypes   98, 167, 173, 178, 184, 187
Sturm-Trigonakis, E.   64

sustainable existential intercultural mindset (SEIM)   24–8, 31, 33–5, 37, 39–40
Swahili and Lingala   35–7
Sweden, gender and LGBTQ+ in
  gender-neutral pronoun *hen*   171
  material and method   171–2
  quantitative and qualitative studies   172
  same-sex partnership and adoptive parents   171
  sexual morality and pathologization   171
  text books   171–2, 178
  third non-binary gender   171
  UN's Human Development Report 2020   170
Swedish as a foreign language   12, 166, 168, *see also* gender and LGBTQ+ in textbooks
Swedish textbooks   175–7
  LGBTQ+ and heterosexual relationships   175–7
  men, women and non-binary   174–5

Tajeddin, Z.   47
Tajmel, T.   221, 224
teacher education, *see also* Austrian primary teacher education, translanguaging in; integrative language learning, primary schools in Vienna and Lower Austria; Palestine (Gaza Strip), critical pedagogy in teacher education; translanguaging in teacher education
  programmes   56, 58, 201, 203–6, 208, 210, 212, 215
teachers' beliefs   47, 52, 56–7, 69, 109, 220, 222, 230
Teaching English as a Foreign Language (TEFL)   6, 211
Telles, E.   150
Temple of Confucius   193
TESOL   6, 207
textbook discourses   1, 184, 187–8, 192, 195–6

in Chinese-language (*see* Chinese-language textbooks)
gender and LGBTQ+ in (*see* gender and LGBTQ+ in textbooks)
Thich Nhat Hanh, philosophy of 237
third-person pronouns 141–3
    gender binary in colonial European languages 143
    gender-binary third person pronouns 142
    inequality and limitations 143
    new pronoun, as female gender visible 141–2
translanguaging 1, 107–9
    in Arabic 109–10
    in Austrian primary teacher education (*see* Austrian primary teacher education, translanguaging in)
    impact of 6
    learners' translanguaging journey (*see* Online Arabic from Palestine (OAfP))
    monolingual ideologies 107–8
    multilingual/plurilingual practices 108–9
    outside-the-classroom setting 110
    pedagogies 6
    semi-structured interviews 109
    in teacher education (*see* translanguaging in teacher education)
translanguaging in teacher education
    collaborative work 209
    contrasting courses and language bans 213–14
    designing of multilingual presentations 210
    establishing students' language profiles 212–13
    ghettoization 209
    inclusion and exclusion experiences 213–14
    integration of migration languages 208
    language prestige 214
    multilingual oral presentations 209–12
    multiple multilingual materials 208–11
    Padlet with pictures, creation of 212–13
    parallel texts or translated texts 209
    strategies for pedagogical translanguaging 208–11
    suggestions for integrating into teacher education 211–12
    TESOL and general education programmes 207
    writing and taking notes 210–11
Trentman, E. 109, 111
Tripp, Charles 238
*Troubling Education: Queer Activism and Anti-oppressive Pedagogy* (Kumashiro) 166
true justice 33, 39, *see also* existential justice
Tubino, F. 38

Ubuntu translanguaging pedagogy (UTP) 14, 205
UN Convention on the Rights of the Child 203, 224
University of Westminster 183–4, 187
upper secondary schools, pedagogical stylistics
    canonical texts 65
    case study (*see* Defoe and Bidisha (case study))
    comparative intertextuality 64–7
    contemporary stylistics 62–4
    follow-up classroom activities 78
    pedagogical stylistics 63–4
    selection of WLE passages 65–6
    ways of dealing with texts 65
    *Weltliteratur* 64
    WL, definition 64
    WLE at classroom 64–7
US-based writing programmes 100
Ushioda, E. 115
Using the Palestinian Arts of Resistance in English Language Teaching (teacher training course) 15, 238–9
US liberal-arts colleges 100

van Oostendorp, Marc   169
*Venetian Masters: Under the
        Skin of the City of Love*
        (Bidisha)   10, 67, 74, 79

Wagner, M.   96
Walcott   67
Walsh, C.E.   37, 47
Wa Thiong'o, N.   37
Weiming, Tu   31
Whitehead, Alfred North   28
Wielander, Gerda   12–13
Wikström, Josef   12–13
Williams, Cen   108

Wink, J.   31
Wolters, Juul   12–13
World Literature in English (WLE)   9, 62–7, 79
World Literature (WL)   62, 64, *see also* upper secondary schools, pedagogical stylistics

Yellow River   194
Younes, M.   107

Zhang, L.   5, 86–8
Zhou Zuoren   141